To the Instructor

The *Study Guide* is designed to assist students in mastering the content of the introductory course in psychology whether the course is taught by conventional lecture methods or by unit mastery methods. For students who are in a unit mastery taught course, a separate introduction is available prior to the first chapter in this *Study Guide*. For instructors using a unit mastery approach, a detailed introduction, rationale, and suggested methods are included in the related *Instructor's Guide*.

In the preparation of the *Study Guide*, consideration was given to three major difficulties students often encounter. First, they may be uncertain about what to learn from each chapter—how to distinguish crucial material from less important details. Second, they may fail to recognize notable figures in the field or to learn the meanings of specific psychological terms and concepts. Third, they may have no satisfactory way of knowing how well they have mastered the material until after an examination (which often is too late).

The four or five sections of each chapter in this *Study Guide* have been designed to help students in each of these areas. The first section is a list of learning objectives to help students focus on what they should learn from the chapter. Next in most chapters is a section containing important names and contributions of selected individuals identifed in the chapter. Following is a section asking for the important terms and details in the chapter. Students should be able to provide brief identifications for each of these. Items missed then become an object for further study. (An answer key is provided at the end of each chapter.) The next section, dealing with more complex ideas and concepts, leads students through the text chapter by highlighting conceptual material, theories, research, and major conclusions, but excluding *Critical Discussions* (except in Chapter 1)—these could be the focus for discussion in class.

There are two levels of questions on ideas and concepts: On one level, about 60 percent of the items refer to "basic ideas and concepts." These are asterisked and designed to draw attention to the chapter's most essential points. On the other level, the remaining 40 percent of the items refer to important but less essential ideas and concepts. In a conventionally taught course, it is left for you to decide the level of detail to which you would like your students to attend and to inform them at the start of the term. In a unit mastery taught course, however, the quizzes that are furnished with the program assume that students have dealt with *all* of the Ideas and Concepts items. Finally, two multiple-choice sample quizzes (and answer keys) provide students with an opportunity to practice taking exams and, at the same time, help point out their areas of weakness.

iii

STUDY GUIDE AND UNIT MASTERY PROGRAM

to accompany

Hilgard's Introduction to PSYCHOLOGY

TWELFTH EDITION

Rita L. Atkinson
Richard C. Atkinson
Edward E. Smith
Daryl J. Bem
Susan Nolen-Hoeksema

Prepared by

John G. Carlson
University of Hawaii at Manoa

Harcourt Brace College Publishers

Fort Worth • Philadelphia • San Diego • New York • Orlando • Austin • San Antonio
Toronto • Montreal • London • Sydney • Tokyo

Address editorial correspondence to:
Harcourt Brace College Publishers
301 Commerce Street, Suite 3700
Fort Worth, TX 76102

Address orders to:
Harcourt Brace & Company
6277 Sea Harbor Drive
Orlando, FL 32887-6777
1-800-782-4479 or 1-800-433-0001 (in Florida)

ISBN: 0-15-503074-4

Printed in the United States of America

5 6 7 8 9 0 1 2 3 4   129   9 8 7 6 5 4 3 2 1

To All Students:
How to Use this Guide

This *Study Guide* is designed to help you in several ways: It tells you what you should learn from each chapter; it introduces the names, terms, and concepts you will encounter in the text; and it provides examination questions that will enable you to determine just how much you have learned. Note that the pages of the *Guide* are perforated to allow you to tear out selected sections for ease of use with your text.

Each chapter in the *Study Guide* parallels one in the text, and there are four or five sections for each chapter. The first section lists the Learning Objectives—the fundamental ideas and facts you should learn from the chapter. After you have looked over the Objectives, take the time to read and enjoy the text chapter your instructor has assigned. That way you will have the opportunity to gain perspectives on the area of psychology presented in *Hilgard's Introduction to Psychology* before you become involved in the details of preparation for further learning and examinations. You may want to refer back to each objective after you have covered the appropriate section in the text. Or you may prefer to complete the chapter and then see if you have mastered all the objectives. In any event, the learning objectives cover the important ideas in each chapter; they include topics you probably will be expected to know on examinations.

From the Important Names section and from the Vocabulary and Details section of the chapters you will acquire an acquaintance with the key figures, important terms, and specific facts presented in the text. (Answer keys are at the back of each chapter in the *Study Guide*.) Although these items are meant to be completed after you read the text and before more in–depth studying, they also may be used profitably later as a review before examinations. There probably is not sufficient room in the blank space within every item to allow you to write the answers. The intention is that you will attempt to answer each item on a separate piece of paper or in the margin of your *Study Guide*. That way, you can cover the answers and use these items for self–review before examinations, making the attempt to state each answer before looking at the correct response. The list of terms may seem long for some chapters, but if you learn them all, you will have a good grasp of the material that is likely to appear on examinations. It is a good idea to complete this section of your *Study Guide* before turning to the Ideas and Concepts section because many of the terms are used in the context of questions in that section.

A word of warning: The Vocabulary and Details items cannot serve as a substitute for the text chapters. Terms do not cover all the ideas presented in the text.

It is from the Ideas and Concepts section of each chapter that you will gain insight into theories and conceptual material in psychology, categories or outlines of text information, methods and results of experiments, and

v

relationships or distinctions between fine points. You will also encounter additional chapter terms that are best defined in the context of conceptual material—these are italicized terms and printed in boldface type. (Note that a term that has been covered in the Vocabulary section will not be italicized again in the Ideas section.)

There are two levels of Ideas and Concepts items. The ones that are marked with an asterisk (about 60 percent of the items) are the basic or main points; the remaining items deal with less essential material. It is for your instructor to decide the level of comprehension he or she expects in the course, determining whether you use some or all Ideas and Concepts items.

It is *not* intended that you write out every answer to the Ideas and Concepts questions, although you may occasionally find tables or blanks convenient to complete in the *Study Guide*. To write out every answer would be a very time–consuming and probably unnecessary task. Rather, it will be to your advantage to prepare for examinations by marking your text in some way—say, with a highlighter or by underlining—the portions that are covered by these items. (Note that, with one exception in Chapter 1, the Ideas and Concepts items do not cover the Critical Discussions. It is left to your instructor to decide whether to include this material in class discussions or examinations.)

Finally, turn to the Sample Quiz sections of the *Study Guide* and answer all the questions on the first quiz. Check your answers against the Answer Key. For questions on which you made an error go back to the text and review the appropriate material. Then turn to the second quiz for further self–evaluation of your mastery of the chapter.

To summarize, there are four or five sections in each chapter of the *Study Guide:* Learning Objectives, Important Names (in some chapters), Vocabulary and Details, Ideas and Concepts, and Sample Quizzes. First look over the learning objectives, read the chapter, and then proceed to the names, vocabulary, and concepts, and finally to the quizzes. These sections are designed to help you gain perspective, identify the names and special terms in psychology, to understand the conceptual material in the text, and to allow you to evaluate your learning. Remember, however, that the *Study Guide* is designed as a supplement, not a substitute, for the text. Used properly, the *Study Guide* is intended to *enhance* your comprehension of the text.

To The Unit Mastery Student

ASSUMPTIONS OF LEARNING

A wise man once likened students to three products of nature: a stone, a sponge, and a spark. Learners who are like "stones" tend to resist learning; new ideas and knowledge tend to "bounce off" and leave no impact. "Sponge" learners soak up knowledge readily, yet retain it passively in its original form. "Spark" learners, however, *actively* pursue knowledge, applying themselves in the process of learning and transforming the knowledge they acquire through ongoing dialogue and interaction with the knowledge source. Active learning reaps maximum rewards and benefits for students, and it is the process emphasized in your *Study Guide.*

In accordance with suggestions made by Carl Rogers, a well–known psychologist whose views are discussed in your text, several assumptions underlie the active learning model used in this *Guide:*

1. Significant learning takes place when the subject matter is seen to have relevance for one's own purposes. In other words, people learn best those things which they perceive are involved in maintaining or enhancing themselves. To the degree that you are interested in and committed to the study of psychology—the useful science of the individual—you will come to know well a body of knowledge about the subject.

2. Learning can proceed more rapidly in a supportive environment. In an environment where personal security is assured and there is little or no threat, differentiation of information can take place, partial meanings can be explored and put together in a variety of ways, and understanding will develop. As you will see, the process used in the *Unit Mastery Program* allows you to explore material in a more predictable environment with fewer sources of anxiety and worry.

3. Learning is facilitated when students direct the learning process. When you choose your own directions, decide your own course of action, determine your own rate of study and learning, and benefit from the consequences of these choices, then significant learning is maximized. This form of participative learning is much more effective and rewarding than is passive, externally directed learning.

4. Significant learning is acquired through doing. The process utilized in this *Study Guide* is action–oriented. You will participate through reading, thinking, writing, answering questions, correcting, and reviewing. This is *not* a passive process; rather it is a behavioral and experiential process in which learning is sparked.

This *Unit Mastery Program* is designed to help you become a master in the art of active learning, to develop such "cognitive" skills as conceptualization, memorization, analysis, comparison, and synthesis. The program will also help you by providing a mechanism for consistent, ongoing feedback. Feedback, as a learning tool, is important in letting you know immediately if you are on the right track. Consider feedback to be a "cue" to tell you that you are on course, or that you need to go back

vii

and review the material again, rather than just a way of determining if you have the "right answer." In other words, think of feedback as part of the learning process, rather than an end in itself.

Finally, beyond training in the "active" approach to learning, this *Guide* is intended to help you explore the fascinating world of psychology, to gain insight as to how psychology is part and parcel of your everyday life, and to afford you a glimpse of how psychological principles impact on your daily interactions with others.

THE UNIT MASTERY METHOD

Objectives of the Program

Unit mastery learning is a positive alternative to traditional methods of college instruction. The very name implies a shift in the concept of instruction—from mere learning to "mastery" learning. This notion means that instruction is segmented into meaningful "units," each of which are studied until a high rate of competency, or "mastery," is achieved. Mastery learning also implies that you can retake examinations on material until you have mastered the information. You move on in the program when you have achieved mastery over the current unit.

Some of the other characteristics and benefits of the mastery learning approach are these:

1. **Objectives of the course are clearly outlined, and the criteria for mastery are clearly defined.** Your final grade is self–selected, in the form of the number of units you complete by the end of the semester. You know in advance what you need to do for a particular grade, and you know where you are going and how you are doing as you progress through the term.

2. **Feedback is a fundamental part of the program.** In the *Unit Mastery Program* you are given timely and specific feedback on your performance. After you have taken a quiz, the course staff will most likely grade your work immediately. This can be an important reward for having completed a chapter. Additionally, the grader will have text references available for each quiz question, and can refer you to the relevant sections of the text so you can look back for information and clarification. Review after a quiz is a key part of the mastery learning process. This "look back" can help

you determine what material you missed, misunderstood, or did not grasp entirely. An advantage of doing this review immediately is that you have the chance to consult with the teaching staff right then and there, while questions are still fresh in your mind.

3. **You select the pace of learning, and you determine the rate of progress you wish to make.** You are tested on a certain amount of material when you decide that you are ready, so that external pressures are kept to a minimum. However, it is important for you to remember that while you have a tremendous amount of freedom in this program, you also carry the major responsibility for learning. It is your job to pace yourself so that you can complete the course on time.

4. **Frequent personal contact with teaching staff is built into the program.** In contrast to some traditional college instruction, there are frequent opportunities for interpersonal contact with your instructor and teaching staff in the *Unit Mastery Program*. When you take quizzes, there is greater availability of instructional staff to assist you with immediate feedback and individualized help if you need it. Some of the course assistants may be former students who have completed a unit mastery course. They can provide both knowledge and emotional support, having been through the program themselves.

Concerns and Cautions

In the *Unit Mastery Program*, there are a number of quizzes for each chapter. Each quiz covers somewhat different aspects of each chapter of the text. For this reason, you should not anticipate that you can pass a second quiz on the chapter by merely reviewing the errors you made on the first quiz. You may need to restudy the entire chapter or selected portions before taking another quiz. There may be times when you find that you miss the mastery criterion for several quizzes in a row. While this can be disheartening, try to keep in mind that **all** students, even the most well–prepared ones, may have difficulty from time to time. It is best if you do not try to compete with or compare your performance to that of friends or classmates. Rather, find a pace and level of comfort that works for you while still allowing you to attain the goal you have set for yourself. Making mistakes is part of the learning process, not a mark of failure.

A caution: Procrastination is a major barrier for students who are enrolled in courses using mastery learning methods. Because exam schedules are not pre–fixed and announced, they are determined by you, according to your level of readiness. This approach demands a level of maturity, planning, and self–discipline from you that may be new and unfamiliar. While you enjoy great personal freedom in this approach, you also must assume a great deal of personal responsibility for the outcomes. It is not a good idea to wait several weeks before taking your first quiz, nor is it wise to take two or three quizzes in a row, and then wait several weeks to start again. Putting off studying and test–taking until the last few weeks of the semester can have serious results in terms of your course grade, in addition to the emotional stress and anxiety you will feel when you realize that you cannot "catch up" after all. One strategy that is recommended is to plan to study a fixed period of time each week. If for some reason you are unable to meet your goal for any one week, then extra study time should be scheduled for the week following. This planning will help keep you on track and up to date.

Some Outcomes for You

By now you may be wondering about your ability to fulfill the requirements for a course using the unit mastery approach. However, there are a number of positive outcomes for the student who studies conscientiously and completes the assigned units.

1. You know what is expected of you. The goals and criteria for course completion and grades are stated up front. You are in a position of certainty at all times, so concern about "How am I doing?" and performance anxiety should be at a minimum.

2. Unit mastery instruction allows you to self–pace your tests. This approach helps you schedule your exams when you feel most prepared and allows you to pace your quizzes to fit into what else may be going on in your life—for instance, other course exams, social obligations, or illness. This experience can serve to help you become more effective in your studying in general, with the result that you may find yourself acquiring better study habits across all your coursework.

3. The ongoing testing and immediate feedback creates a reward schedule that contributes to a sense of success and confidence. Because the opportunities to retake quizzes and obtain help from the staff are built into the program, test–taking anxiety and fear of failure should be greatly reduced as you make your way through the course. Moreover, as you progress through the assigned chapters, you will experience a systematic improvement in your studying and test–taking skills. The actual process of working through material using the unit mastery approach has benefits beyond mere practice and repetition.

4. A sense of "self–efficacy" develops as you work through the *Unit Mastery Program*. As you progress through the term, you begin to experience a sense of personal control and competence that is a direct result of your own actions, decisions, and performance. You will learn more, and you will know you are learning more. Perhaps this sense of personal mastery over your own educational environ–ment is the most powerful outcome of the *Unit Mastery Program*.

BEGINNING THE PROCESS

The initial or introductory study of any discipline requires a two–pronged approach to knowledge: the first is the study of basic vocabulary and the basic facts of the field, as well as knowing the major contributors to the subject matter. The second focus of knowledge is the study of the more complex ideas and concepts of the field, the pulling together of larger units of information that have meaning beyond the individual facts and specifics. These two components, basic "vocabulary and details" and "ideas and concepts," form the main structure for the design of this *Guide*. Careful study and attention to *both* components will reap maximum rewards for you as you learn about the field of psychology.

Mastering Vocabulary and Details

What are they? The Vocabulary and Details section includes terms and language specific to the field and basic facts of the discipline. (Prior to this section, the names of major researchers and theorists who have contributed to the field may also be called for, depending on the focus of the particular chapter.)

When and how do I fill out this section of the guide? For most students, the best time to go through the guide is right after reading the entire chapter. However, the *Study Guide* is segmented into subsections corresponding to the text, so you can read your text and complete portions of the *Guide* at the same time, rather than attempting all of the questions at once, depending on your preference.

Complete each blank before going on to the next one. (As noted in *To all Students,* it may be best to write your answers on a separate sheet of paper or in the margin of the *Guide*.) It is important that you do the items in order because one item may contain material that assumes you have answered a previous item. If you cannot think of the answer, or if you discover later that your answer does not match the one in the key, go back to the page of your text that is referred to in the item. After you have completed your answers, refer to the key at the end of each chapter to check your answers against the correct ones. While it is important to answer items correctly the first time through, *the critical thing is that you understand the items when you are finished with the process.* Merely finding the right answer in the key and filling in the correct blank of the guide is a much less effective way to develop your understanding of the material.

Why should I fill out this section of the guide? Working through the Vocabulary and Details section of the *Study Guide* systematically and completely will help you identify areas of strength and weakness, thereby helping you target terms and details needing more study. Moreover, approximately one-half of your chapter quiz items will be drawn from the Vocabulary and Details items.

Mastering Ideas and Concepts

What are they? Concepts are abstract ideas that help to generalize specific units of information. As discussed in your text, ideas and concepts are important for you to know because they are the melding of many bits of information into a larger whole, which has meaning of its own. This larger unit of knowledge helps us understand and grasp meanings that go beyond concrete, specific knowledge, and helps us see patterns in everyday life.

When and how do I fill out this section of the guide? It is probably a good idea to complete this section of the guide after you have done the Vocabulary and Details portion. A strong foundation of basic knowledge will help you work through this section of the guide; building on that knowledge will assist you in completing it.

The items that are found in this section may require that you answer essay questions, fill in charts and tables, or complete diagrams. Some items will ask you to remember explicit information from the chapter, while others will call for higher-order thinking processes, such as comparing and contrasting ideas, generating new examples of a particular concept, or integrating new material with information you already have. Because you are being asked to analyze and synthesize material, rather than merely to recall information, there is no answer key for this section of the guide. However, text page numbers are given for reference to the section of the chapter where related material is presented. Refer to these text pages for feedback regarding your answers.

Why should I fill out this section of the guide? The main point of this section is to provide you with a mechanism for organizing material into a coherent whole, while at the same time relating the parts of the whole to each other. This process helps new information "fit into" a meaningful framework. You will learn in your text that this is an important aspect of long-term memory. Approximately one-half of the Unit Quiz items will be taken from the Ideas and Concepts section of the guide, including items without asterisks. (While, as noted above, 60% of the Ideas and Concepts items are considered "basic" to understanding of the chapter, the Unit Mastery Program assumes mastery of all of the items.)

Sample Quizzes

As discussed earlier, self-evaluation in a "safe" environment is a major component of the active learning process. Sample quizzes are provided in the *Study Guide* for you to test your mastery of the material you have read. Two Sample Quizzes are provided for each chapter. Taking the time to go through these quizzes and checking your answers with the key at the end of the chapter gives you the opportunity to assess your level of knowledge immediately after working through the *Study Guide* sections, and gives you a chance to determine how much material you have retained over time. The Sample Quizzes also help you assess your readiness level for taking the Unit Quizzes in class.

x

Contents

Each chapter in this *Guide* consists of Learning Objectives, Vocabulary and Details, Ideas and Concepts, two Sample Quizzes, and an Answer Key. Some chapters contain Important Names.

1

Nature of Psychology

Learning Objectives

1. Be able to name and define the five perspectives in psychology described in the text. Know what characterizes each and how each approach differs from the other four.

2. Be familiar with the historical roots of the biological, behavioral, and cognitive perspectives and the way in which contemporary versions of these approaches differ from earlier ones.

3. Understand some possible relations between psychological and biological perspectives and the related concept of reductionism.

4. Know what is meant by "generating hypotheses" and from where they are derived.

5. Know what distinguishes the experimental method from other methods of scientific observation. Be able to define, and to differentiate between, an independent variable and a dependent variable.

6. Know what is involved in the designing of an experiment. Be able to define, and to differentiate between, an experimental group and a control group.

7. Understand the use of measurement in experimental design, including the use of group means and tests of the significance of a difference between means.

8. Know when correlation is an alternative to experimentation and understand its advantages and disadvantages.

9. Know the meaning of differences in the size and the arithmetic sign of a coefficient of correlation. Be able to show, with an example, why correlation does not establish cause–and–effect relationships.

10. Be familiar with direct, survey, and case–history methods of observation. Understand when and why each is used and the advantages and disadvantages of each.

11. Be familiar with four interdisciplinary approaches within psychology.

Important Names

1. The view that behavior should be the sole subject matter of psychology was maintained in the early 1900s by the American psychologist _____. (12)

2. At about the same time, the European physician _____ was developing the psychoanalytic conception of human behavior that blended unconscious cognitive processes with biologically based instincts. (13)

Vocabulary and Details

SCOPE OF PSYCHOLOGY

1. Psychology can be defined as the _____. (8)

PERSPECTIVES IN PSYCHOLOGY

1. An inability to recognize familiar faces is termed _____. (8)

2. Some behavioral functions, like face recognition, are controlled or _____ in specific areas of the brain. (8)

3. A biased tendency to underestimate situational influences on behavior and to interpret acts as an expression of an individual's personality is referred to as the _____. (8)

4. The nineteenth–century "cognitive" perspective made use of data obtained through an individual's observation and recording of his or her own perceptions, thoughts, and feelings in the method called _____. (11)

5. The _____ perspective in psychology seeks to specify the _____ (electrical and chemical) processes that underlie behavior and mental processes. (11)

6. _____ are chemicals produced in the brain that make possible the communication between _____ (nerve cells). (11)

7. By contrast with the biological perspectives, the _____ approach in psychology studies the activities of an organism that can be directly _____. (12)

8. The position taken by the behavioral perspective, termed _____, gave rise to the study of eliciting stimuli, responses, and rewards and punishers for behavior; the offspring of this approach is called _____ psychology, or _____ for short. (12)

9. The _____ perspective in psychology is concerned with _____, such as perceiving, remembering, reasoning, decision making, and problem solving. (13)

10. In the _____ approach, the basic assumption is that much human behavior is caused or motivated by _____ processes, that is, by beliefs, fears, and desires of which a person is unaware. (13)

11. The _____ perspective focuses on subjective experience—the individual's personal view of events, that is, his or her _____. (14)

12. Some phenomenological theories are said to be _____ in the sense that they emphasize qualities that are unique to humans (as opposed to animals), including the drive toward _____. (14)

13. Reducing psychological concepts to biological ones is the kind of explanation called _____. (15)

METHODS OF PSYCHOLOGY

1. The first step in any research project is _____. (16)

2. The term "scientific," as used in the definition of psychology above, means that the research methods of psychology are _____—that is, they do not favor one hypothesis over another—and they are _____, in that they allow for repetition of observations and results. (17)

3. In the prototypical scientific method, called the _____ method, the researcher (a) carefully introduces _____ of variables (conditions), and (b) takes measurements to discover _____. (17)

4. A _____ is defined as something that can vary or occur with different values. (17)

5. The _____ is manipulated by the experimenter independently of what a subject does, whereas the _____ is a measure of the subject's behavior that is observed; we say that the latter is a _____ (dependent upon) the former. (18)

6. The term _____ refers to the procedure used in collecting data. (19)

7. An experimental design might consist of a single independent variable that is present for some subjects, in the _____, and absent for other subjects, in the _____. (19)

8. Alternatively, an experimental design may involve the manipulation of several independent variables at the same time; this type of experiment is termed _____. (19)

9. _____ means a procedure for assigning numbers to variables. (19)

10. The discipline that deals with sampling data from a population and drawing inferences about the population from the sample is called _____. (19)

11. The most common statistic is the _____, an arithmetic average of a set of values. (19-20)

12. To say that a statistical test has been applied to an observed difference and that difference is trustworthy is to also to say that the difference is _____. (20)

13. When the experimental method is not practical, the _____ may be applied to determine whether some variable that is not under experimental control is associated or _____ with another variable. (20)

14. The statistic that is used in the correlational method is the _____, symbolized by the letter _____, defined as an estimate of the degree to which two variables are related. (20)

15. A correlation coefficient is a number between _____ and _____. No relation is indicated by _____; as the value of r goes from 0 to 1, the strength of the relation _____ (increases/decreases); a perfect relation is indicated by a value of_____. (20)

16. In cases in which r is preceded by a + sign, the variables are said to be _____ (positively/negatively) related; in cases in which r is preceded by a - sign, the variables are _____ (positively/negatively) related. (21)

17. We may carefully record human or animal behavior as it occurs naturally in the observational method termed _____. (22)

18. In another (indirect) observational method, termed the _____, psychologists may use questionnaires or interviews. (23)

19. In yet a third type of observational method, indirect observations may be made of individuals, groups, or institutions by obtaining biographies, or _____, for scientific use. (23)

INTERDISCIPLINARY APPROACHES

1. A new biological movement in psychology, called _____, uses human subjects, focuses on cognitive processes, and relies heavily on the methods and findings of neuroscience (the branch of biology dealing with the nervous system). (24)

2. New techniques in this approach used for studying brains of normal subjects while engaged in a cognitive task are called _____ or _____. (24-25).

3. Another interdisciplinary area of psychology more concerned with the biological *origins* of cognitive and other psychological mechanisms is _____. (26)

4. The term _____ describes those areas of research in psychology that a) are concerned with _____, such as perceiving, remembering, and problem solving, and b) overlap with other disciplines that have interests in these processes. (28)

5. A branch of computer science that is concerned with developing computers that act intelligently and computer programs that simulate human thought processes is called _____. (28)

6. An interdisciplinary movement in the social sciences that is concerned with how the culture of the individual influences mental representations and psychological processes is _____. (29)

Ideas and Concepts

1. What are the two things you need to know to judge the truth of claims made in the name of psychology? (7)

SCOPE OF PSYCHOLOGY

* 1. For each of the representative problems in psychology in the table below, indicate a major experimental result or phenomenon and, if possible, its significance. Be sure you can define the related terms noted in italics. (8-9)

Problem	Results or Phenomena	Significance
Brain damage and face recognition		
Attributing traits to people		
Childhood amnesia		
Obesity and *anorexia*		
Expression of aggression		

PERSPECTIVES IN PSYCHOLOGY

* 1. List the five perspectives by which a topic in psychology can be described. Be able to apply three of them to a common example, such as crossing the street or reading a study guide. (10)

* 2. a) To what period of history and to what individuals can the roots of cognitive psychology be traced? With what did their questions deal? (Be able to give some examples.) (10)

*Basic ideas and concepts

*   b)   Outline some historical high points of the biological perspective in psychology citing an important figure. (10)

*   c)   When was scientific psychology born, and what was its fundamental idea? (10)

3.   a)   In what major respect did the nineteenth–century biological perspective differ from the modern one? (11)

    b)   On what did the nineteenth–century cognitive approach focus and how was data obtained? (11)

    c)   Was introspection an effective method? Explain. (11)

* 4.   a)   In principle, to what do all psychological events correspond? Give an example. (11)

    b)   For each of the following topics, indicate a main contribution of the biological perspective to its understanding. (11-12)

—face recognition:

—memory (use the term *hippocampus* in your answer):

—motivation and emotion:

5.   Apply the behavioral approach to each of the following sample problem areas. (12)

—obesity:

—aggression:

* 6.   a)   Discuss the role that mental processes play in the behavioral perspective. (12)

    b)   How many psychologists still profess to be "strict behaviorists"? (13)

* 7.   a)   In what respects was the development of the modern cognitive approach a reaction to behaviorism and S–R psychology? (13)

*   b)   How does the modern cognitive approach differ from its nineteenth–century version? Cite two assumptions of today's cognitive perspective. (13)

8.   a)   What is the special analogy that cognitive psychologists rely upon? Cite an example. (13)

    b)   Again, as you did with the other perspectives, apply the cognitive approach to the sample problems that follow. (13)

—fundamental attribution error:

—childhood amnesia:

6   Chapter 1

—aggression:

* 9. a) In Freud's psychoanalytic conception, what is the origin of impulses for human actions? What does society attempt to do with such impulses and what are the main results? (13)

* b) Did Freud view the causes of actions to be our rational reasons for what we do? Explain, citing man's two basic instincts, and indicate the view of human nature that this approach supports. (14)

c) Do most psychologists accept Freud's view of the unconscious? On what would they agree? (14)

d) Apply the psychoanalytic approach to these sample problem areas. (14)

—childhood amnesia:

—obesity:

—aggression:

* 10. a) In part, why did the phenomenological approach develop, and what aspects of other perspectives in psychology did it reject? (14)

* b) In what respects do the goals of phenomenologically–oriented psychologists differ from those of psychologists who represent other perspectives? (14)

* c) Using an example, explain what is meant by the "tendency toward growth and self–actualization" that provides a major motivational force in humanistic theories. (14-15)

11. a) Indicate the fields with which humanistic psychology is more closely aligned and what this fact means for the application of this perspective to the sample problems in this chapter (such as face recognition and childhood amnesia). (15)

* b) Discuss the pros and cons of the position of some humanistic psychologists that psychology should not be a science at all. (15)

12. a) When are the various perspectives in psychology compatible and when are they competitive? (15)

* b) In what sense is the biological perspective partly at a different level than other perspectives? (15)

* c) How does the biological perspective "make contact" with the more psychological perspectives? Cite an example and use the term *reductionism* in your answer. (15)

* 13. What is your authors' answer to the question, "Is psychology just something to do until the biologists get around to figuring everything out?" Give two reasons why or why not and be sure you understand the related examples in your text. (15-16)

14. Do your authors maintain that the interplay between psychological and biological explanations is one of "biology versus psychology"? Explain. (16)

METHODS OF PSYCHOLOGY

* 1. a) Indicate the two steps of research in psychology. (16)

   b) With respect to the first step, cite two general sources for research hypotheses. (17)

   c) What do your authors mean when they say that a scientific hypothesis goes beyond common sense? (17)

* 2. a) What distinguishes the experimental method from other methods of scientific observation? Give an example. (17-18)

   b) In this example, indicate the independent and dependent variables, respectively. (18)

* 3. Using the experiment in your text that investigated the effects of marijuana on memory as a prototype, can you design a study to investigate the relationship between amount of caffeine consumed while studying and later performance on a mid–term examination? What is the independent variable? What could serve as the dependent variable? What sorts of variables should be controlled? (18)

* 4. Why are most experiments conducted in laboratories? (19)

5. What kinds of general statements (in terms of X's and Y's) can be made when the effects of a single independent variable are observed in a controlled experimental design? Give some illustrations. (19)

6. a) What must be done when experiments make measurements on a sample of subjects rather than on just one subject? How is this accomplished? (19)

* b) Describe what happens when the difference between the means of two samples is large. What happens if it is small? Use the terms *significance of a difference* and *statistically significant* in your answer. (20)

* c) What does it mean when a statistical test indicates that a difference is significant? If a difference is not significant, then to what may it be due? (20)

* 7. Look at Figure 1–6 in your text describing data obtained from patients with prosopagnosia on a face recognition test and be able to answer the following questions. (20-22)

   a) Why are the data points in Figure 1–6a "scattered" to some degree rather than in a straight line? What is r for these data? In your authors' words, what does a correlation coefficient of this magnitude mean?

   b) What would it have meant if the data points had all fallen in a straight line? What would the value of r have been?

   c) What is the difference between the scatter diagrams in Figures 1–6a and 1–6b?

8   Chapter 1

d) What is *r* for the data in Figure 1–6c and what does it mean for these data?

8. In psychological research, what does it mean when the value of a correlation coefficient is: (22)

—.60 or higher?

—.20 to .60?

—0 to .20?

* 9. a) Indicate one common use of the correlation method. (22)

   b) What can be done with the variation in scores on two tests? Cite an example. (22)

* c) Why are tests important in psychology? (22)

* 10. When two variables are correlated (even highly), does this necessarily mean that there is a *cause–and–effect* relation between them? Explain using an example in your answer. (22)

* 11. a) When do we use the method of direct observation in psychology? (22)

   b) When making observations of natural behaviors, why must investigators be specially trained? (23)

   c) Are laboratories ever used when making direct observations? Cite the example from the Masters and Johnson laboratory and indicate the three types of data that were gathered in this instance. (23)

* 12. a) What specific kinds of observations have been made with survey methods? Which of these are probably the most familiar? (23)

* b) Why is this method more open to bias than direct observation? (23)

   c) Indicate a feature of an adequate survey. (23)

* 13. a) How are most case histories prepared and why is this method useful? Use the term *reconstructing the biography* in your answer. (23)

* b) Cite a risk in the use of retrospective methods of data gathering. (23)

* 1. a) What is the key idea of bringing together cognitive psychology and neuroscience? In your words, what is meant that this is a form of "reductionism"? (24)

* b) Cite an example of the application of neuroimaging techniques in the distinction between short– and long–term memory. (25)

2. a) List some of the major disciplines involved in evolutionary psychology. (26)

* b) Discuss the key idea underlying evolutionary psychology and give an example. (26–27)

c) Outline two ways in which an evolutionary perspective can impact on the study of psychological issues. Where it is helpful, cite examples. (27-28)

* 3. a) List three main objectives of the new field of cognitive science. (28)

b) Be able to recognize some of the disciplines that are relevant to cognitive science. (28)

* 4. a) Discuss the central idea of cognitive science, that various parallels exist between the human cognitive system and a computer engaged in complex calculations. Include the terms *mental computation* and *levels of analysis.* (28)

* b) What is meant by *connectionism* in cognitive science? Be sure you understand your authors' meaning that there are at least two levels of analysis in this approach. (28-29)

* 5. a) Using the approach of cultural psychology, discuss some differences between Eastern and Western cultures and how these impact on the phenomenon of the fundamental attribution error. (29)

b) Similarly, indicate some educational implications of East–West differences. (29)

* 6. It is important to be able to make distinctions among some major types of psychologists. Return to the *CRITICAL DISCUSSION, Specializations in Psychology*, on pp. 26-27. For each of the fields of psychology in the table on the following page be able to properly identify the types and activities of psychologists in the profession:

Field of Psychology	Psychologists: Types	Psychologists: Activities
Biological		
Experimental		
Developmental, social & personality		
Clinical & counseling		
School & educational		
Industrial & engineering		

Sample Quiz 1.1

1. The fundamental attribution error is: a) the tendency of phenomenological psychologists to underestimate the importance of the scientific method; b) a tendency of humans to underestimate the importance of the situation and overestimate the importance of personality in behavior; c) the statistical error committed when two groups are believed to be different despite a lack of statistical significance; d) Freud's mistaken attribution of human motivation to unconscious processes.

2. That particular regions of the brain are specialized for face recognition and that the hippocampus appears to be involved in human memory are examples in your text of: a) the idea that all psychological events correspond to activity of the brain and nervous system; b) the biological perspective; c) attempts to specify the neurobiological processes that underlie behavior; d) all of the above.

3. S-R psychology is to behavioral as _____ is to phenomenological: a) humanistic; b) neurobiological; c) unconscious processes; d) introspection.

4. Which of the following is *true* of a dependent variable? a) We say that it is a function of the independent variable. b) It is a measure of a subject's behavior. c) It is manipulated by the experimenter. d) Both a and b.

5. The term that best summarizes the reason why most experiments are done in laboratories is: a) economics; b) control; c) bureaucracy; d) status.

6. To say that a difference is statistically significant is to say that: a) an experiment was conducted with an experimental group and a control group; b) a statistical test has been applied to a difference and it is trustworthy; c) a correlation coefficient has been statistically derived and it has a value greater than .60; d) a graph has been drawn and the differences between two groups appear very large.

7. An estimate of the degree to which two variables are related is: a) the mean; b) r; c) a common result of the case history method; d) not often studied in psychology.

8. *In general*, tests are useful in psychology because they: a) help in screening people for employment; b) enable psychologists to obtain large amounts of data with minimal disturbance of their subjects; c) provide the basis for conducting experimental research; d) establish cause-and-effect relationships.

9. Evolutionary psychology is: a) an interdisciplinary area concerned with the origins of psychological mechanisms; b) a branch of computer science; c) an area that originally developed in Germany in the late 1800s; d) the field that currently employs the largest number of psychologists.

10. From a cultural perspective, relative to Westerners, people from Eastern cultures: a) are more likely to make the fundamental attribution error; b) are less likely to make the fundamental attribution error; c) are less likely to attribute behavior to social situations; d) both b and c.

Sample Quiz 1.2

1. Which of the following has *not* been a finding of psychological research? a) Virtually no one remembers events occurring prior to the age of three. b) Prior deprivation of food leads to later overeating when food is abundant. c) Aggression usually can be controlled by allowing individuals to express aggressive feelings either directly or vicariously. d) Under certain circumstances, the right half of the brain might not know what the left side of the body is doing.

2. The study of eliciting stimuli, responses, and rewards characterizes the _____ perspective in psychology: a) biological; b) behavioral; c) phenomenological; d) humanistic.

3. Your authors make the point that some fields of psychology are "at the same level," while one approach is not. Which of the following fields below are in the same category? a) behavioral, cognitive, phenomenological; b) biological, behavioral, psychoanalytic; c) behavioral, biological, phenomenological; d) biological, psychoanalytic, phenomenological.

4. The first step in any research project is: a) conducting an experiment; b) conducting statistical tests; c) measurement; d) generating hypotheses.

5. If all the points in a scatter diagram fall on a straight line, the correlation coefficient would be: a) around .50; b) low; c) 1.00; d) 0.

6. You repeatedly observe that the *greater* the amount of studying you do between midnight and 5 am the *lower* your grade on a test that morning. If that same relationship were true of many (but not all) students, it probably would be characterized by a correlation coefficient that would be: a) close to zero; b) very low; c) negative; d) equal to 1.00.

7. According to your text, of the various methods for conducting research in psychology, which one(s) are more open to bias or distortions on the part of subjects or researcher? a) case histories; b) direct observation; c) survey methods; d) both a and c.

8. A new technique used in the field of cognitive neuroscience is: a) the survey method; b) brain scanning; c) neuroimaging; d) both b and c.

9. The interdisciplinary approach that has as its key idea that natural selection plays a role in the origin of psychological mechanisms is: a) evolutionary psychology; b) cultural psychology; c) cognitive neuroscience; d) behavioral psychology.

10. How the culture of the individual influences psychological processes is the subject matter of the interdisciplinary field called: a) evolutionary psychology; b) societal psychology; c) cultural psychology; d) cognitive science.

Answer Key, Chapter 1

Important Names

1. John B. Watson
2. Sigmund Freud

Vocabulary and Details

SCOPE OF PSYCHOLOGY

1. scientific study of behavior and mental processes

PERSPECTIVES IN PSYCHOLOGY

1. prosopagnosia
2. localized
3. fundamental attribution error
4. introspection
5. biological; neurobiological
6. neurotransmitters; neurons
7. behavioral; observed
8. behaviorism; stimulus–response; S–R psychology
9. cognitive; mental processes
10. psychoanalytic; unconscious
11. phenomenological; phenomenology
12. humanistic; self–actualization
13. reductionism

METHODS OF PSYCHOLOGY

1. generating hypotheses
2. unbiased; reliable
3. experimental; control; relations among variables
4. variable
5. independent variable; dependent variable; function of
6. experimental design
7. experimental group; control group
8. multivariate
9. measurement
10. statistics
11. mean
12. statistically significant
13. correlational method; correlated
14. coefficient of correlation; r
15. -1; 1; 0; increases; 1
16. positively; negatively
17. direct observation
18. survey method
19. case histories

INTERDISCIPLINARY APPROACHES

1. cognitive neuroscience
2. neuroimaging; brain scanning
3. evolutionary psychology
4. cognitive science; cognitive processes
5. artificial intelligence
6. cultural psychology

Sample Quiz 1.1

1. a, 4
1. b, 8
2. d, 11
3. a, 14
4. d, 18
5. b, 19
6. b, 20
7. b, 20
8. b, 22
9. a, 26
10. b, 29

Sample Quiz 1.2

1. c, 8-9
2. b, 13
3. a, 15
4. d, 16
5. c, 20
6. c, 21
7. d, 23
8. d, 24
9. a, 26-27
10. c, 29

Neurobiological Basis of Psychology

Learning Objectives

1. Be able to identify the major components of a neuron. Know the functions of sensory neurons, motor neurons, and interneurons and the difference between neurons and nerves. Understand the nature of axon potentials.

2. Be able to identify the main features of a synapse and to describe synaptic transmission. Understand the role of neurotransmitters and the difference between excitatory and inhibitory synapses.

3. Be able to name and to diagram the relationships among the major components of the nervous system. Be able to explain the functioning of a spinal reflex.

4. Know what structures comprise each of the three concentric layers of the human brain. Be able to describe, in general, the functions of these structures.

5. Be able to define and describe the cerebral cortex. Be able to describe its major areas and know approximately where each is located.

6. Be familiar with the right/left differences typically found in humans. Know what functions usually are controlled by each of the two hemispheres.

7. Be able to describe, in general, the differing structures and functions of the two divisions of the autonomic nervous system.

8. Be familiar with the major endocrine glands and their hormones. Understand the interrelationships between the endocrine system and the autonomic nervous system.

9. Be able to define and differentiate between genes and chromosomes. Understand what is meant by dominant, recessive, and sex-linked genes. Be familiar with the several chromosomal-abnormality syndromes discussed in the text.

10. Understand the multiple contributions to human traits, including polygenic transmission and environmental interaction. Be familiar with the use of selective breeding and twin studies.

Important Names

1. The Nobel Prize winner who is known in part for his pioneering research on effects of the split–brain operation is _____. (55)

Vocabulary and Details

PROPERTIES OF NEURONS

1. The basic unit of the nervous system is a specialized cell called a _____. (37)

2. Neural impulses are received by the neuron on its _____ and on a number of short branches that project from the cell body called _____. (37)

3. Neural impulses are transmitted from the neuron to other neurons, muscles, or glands by way of a slender tube–like extension called an _____. (37)

4. At the end of the axon are fine collaterals that end in small swellings called _____ that _____ (do/do not) touch the neuron they will stimulate. (37)

5. This junction between two neurons is termed a _____; the gap between the synaptic terminal and the dendrites of the receiving neuron is called the _____. (37-38)

6. Transmission across the synaptic gap is made possible by a chemical called a _____ that is stimulated by arrival of a neural impulse at the synapse. (38)

7. A _____ is a group of specialized cells in the sense organs, muscles, skin, and joints that detects physical or chemical changes due to stimulation and translates these into neural impulses. (38)

8. In turn, these events are transmitted *to* the central nervous system (the brain or spinal cord) by the first of three types of neurons, termed the _____. (38)

9. *In* the central nervous system (plus in the eyes), the second type of neurons, the _____, receive signals from the sensory neurons and transmit them either to other interneurons or to neurons leading out. (39)

10. *From* the central nervous system, the third type of neurons, the _____, transmit outgoing signals to the _____, that is, the muscles and glands. (39)

11. A _____ is a bundle of elongated axons that may contain both sensory and motor neurons. (39)

12. Besides the neurons, another type of cells in the nervous system is referred to as the _____; these cells are specialized for "gluing" or holding the neurons in place and for other functions (rather than for reception or transmission of impulses). (39)

13. The electrochemical impulse that moves along a neuron from the dendrites to the axon is termed _____. (39)

14. Donut–shaped protein molecules that form pores across the cell membrane and selectively regulate the flow of electrically charged ions are called _____; separate protein structures, called _____, help to maintain an uneven distribution of ions across the cell membrane by pumping them into or out of the cell. (39)

15. When a neuron is stimulated, positively charged sodium ions, abbreviated _____, enter the cell in the process called _____, during which the inside of the cell membrane becomes _____ (more/less) positive than it was when at rest. (40)

16. The process of depolarization repeating itself successively along an axon's length gives rise to the _____. (40)

17. The _____ is a thin fatty sheath, in segments separated by gaps, that insulates the axons of most neurons; the sheath allows nerve impulses to jump from one gap to the next, thereby _____ (increasing/decreasing) the speed of axonal conduction. (40)

18. In accordance with the _____ of action, a neuron discharges at a constant level when stimulation from multiple synapses reaches a specific _____. (40)

19. When a nerve impulse travels down an axon, it stimulates small spherical or irregularly shaped structures in the synaptic terminal termed the _____ that, in turn, discharge neurotransmitters. (40)

20. One neurotransmitter that is normally excitatory is _____ (abbreviated _____), particularly prevalent in the portion of the brain important in _____, called the hippocampus, and also in neural transmission to the cells of skeletal muscles. (42)

21. Another neurotransmitter, _____, (abbreviated _____), produced mainly by neurons in the brain stem, causes _____ (stimulating/depressing) psychological and mood effects ("arousal"). (42-43)

22. A third neurotransmitter, _____, has a(n) _____ (inhibitory, stimulating) effect on muscle movement and also may be involved in the _____ (tranquilizing/ stimulating) effects of certain drugs used to treat anxiety. (43)

23. The most common excitatory neurotransmitter in the central nervous system is _____. (43)

24. In the brain structure, the hippocampus, one type of glutamate receptor called the _____ may play a role in the formation of new _____ . (43)

25. An influx of calcium ions into the membrane of a neuron due to action of the NMDA receptor may result in a long–term change, making the neuron _____ (more/less) responsive to a signal when it reoccurs; this phenomenon is termed _____. (44)

DIVISIONS OF THE NERVOUS SYSTEM

1. All of the neurons in the brain and spinal cord comprise the _____. (44)

2. The _____ consists of the nerves connecting the central nervous system to the other parts of the body. (44)

Neurobiological Basis of Psychology   17

3. The peripheral nervous system is in two divisions, one of which, the _____, transmits information to and from the muscles (as well as sensations from the skin and joints). (44)

4. The other part of the peripheral nervous system, the _____, that functions in internal regulation and emotion, consists of neurons running to and from the internal organs. (44-45)

5. Most of the nerve fibers connecting various parts of the body to the brain are gathered together to form the _____. (45)

CENTRAL CORE AND LIMBIC SYSTEM

1. The brain may be described as consisting of three concentric layers: the _____, that includes most of the brain stem, the _____, closely interconnected with the hypothalamus and having some control over both this structure and the brain stem, and the _____ (or _____). (45, 47)

2. The normal level of functioning characteristic of the healthy organism is called _____. (46)

THE CEREBRUM

1. The outer layer of the cerebrum termed the _____, or simply _____, is _____ (more/less) highly developed in humans than other animals. (50)

2. Specific areas of the cortex are involved in reception of information from the _____ systems and control of movements of the body, or _____ responses. The remaining largest areas, _____ areas, are concerned with memory, thought, and language. (50)

3. The primary anatomical division of the cerebrum is into two roughly symmetrical _____, referred to simply (in accordance with the side of the body) as the _____ and _____, separated by a deep longitudinal "fissure." (50)

ASYMMETRIES IN THE BRAIN

1. _____ is the area of the frontal lobe of the left hemisphere just above the lateral fissure that is important in the production of speech in most people. (53)

2. The broad band of nerve fibers connecting the two hemispheres that allows the immediate transmission of information between them is termed the _____. (53)

3. The procedure sometimes performed on epileptics that involves severing the corpus callosum, leaving the two hemispheres functionally separate, is termed the _____ operation. (54–55)

4. In some research with split–brain patients, investigators have taken advantage of the fact that when the eyes are fixated straight ahead, images to the left of the fixation point (the left visual field) go through both eyes to the _____ (right/left) hemisphere; whereas images in the right visual field, go to the _____ (right/left) hemisphere. (55)

AUTONOMIC NERVOUS SYSTEM

1. The portion of the peripheral nervous system that controls the _____ and _____ is called the *autonomic nervous system* because its activities are _____ or self-regulating. (58)

2. The autonomic nervous system is itself in two parts that are often antagonistic—the _____ division tends to activate the internal organs as a unit during times of _____; the _____ division tends to affect internal organs individually during times of _____. (58, 60)

ENDOCRINE SYSTEM

1. The _____ consists of a number of glands throughout the body that indirectly control cells by way of chemicals, called _____, that are secreted into the bloodstream. (60)

2. One endocrine gland, the _____, located below the hypothalamus in the brain, is sometimes called the "master gland" because it produces many different hormones that have a variety of functions and that influence other glands. (60)

3. One hormone produced by the pituitary gland is _____ (abbreviated _____), the body's main stress hormone. (60)

4. In turn, ACTH acts upon the _____, (located at the top of the kidneys), which play an important role in mood, arousal, and coping with stress. (60)

5. The adrenals secrete one hormone called _____ (also known as _____), and a second hormone called _____ (also known as _____), both of which are important in the activities of the sympathetic nervous system (and other glands) during times of emergency and stress. (60-61)

GENETIC INFLUENCES ON BEHAVIOR

1. The field of _____ combines the methods of genetics and psychology to study the inheritance of behavioral characteristics. (62)

2. Hereditary units are carried from parents to offspring by structures called _____ found in most body cells; at conception _____ (how many?) of these units are contributed each by the human mother and the father, for a total of _____, that are duplicated in the cells. (62)

3. Each chromosome is composed of hereditary units called _____ made up of a segment of _____ that actually carries the genetic information. (62)

4. A gene is said to be _____ when it determines the form of the trait it specifies in a gene pair with either a dominant or a recessive gene; a _____ gene determines the form of a trait only in a gene pair with another recessive gene. (63)

5. The disorder _____, a genetically caused deterioration of the nervous system accompanied by behavioral and cognitive problems, results from a _____ (dominant/recessive) gene transmitted from each parent. (63)

Neurobiological Basis of Psychology   19

6. The disorder _____ is caused by a single _____ (dominant/recessive) gene and involves deterioration of certain areas of the brain accompanied by a loss of memory and mental ability beginning around age 30 or 40. (63)

7. A person's sex is determined by the _____ pair of chromosomes distinguished by their appearance; the male pair contains the chromosomes represented by the symbol _____, while the female pair contains the chromosomes represented by the symbol _____. (64)

8. Because it is chromosome pair 23 that determines a number of genetic disorders owing to abnormal or recessive genes, such problems are called _____. (64)

9. To say that most human characteristics are determined by many genes is to say that they are _____. (64)

10. Two humans who develop from a single fertilized egg (or _____) are called _____, or said to be _____. (65)

11. Twins who develop from different egg cells are called _____, or said to be _____. (65).

Ideas and Concepts

PROPERTIES OF NEURONS

* 1. Be able to identify the parts of the neuron below using appropriate terms from the key to the related items in your *Vocabulary and Details* section. (See especially items 1–5). (37-38)

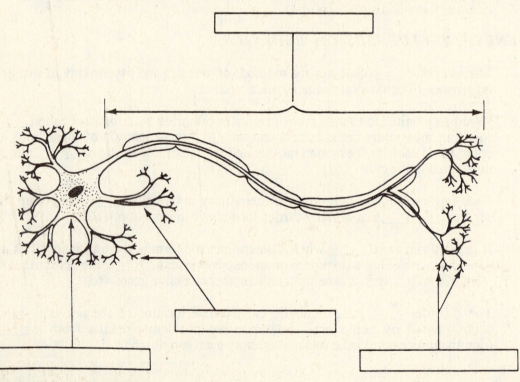

*Basic ideas and concepts

20   Chapter 2

2. a) Are all neurons alike in terms of size and shape? Explain. (38)

    b) Are there just a few neurons and glial cells? Give some estimates. (39)

    c) Discuss the functions of the glial cells. (39)

*   3. Describe in detail the mechanism of action potentials, discussing in particular the role of ion channels and pumps. (39-40)

*   4. Why does depolarization occur and what is the process by which the cell membrane returns to its resting state? (40)

*   5. a) What two factors determine the speed of the action potential? (40)

    b) What is the relationship between phylogenetic level and presence of the myelin sheath? (40)

    c) As one indication of its significance, what may result from degeneration of areas of the myelin sheath and what is this disease called? (40)

*   6. a) Why is the synaptic junction between neurons so important? (40)

*   b) Describe the all–or–none process of discharge of a neuron. (40)

*   c) In the usual case, when neurotransmitters are involved in neural transmission, how does the process work? Use the terms *synaptic vesicles, neurotransmitter* and *receptor molecules*, and *lock–and–key action* in your discussion. (40-41)

*   7. Must a neuron receive impulses from only one or a few synapses? What determines when the neuron will fire? (41)

*   8. a) Why must the effects of a neurotransmitter be very brief? (41)

*   b) Detail two ways in which this brevity is achieved; use the terms *reuptake* and *degradation* in your answer. (41)

    9. How many different neurotransmitters are known to date? Is a given neurotransmitter always excitatory or inhibitory? Explain. (41-42)

   10. a) What is Alzheimer's disease? Discuss the role of ACh in this disorder. (42)

    b) Describe the mechanism by which ACh may be involved in certain instances of muscle paralysis. (42)

* 11. In terms of effects on the neurotransmitter, NE, how do the drugs *cocaine* and *amphetamines* produce their stimulating effects? How does the drug *lithium* depress a person's mood level? (42-43)

* 12. With respect to the neurotransmitter *dopamine*, explain the symptoms of the disorders of schizophrenia and Parkinson's disease. (43)

13. a) Explain in detail how the NMDA receptor differs from others and how it might play a role in determining how memories are stored. Use the terms long–term potentiation and glutamate. (44)

b) In the terms you used in answering 13a), discuss a possible mechanism for how separate events may become associated in memory. (44)

DIVISIONS OF THE NERVOUS SYSTEM

* 1. Be able to fill in the blanks in the diagram below to show the overall organization of the nervous system. (44)

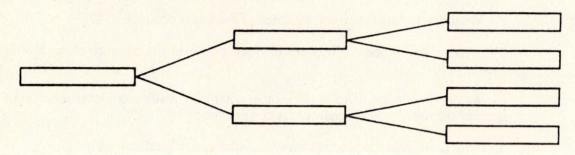

* 2. Discuss the functions of the somatic and autonomic nervous systems. (44-45)

* 3. a) Describe the sequence of events in the knee jerk reflex and its function. (45)

b) Is the brain necessary in this sequence or is the spinal cord sufficient? Explain what role the brain may serve. (45)

CENTRAL CORE AND LIMBIC SYSTEM

* 1. For each of the structures of the central core, indicate major functions in the table below. (45-47)

Structure	Functions
brain stem and medulla	
cerebellum	
thalamus	
hypothalamus	(Include the term homeostasis)
reticular formation	

*   2. In the diagram below, identify the location of each of the brain structures listed in the preceding table. (See also Figures 2-8 and 2-9 in your text.) (46)

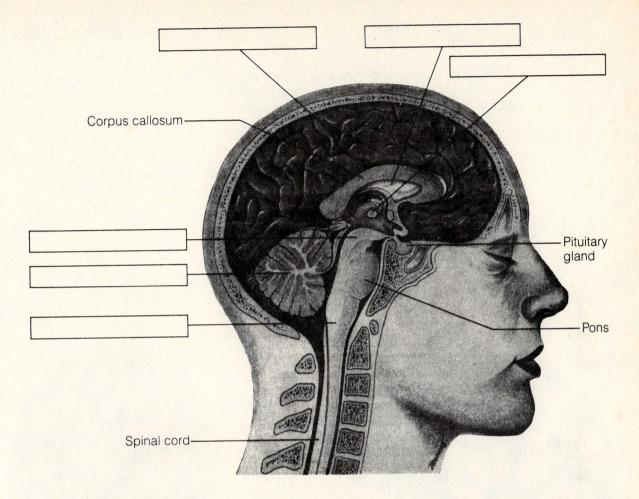

Corpus callosum

Pituitary gland

Pons

Spinal cord

3. What happens to the major nerve tracts that come up through the brain stem when they reach the medulla? (45-46)

4. a) Indicate the role played by the hypothalamus during stress with respect to homeostasis. (47)

    b) What two things may happen when the hypothalamus is given electrical stimulation? (47)

*   c) How does the hypothalamus exert control over the endocrine system and when is this control particularly important? Therefore, what has the hypothalamus been called? (47)

5. a) Indicate the effects of electrical stimulation in the region of the reticular formation. (47)

    b) In what way may the reticular formation act as an attentional filter? (47)

*   6. a) Discuss the different roles served by the limbic system in instinctive behaviors in lower animals and mammals. (47)

Neurobiological Basis of Psychology   23

b) Indicate the part of the limbic system that has a role to play in memory. What happens at the time of injury or removal of this structure? What happens during recovery? Cite examples. (47)

c) Discuss some of the evidence that suggests the importance of the limbic system in emotional behavior. (47)

* 7. Do the three "concentric" brain structures operate independently of one another? Discuss in detail the "interrelated computers" metaphor used by your authors to describe the functions of these structures. (47, 50)

THE CEREBRUM

* 1. If you have not already, be sure to label the cerebral cortex in the figure in item 2 on the preceding page. In addition, be sure that you can identify the parts of the cerebrum shown in the figures below. (51, also Figure 2-10.)

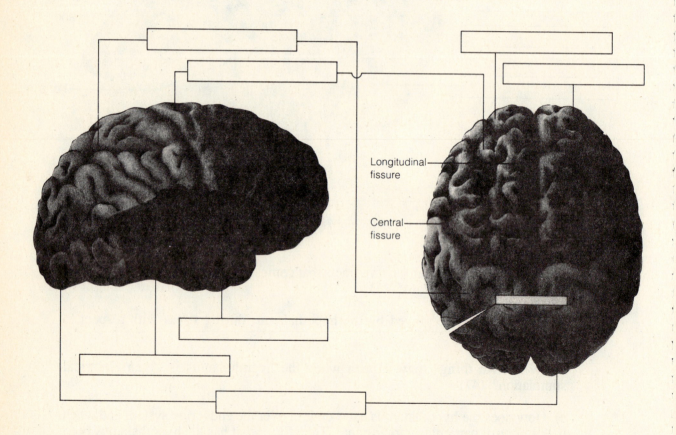

Longitudinal fissure

Central fissure

24   Chapter 2

* 3. In the table below, for each of the cortical areas, be able to indicate its location and functions. (50-53)

Cortical area	Location (in your words)	Functions
primary motor area		
primary somato-sensory area		
primary visual area		
primary auditory area		
frontal and *posterior association areas*		

4. a) What happens to motor responses when a point on the motor area is electrically stimulated? When it is injured? (50)

* b) How is the body represented in the motor cortex? How is it represented in the two hemispheres? (50)

* 5. a) How are sensory impulses represented in the two hemispheres of the cortex? (50)

* b) In general, what is the relationship between the sensitivity and use of a body part and its amount of representation in the cortex? Give some examples. (50, 52)

* 6. a) Discuss the relationship between the eyes and where the optic nerves go in the two hemispheres. Use the term *optic chiasma* in your response. (52-53)

b) What does this relationship mean with respect to the effects of damage to the hemispheres and how might this relationship be helpful? (53)

7. Discuss the effects of cerebral lesions in each of the following cases. (53)

—frontal association area in monkeys:

—posterior association area in humans:

ASYMMETRIES IN THE BRAIN

1. Are the two hemispheres of the brain perfectly symmetrical? What are some of the structural differences? (53)

* 2. a) What was Paul Broca's important discovery regarding the frontal lobe? What happens if the corresponding area in the other hemisphere is damaged? (53)

* b) Besides speaking, what other language functions usually are located in the left hemisphere? How does this relate to the effects of strokes? (53)

c) What is the relationship between handedness and the location of the speech center? (53)

* 3. a) Why does the brain normally function as an integrated whole despite its two hemispheres? When may this become a problem? (53)

* b) Therefore, what procedure may alleviate generalized seizures in some epileptics and what other aftereffects may be expected? (53-54)

4. a) Describe three of Sperry's procedures for investigating sensory and speech effects in split–brain subjects outlined in your text and in Figure 2-14. (55-57)

* b) Discuss the results obtained in each of the types of studies outlined in 4a). (55-57)

c) Why is it important when presenting visual material that it be flashed for only one–tenth of a second? What does this imply with respect to the usual effects of the split–brain operation? (In these terms, what do you think would happen if auditory material is presented?) (55-56)

* 5. a) For each of the following functions, indicate whether the left or right hemisphere appears to be dominant. Be able to illustrate with examples where possible. (58)

—expression in language:

—logical and analytical activities:

—mathematical computations:

—comprehension of abstract linguistic forms:

—spatial and pattern comprehension:

26   Chapter 2

*   b) From the distinctions in item 5a), which hemisphere should be able to identify verbal information more quickly and accurately? Which hemisphere should be able to recognize faces, expressions of emotions, and characteristics of lines or dots more readily? Cite the related experimental evidence. (58)

*   6. Should one infer from the evidence regarding the functions of the two hemispheres that they work independently of one another? Explain. (58)

AUTONOMIC NERVOUS SYSTEM

1. How does the physiologist distinguish in appearance and function between the muscles controlled by the autonomic system from those controlled by the somatic system? (58)

*   2. a) From Figure 2-15, be able to identify some of the antagonistic actions of the two portions of the autonomic nervous system. (Can you see the role the neural *ganglia* may play in the unitary action of the sympathetic division?) (59)

    b) What is the "normal" state of the body and how is this state maintained? (60)

*   3. Are the sympathetic and parasympathetic systems always antagonistic to one another? Cite two examples to support your answer. (60)

ENDOCRINE SYSTEM

1. a) How does the speed of the endocrine system compare with that of the nervous system? (60)

    b) Describe the mechanism by which target cells react to their respective hormones. (60)

    c) Indicate two mechanisms for the activation of the endocrine glands. (60)

*   2. List several functions of the pituitary gland. (60)

*   3. a) Describe the sequence of events that takes place between the hypothalamus and the pituitary gland in response to stress. Use the term *corticotropin–release factor (CRF)* in your answer. (60)

    b) What indicates that the endocrine system is under the control of the hypothalamus and other brain centers? (60)

*   4. List some of the specific effects of each of the following hormones. (60-61)

    —epinephrine:

    —norepinephrine:

*   5. a) In what way are hormones and neurotransmitters similar? Cite an example. (61)

*   b) In what way do hormones and neurotransmitters differ? (61)

* 1. a) What does the DNA molecule look like and what holds its two strands apart? (62)

*   b) How is the "genetic code" determined and, in terms of the chemical composition of the molecule, what gives DNA the ability to express many different genetic messages? (62)

   2. a) If all cells carry the same genes, how is it that different cells perform different functions? Give an example. (62)

*   b) Where do the two genes in each pair originate from? Then, why is it so unlikely that two human beings have the same heredity, even if they have the same parents? (62)

        c) Indicate one exception to your answer to 2b). (62)

   3. a) Explain the mechanism of gene dominance and recessiveness as it applies to eye color. (63)

*   b) Do all gene pairs follow the dominant–recessive pattern? What is the usual basis for human characteristics? (63)

   4. a) What is the actual cause of damage in the disease PKU? (63)

        b) How is this disorder now alleviated by making use of genetic information? (63)

   5. How is Huntington's disease now diagnosed and what eventually will provide the mechanism for treating this genetic disorder? (63–64)

* 6. Whose chromosome, the mother's or the father's, determines their child's sex? Explain. (64)

* 7. Why is it that the male X chromosome often is responsible for expression of recessive characteristics? Give an example of one such sex–linked disorder. (64)

   8. Illustrate with an example the polygenic aspect of most human traits. (64)

* 9. a) Describe the method of selective breeding as it has been used to study the inheritance of learning ability in rats. (65)

*   b) From Figure 2-20, describe the results of this procedure. (65)

        c) List some other examples of selective breeding. (65)

        d) When should a trait be modifiable through selective breeding and what can we conclude if it is not? (65)

* 10. a) Since selective breeding cannot ethically be carried out with humans, what alternative method is used to study the heritability of traits? (65)

        b) What difficulty is encountered in this method? Give some examples. (65)

28   Chapter 2

c) In order to overcome this problem, to what do psychologists turn? (65)

* d) To demonstrate the importance of heredity, cite some characteristics on which identical twins are more similar than fraternal twins. (65)

11. Discuss the role of the environment in influencing gene action in both of the following cases. (66)

—diabetes:

—schizophrenia:

Answer Key, Chapter 2

Important Names

1. Roger Sperry

Vocabulary and Details

PROPERTIES OF NEURONS

1. neuron
2. cell body; dendrites
3. axon
4. synaptic terminals; do not
5. synapse; synaptic gap
6. neurotransmitter
7. receptor
8. sensory neurons
9. interneurons
10. motor neurons; effector organs
11. nerve
12. glial cells
13. action potential
14. ion channels; ion pumps
15. Na+; depolarization; more
16. neural impulse
17. myelin sheath; increasing
18. all–or–none principle; threshold level
19. synaptic vesicles
20. acetylcholine (ACh); memory
21. norepinephrine (NE); stimulating
22. gamma–aminobutyric acid (or GABA); inhibitory; tranquilizing
23. glutamate
24. N–methyl D–aspartate (NMDA) receptor; memories
25. more; long–term potentiation (LTP)

DIVISIONS OF THE NERVOUS SYSTEM

1. central nervous system
2. peripheral nervous system
3. somatic system
4. autonomic system
5. spinal cord

CENTRAL CORE AND LIMBIC SYSTEM

1. central core; limbic system; cerebral hemispheres (cerebrum)
2. homeostasis

THE CEREBRUM

1. cerebral cortex; cortex; more
2. sensory; motor; association

3. cerebral hemispheres; left hemisphere; right hemisphere

ASYMMETRIES IN THE BRAIN

1. Broca's area
2. corpus callosum
3. split–brain
4. right; left

AUTONOMIC NERVOUS SYSTEM

1. glands; smooth muscles; autonomous
2. sympathetic; excitement; parasympathetic; quiescence

ENDOCRINE SYSTEM

1. endocrine system; hormones
2. pituitary gland
3. adrenocorticotrophic hormone (ACTH)
4. adrenal glands
5. epinephrine (adrenaline); norepinephrine (noradrenaline)

GENETIC INFLUENCES ON BEHAVIOR

1. behavior genetics
2. chromosomes; 23; 46
3. genes; deoxyribonucleic acid (or DNA)
4. dominant; recessive
5. phenylketonuria (or PKU); recessive
6. Huntington's disease (or HD); dominant
7. 23rd; XY; XX
8. sex–linked disorders
9. polygenic
10. (zygote); identical twins; monozygotic
11. fraternal twins; dizygotic

Sample Quiz 2.1   Sample Quiz 2.2

Sample Quiz 2.1	Sample Quiz 2.2
1. b, 39	1. b, 39
2. c, 40-41	2. a, 41
3. b, 42	3. d, 43
4. d, 44-45	4. a, 46
5. b, 60	5. d, 50
6. c, 55	6. a, 56
7. c, 58	7. a, 61
8. d, 60	8. b, 62
9. c, 62	9. c, 64
10. c, 63	10. b, 65

3

Psychological Development

Learning Objectives

1. Understand how heredity and environment interact to determine human development. Be able to define the concept of maturation and show how it relates to this interaction, using motor development as an example.

2. Be familiar with what psychologists mean by developmental stages and by the related concept of critical periods.

3. Be able to describe the capacities of the newborn and the procedures used to assess these capacities.

4. Know the sequence of Piaget's stages of cognitive development and the major events that characterize each stage. Be familiar with some difficulties with Piaget's theory and with alternative views, including Kohlberg's work on moral reasoning.

5. Be familiar with characteristics of personality development and early social behavior, including the research on attachment in animals and a model for categorizing types of attachment in human babies.

6. Understand what is meant by gender identity and sex typing and be able to describe some of the influences that create and maintain sex–typed behavior in terms of four alternative theories.

7. Be familiar with Erikson's psychosocial stages and how they relate to the problems faced by people at different times in their lives.

8. Be able to describe the biological developments that characterize adolescence and the psychological changes that accompany these developments, including the research on early and late maturers. Be familiar with the data concerning the sexual behavior of adolescents.

9. Understand the problems and confusion involved in adolescent–family relation–ships and the adolescent's search for personal identity.

10. Be familiar with some of the problems of early and middle adulthood and the aging years in relation to Erikson's psychosocial stages.

Important Names

1. The question of whether nature or nurture determines human development was answered by the seventeenth–century British philosopher _____, who maintained that the mind of an infant is a "blank slate," or *tabula rasa,* in the sense that its contents are determined entirely by the baby's sensory experiences. (70)

2. Another important figure in the historical background of developmental psychology was _____, whose nineteenth–century theory of evolution, by contrast with John Locke's view, emphasized the biological bases of human development, or heredity. (70)

3. A third important historical period for developmental psychology began in the twentieth century, during which behavioral psychologists such as _____ and _____ maintained an *environmentalist* position, asserting that human nature is influenced completely by early training and continuing interactions with the environment. (70)

4. The Swiss psychologist _____ is noted in part for his studies and his theory of cognitive development in children. (78)

5. From original efforts by Piaget, work on the development of moral reasoning was extended to adolescents and adults by the American psychologist _____. (83)

6. Most of the work on attachment in human infants originated in the 1950s and 1960s with the psychoanalyst _____. (92)

7. The first comprehensive account of gender identity and sex typing was in a theory of psychosexual development by the psychoanalyst _____. (96)

8. The notion that development throughout life could be characterized in a series of eight psychosocial stages was proposed by _____. (104)

Vocabulary and Details

1. In the field of _____, psychologists are concerned with how and why different aspects of human functioning develop and change across the life span. (70)

2. One of the most basic issues in developmental psychology is whether _____ (_____) or _____ (_____) is more important in determining the course of human development. (70)

3. The other basic question that underlies theories of human development is whether development is a _____ process of change or a series of qualitatively distinct _____. (70)

INTERACTION BETWEEN NATURE AND NURTURE

1. Genetic determinants of development are expressed through _____, innately determined sequences of growth or bodily change that are relatively independent of the environment. (71)

STAGES OF DEVELOPMENT

1. As used by psychologists, the concept of *developmental stages* implies that (a) behaviors at a given stage are organized around a _____, (b) behaviors at one stage are _____ from behaviors in earlier or later stages, and (c) all children go through the same stages _____. (72)

2. Closely related, crucial time periods in a person's life during which specific events must occur for physical development to proceed normally are called _____. (72)

3. With respect to psychological development, it is probably more accurate to speak of _____ periods that are optimal for a behavior to develop if it is to reach its full potential. (72)

COGNITIVE DEVELOPMENT IN CHILDHOOD

1. In Piaget's view, children conduct miniature experiments on the world and form theories or _____ (singular, _____) regarding how the physical and social worlds operate. (78)

2. The child's attempt to understand new objects or events in the world in terms of pre–existing schema is the process of _____. Alternatively, if new events do not fit the existing schema, the child will modify and thereby extend the theory in the process called _____. (78)

3. Piaget designated the first _____ years of life as the _____. (78)

4. During the sensorimotor stage, Piaget maintained that children develop the concept of _____, an awareness that an object continues to exist even when it is not present, a phenomenon that suggests that the child possesses a _____ of the missing object. (79)

5. The next period of development, between the ages of _____ and _____, Piaget calls the _____ because the child can think in symbolic terms but does not yet comprehend certain rules. (80)

6. These rules or _____ are mental routines for transforming information. (80)

7. As children approach the end of the preoperational stage, they may begin to develop an understanding of the principle of _____, that the total amount or weight of a substance does not change when the shape or number of parts of the substance is altered. (80)

8. Piaget held the position that in the second stage of development of moral judgments, children confuse moral with physical laws—in the sense that moral laws are seen to be predetermined and permanent—a view of morality termed _____. (81)

9. In Piaget's stage termed the _____, between the ages of _____ and _____, children use abstract terms and operations, but only in relation to objects to which they have direct sensory access (concrete objects). (82)

10. In Piaget's fourth stage, the _____, beginning around age _____, youngsters are able to reason in purely _____ terms, that is, without direct reference to concrete objects. (82)

PERSONALITY AND SOCIAL DEVELOPMENT

1. Mood–related personality characteristics are called _____. (88)

2. One example of a temperament is an infant's wariness or distress at the approach of a stranger, termed _____. (90)

3. _____ is an infant's tendency to seek closeness to particular people and to feel more secure in their presence. (91)

4. A laboratory procedure for assessing attachment consisting of a series of episodes in which a child is observed as the primary caregiver leaves and returns to the room is called the _____. (92)

5. The acquisition of a clear sense of oneself as either male or female is the acquisition of _____. (95)

6. The acquisition of behaviors that the culture considers sex–appropriate is called _____. (95)

7. _____ refers to the understanding that a person's sex remains the same despite changes in age and appearance. (99)

8. The notion that children are encouraged to view everything as somehow gender related—that is, to look at the world through "lenses" of gender—is the learning of a _____. (102)

DEVELOPMENT AFTER CHILDHOOD

1. Erikson called his eight stages of development _____ because he believed that psychological development depends upon the social relations a person forms at different points in life. (104)

2. The period of transition from childhood to adulthood is called _____. (104)

3. The period of sexual maturation that transforms a child into a biological adult, capable of sexual reproduction, is termed _____ and lasts three or four years. (105)

4. This period begins with a time of very rapid physical growth, called the _____, which is accompanied by the gradual development of the reproductive organs and the appearance of _____, such as breast development in girls, beard development in boys, and pubic hair in both sexes. (105)

5. A girl's first menstrual period is termed _____ and occurs relatively _____ (early/late) in puberty. (105)

6. The active process of self–definition during adolescence was called _____ by Erikson. (106)

7. The term _____ was used by Erikson to describe the concern that people in middle age have for guiding and providing for the next generation. (119)

Ideas and Concepts

1. Discuss the relationship between an organism's level on the phylogenetic scale and the time required for the development of maturity. (70)

* 2. Be able to distinguish by way of example between *physical, cognitive,* and *personality and social development.* (70)

INTERACTION BETWEEN NATURE AND NURTURE

* 1. Today, what is the view of most psychologists on the nature–nurture issue in human development and how does this contrast with earlier views? (70)

2. a) Discuss the role of maturation in fetal development, citing examples. What kinds of factors may disrupt the regularity of development before birth? (70-71)

* b) Describe the role of maturation in one developmental process after birth. Do all children go through the stages in the same order? At the same rate? To what question did the differences lead? (71)

3. a) Describe a recent study that supports the conclusion that learning and experience *do* affect the rate at which children move through developmental sequences in the area of motor development. (71)

b) Similarly, be familiar with an example in the area of speech development that further demonstrates the interaction between nature and nurture. (71)

STAGES OF DEVELOPMENT

1. Indicate some of the ways the concept of stages of development is used. (72)

* 2. What are the two positions on the usefulness of stage theories and at least two reasons why some psychologists take a negative stance on this issue? (72)

3. a) Cite two examples of critical periods in human development. (72)

* b) What is the current status of the existence of critical periods? Use an example. (72)

CAPACITIES OF THE NEWBORN

* 1. a) What do we know about the functioning of infant sensory systems? (72-73)

b) Why are ingenious procedures necessary for the study of infants? Indicate the basic method used to study infant sensory capacities. Cite an example and a variation on this method. (73)

*Basic ideas and concepts

* 2. For each of the following sensory processes, indicate typical responses of newborn infants. (73-74)

   —Vision:

   —Hearing:

   —Taste and smell:

  3. a) Are newborns near–sighted or far–sighted? When can they see about as well as adults? (73)

*   b) To what characteristic of objects are infants particularly attracted? What kinds of patterns do newborns prefer in the sense that they look longer at them? (73)

*   c) Do newborns have a preference for looking at human faces because they are human? Explain and indicate what part of the face is generally attended to. (73)

* 4. a) Can infants distinguish the sound of the human voice from other sounds? (74)

*   b) What capacities do infants have that adults do not with respect to speech sounds? Therefore, what may be concluded with regard to the perceptual mechanisms of hearing in human infants? (74)

* 5. a) What was once thought regarding whether infants could learn or remember? Describe an experiment to show that infants can learn to discriminate between auditory stimuli. (74)

     b) Cite a demonstration that infants as young as three months have very good memories. (74-75)

* 6. a) Discuss some of the evidence showing that basic sound preferences develop through learning even during pre–birth experiences in the uterus. (75)

     b) Outline a dramatic experiment showing preferences of newborns for familiar story material. (76-77)

* 7. From this kind of research, what is your authors' conclusion with regard to John Locke's notion that the infant's mind is a "blank slate"? (77)

COGNITIVE DEVELOPMENT IN CHILDHOOD

* 1. a) In what respects did Piaget's focus differ from the prior two dominant trends in theories of cognitive development? How did Piaget view the child in this process? (78)

*   b) In what other respect did Piaget differ from other early psychologists in this field? Specifically, what methodology did he use? (78)

     c) Discuss the lasting impact of Piaget's approach on aspects of theory and methodology of contemporary developmental psychologists. (78)

38   Chapter 3

*   2. Be able to recognize the characteristics of Piaget's sensorimotor, preoperational, concrete operational, and formal operational stages, as outlined in Table 3-1. (79)

    3. a) What are infants discovering during the sensorimotor stage? What is the outcome of their "experiments" with the environment? Give an example. (78-79)

        b) To illustrate the concept of object permanence, indicate how a child early in this stage reacts differently to a cloth covering a toy than a child late in this stage. (79)

    4. a) Can you cite an example other than that in your text to be sure that you understand the way in which conservation principles operate? (80)

        b) Conversely, describe a situation in which there is a lack of conservation in the behavior of a child. (80)

*   c) In Piaget's view, what are two reasons why the majority of children younger than about seven years of age have such difficulties in the preoperational stage? Cite an example. (80-81)

*   5. a) Why did Piaget develop an interest in the development of morality in children and what unusual basis did he use for his theory? (81)

*   b) For each of the two preoperational stages of moral development, indicate the major features of the child's behavior and "rules" of conduct. Cite examples and use the term *moral realism* in your answer. (81)

        c) Be sure you know what is meant in the characterization of the second stage of moral development that "children judge an act more by its consequences than by the intentions behind it." (82)

    6. a) Describe some of the specific things that children between about seven and twelve years of age (in the concrete operational stage) can do and relate these activities to what can be accomplished in the previous stage. (82)

*   b) What stage of moral understanding begins about this time and what are some of the specific characteristics of this period of moral development? (82)

        c) Give an example of what a youngster in the formal operational stage is able to do when presented with a problem by contrast with a child in the concrete operational stage. What, then, is the essence of formal operational thought? (82-83)

*   d) Indicate the characteristics of Piaget's fourth and final stage of moral development, which emerges during the formal operational period. (83)

    7. a) Describe Kohlberg's technique for studying the development of moral reasoning. What was Kohlberg attempting to determine with these methods? (83)

*   b) In the table below, indicate the basis for resolving moral dilemmas for each level of moral development and suggest a possible explanation that might be offered for why it is wrong to cheat on a classroom examination that would be characteristic of each level. (83)

Level	Basis for Judgment	Sample Explanation
Preconventional Morality (Level I)		
Conventional Morality (Level II)		
Postconventional Morality (Level III)		

c) Cite three bases on which Kohlberg's theory has been criticized, including two that stem from evidence. (83-84)

* 8. a) Cite several positive contributions of Piaget's theory and one of its major difficulties. (84)

b) As one example of the latter, what possibility did Piaget overlook when maintaining that children under about eight months fail to demonstrate object permanence? (84)

* c) Outline an ingenious set of experiments by which it was shown that object permanence appears in very young infants, provided that they do not have to perform an *activity* that is too advanced for their motor abilities. (84-85)

* 9. a) Turning to an evaluation of the notion of conservation, what specific manipulation will result in a demonstration of number conservation in children much younger than Piaget presumed capable? (85)

b) Describe a related experiment showing a remarkable degree of number conservation in five–year–old children. (85)

10. Discuss a few of the results of a study of "preoperational" children to show that their level of moral judgment may be somewhat more advanced in at least two respects than Piaget's theory suggested. (85-86)

* 11. For each of the following alternatives to Piaget's theory, indicate the fundamental tenets of the position and the main point(s) of difference between the approach and Piaget's. (86-88)

—information–processing approaches:

—knowledge–acquisition approaches:

—sociocultural approaches:

40   Chapter 3

PERSONALITY AND SOCIAL DEVELOPMENT

1. a) Give some instances of temperament differences among infants. (88)

   * b) What has been the traditional view of the origin of temperament differences and how has research altered this view to some extent? Cite some examples. (89)

2. a) Discuss a pioneering study that provided mixed results on the continuity of temperament. (89)

   b) What conclusion did these researchers come to regarding continuity and discontinuity of temperament? Cite an example and use the terms *genotype* and *goodness of fit* in your answer. (89)

   * 3. a) Describe the early mutually reinforcing social interactions between parents and their children. (89-90)

   b) Cite evidence to indicate that infant smiling is maturational and innate. (90)

   c) How do three– and four–month–old infants demonstrate recognition and preference for familiar people, and what begins to happen around seven or eight months? (90)

   * 4. a) Describe the time course and pattern of reactions in infant "stranger anxiety" and distress over separation from parents, noting also when these behaviors decline. (90)

   * b) What evidence suggests that conditions of child rearing have little effect on these behaviors? (90)

   * c) Explain in detail two factors important in the onset and decline of stranger anxiety and separation distress. Use the term object permanence in your answer. (90-91)

5. a) Cite some examples of attachment. What adaptive value does attachment have? (91)

   b) Indicate both the first view that psychologists held regarding the source of attachment and a conflicting piece of evidence. (91)

   * 6. a) Describe the basic procedures of the classic Harlow experiments on attachment in monkeys. What was the question being asked in the study cited by your authors? (91)

   * b) Indicate the clear–cut results of this research. What is the most important attribute of the mother? (91)

7. Is attachment to an artificial mother and contact comfort sufficient for early social development in infant monkeys? Explain, citing typical responses. (91-92)

   * 8. What was Bowlby's hypothesis regarding the failure to form secure attachments in human infants? (92)

9. a) Be familiar with the episodes in Ainsworth et al.'s Strange Situation and the measures recorded. How are babies categorized in this procedure? (92-93)

   * b) By completing the following table, characterize each of the following types of babies and its primary caregiver that were distinguishable in the Strange Situation, including the fourth category that was added to Ainsworth's types. (93)

Types of Babies	Behaviors of Babies	Behaviors of Primary Caregiver
Securely attached		
Insecurely attached: Avoidant		
Insecurely attached: Ambivalent		
Disorganized		(Not applicable)

* 10. a) What is the main finding regarding the primary caretaker in the development of a baby's secure attachment? (93)

   b) Do all developmental psychologists agree that a caregiver's responsiveness is the major cause of infant attachment behaviors? What is an alternative possibility? (94)

   c) Cite evidence on both sides of the debate outlined in b, including that which may give a resolution. (94)

* 11. How stable are results obtained in the Strange Situation procedure and what may influence them? (94)

12. a) Cite a study that showed a relationship between the pattern of early attachment and later coping with new experiences. (94-95)

   b) Similarly, indicate the results of a study on social behavior in children as a function of early attachment styles. (95)

   * c) What conclusions may be drawn from these studies? However, what may be an additional *ongoing* variable to consider? (95)

* 13. Are gender identity and sex typing the same thing? Explain by citing an example. (95)

* 14. Contrast the following approaches by indicating the major theoretical variables used to account for gender identity and sex typing. (If a given approach deem-

42   Chapter 3

phasizes one of these concepts, so indicate.) Also be able to cite your authors' criticisms of each approach. (96-103)

Theory	Explanation	Critique
Psychoanalytic (Psychosexual Stages)	Use the terms *phallic stage, Oedipal conflict,* and *identification*	(96)
Social Learning		(98)
Cognitive–Developmental		(99)
Gender Schema		Not applicable

15. a) Indicate two broad points about social learning theory by contrast with the psychoanalytic view. (96)

* b) Discuss some of the evidence that has been generated by the social learning approach with regard to each of the following: (96-98)

—differential reward and punishment of sex–appropriate and –inappropriate behaviors:

—stereotyped expectations of sex on the part of mothers and fathers (noting differences):

—sex stereotyping on the part of other children and different strengths of taboos:

—the role of books and television programs and attempts to reverse sex typing:

* 16. a) Cite some data on gender constancy obtained by Kohlberg. Therefore, from the perspective of the cognitive–developmental approach, why do preoperational children seem to be particularly sexist and intolerant of gender nonconformity, as well as resistant to nonsexist childrearing? (99)

b) By contrast, cite a study to show limitations on the notion of conservation with respect to gender constancy. (99)

c) Discuss in detail the methods and results of a study that supports the knowledge acquisition approach to cognitive development in general and the notion of conservation (in the form of gender constancy) in particular. (99-102)

Psychological Development   43

17. a) Cite some examples of the teaching of gender schema. (102-103)

*   b) How does gender schema theory address the question: "Why should children organize their self–concepts around their maleness or femaleness?" (103)

DEVELOPMENT AFTER CHILDHOOD

1. In what ways is development to be viewed as a continuous process? (104)

*   2. a) What was Erikson's belief regarding passage from one psychosocial stage to the next? (104)

b) Look at Table 3-3. Be able to recognize the psychosocial crises associated with Erikson's eight stages of psychosocial development and the favorable outcome associated with successful negotiation of each stage. (104)

*   3. List two major tasks accomplished during adolescence. (104)

4. a) Are boys and girls immediately able to reproduce with the onset of puberty? Illustrate your answer by describing the menstrual cycles and ejaculations of young adolescents. (105)

b) Cite some statistics to illustrate the variation in duration and age of onset of puberty. In general, which sex enters puberty first and by how many years? (105)

5. Describe the general findings of studies examining psychological effects of puberty, noting in particular the nature of the experience for each sex on the dimensions listed below. Do these results support the notion of adolescence as a period of "storm and stress" for everyone? (105-106)

—body image:

—self–esteem:

—mood:

—relationships with parents:

*   6. a) In Erikson's view, what is the major task of the adolescent and what is the related view of most developmental psychologists? (106)

b) What makes the task of the adolescent especially difficult in our society? (106)

*   c) When should the identity crisis be resolved and what are the outcomes when the process is successful or unsuccessful (that is, unresolved)? (106)

7. a) How did Marcia research Erikson's ideas concerning the development of adolescent identity? (106)

44   Chapter 3

* b) Using the following table, be able to categorize correctly Marcia's four identity statuses, *identity achievement, foreclosure, moratorium, and identity diffusion*. In addition, be sure you can describe the characteristics of an adolescent at each of these positions in the identity–formation continuum. See also Table 13-2. (106-107)

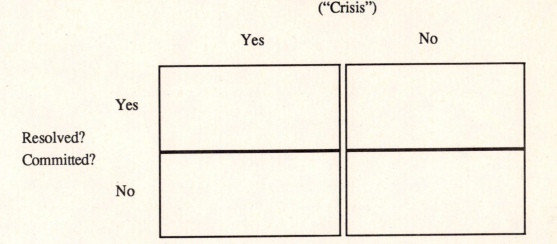

Perceived as an Issue?
("Crisis")

8. a) During which psychosocial stage do most people marry or form other types of intimate relationships? (107)

* b) For this time of life, contrast Erikson's and Sullivan's views in relation to which is primary, a search for identity or the need for intimacy. What is your authors' view on this issue? (107)

9. a) Describe how middle adulthood is the most productive period for many people. (107)

b) From Erikson's view, what are the sources of the feelings of satisfaction that occur during middle adulthood? (107)

10. a) By contrast, characterize the emotional turmoil during "midlife crises" found in several longitudinal studies. To what earlier psychosocial stage has the transition to middle adulthood been compared according to this view? (107-108)

* b) Is the notion of midlife crisis as a developmental stage accepted by everyone? Cite some evidence to support your answer. (108)

c) Nevertheless, in what ways is middle age a period of transition? (108)

11. a) Cite some of the statistics on our aging population. (108)

* b) Does aging result in inevitable physical and mental deterioration? To what three classes of factors can extreme debility in the later years be attributed? (108-109)

* c) Summarize what is known about changes in cognitive ability associated with aging. (109)

Psychological Development   45

12. a) What are some of the variables that can make the later years a period of happiness or unhappiness? (109)

* b) According to Erikson, with what is the final psychosocial crisis concerned? (109)

Sample Quiz 3.1

1. Which of the following is *true* regarding the motor development of walking? a) Not all children go through the same sequence of motor behaviors. b) Children go through the sequence of motor behaviors at different rates. c) Learning and experience play no role in the process. d) All of the above.

2. In your authors' view, it is probably most accurate to speak of _____ that are optimal for behavior to develop. a) psychosexual stages; b) critical periods; c) sensitive periods; d) preoperational stages.

3. By the beginning of a child's preoperational phase, if a parent playfully hides a teddy bear: a) the child will act as though the bear no longer exists; b) the child will act as though the bear is hiding; c) the child will demonstrate object permanence; d) both b and c.

4. Moral realism is: a) the notion that moral principles should evolve across one's lifetime experiences and emerge only after maturity is attained; b) the view that moral laws are permanent and predetermined; c) Kohlberg's theory that morality is best founded on reality; d) the highest form of morality reached during the formal operational stage.

5. John Bowlby was important for: a) studies of cognitive development in children and a related stage theory; b) work on attachment begun in the 1950s; c) the first comprehensive account of gender identity and sex typing; d) the *tabula rasa* view of the infant's mind.

6. "Strange Situation" refers to a procedure for assessing: a) cognitive development in the concrete operational stage; b) early psychosexual development; c) attachment; d) moral realism.

7. From the social–learning view, sex typing owes critically to: a) reward, punishment, and observation; b) discovery of genital differences and identification with the same–sex parent; c) the motive to behave consistently with one's gender identity; d) evaluating behavioral alternatives through the "lenses" of gender.

8. The idea that psychological development depends upon the social relations that a person forms at different stages of life underlies: a) Piaget's cognitive development theory; b) Kohlberg's theory of morality; c) Bem's schema theory; d) Erikson's psychosocial stage theory.

9. In Erikson's view, a person's identity crisis is most likely to be experienced during: a) the third through the fifth years of life; b) adolescence; c) early adulthood; d) middle adulthood.

10. Research on psychological effects of puberty shows that: a) early maturation in girls is related to lower self–esteem; b) early maturation in boys is related to positive self–image; c) early maturation in girls is related to emotional and behavioral problems; d) all of the above.

Sample Quiz 3.2

1. Heredity is to environment as: a) Darwin is to Locke; b) Locke is to Piaget; c) Piaget is to Kohlberg; d) Watson is to Darwin.

2. Which of the following sets of terms do *not* characterize a basic issue in developmental psychology? a) sexual identity vs. sex typing; b) nature vs. nurture; c) continuous process vs. stages; d) environment vs. heredity.

3. Which of the following is *true*? a) Young infants do not have very good memories. b) Newborns prefer looking at human faces because they are faces. c) Infants can distinguish the human voice from other kinds of sounds. d) Infants are not born with the perceptual mechanisms that enable them to distinguish speech sounds.

4. Which of the following is cited in your text as a difficulty for Piaget's theory? a) Piaget underestimated children's abilities. b) The theory has not generated much research on cognitive development. c) The theory was mainly a rehash of old ideas. d) All of the above.

5. The alternative to Piaget's theory that argues that a child is embedded in and influenced by his or her particular environment of rules and norms is the: a) information–processing approach; b) sociocultural approach; c) knowledge–acquisition approach; d) psychosocial stage approach.

6. Current research on temperament challenges the traditional view that: a) all infant behaviors are genetically–determined, mood–related personality characteristics; b) all infant behaviors are shaped by the early environment; c) temperamental differences account for all adult behaviors; d) there is a continuing interaction between genotype and the environment.

7. The most clear outcome of the Harlow research on attachment in monkeys is that: a) it is the association of a mother with food that mainly determines attachment; b) artificial mothering is sufficient for satisfactory development; c) it is the soft–contact of an artificial mother that is critical to attachment; d) both b and c.

8. Babies who seek consistently to interact with their mother when she returns in the Strange Situation are termed: a) insecurely attached: avoidant; b) insecurely attached: ambivalent; c) attached: codependent; d) securely attached.

9. Sex typing is: a) the acquisition of behaviors that the culture feels is appropriate; b) the acquisition of a clear sense of self as either male or female; c) the notion that children are encouraged to view everything as gender–related; d) the idea that a person's sex remains the same despite changes in age and appearance.

10. Marcia reserves the term _____ for adolescents who are in the midst of an identity crisis. a) foreclosure; b) moratorium; c) identify diffusion; d) operational.

Answer Key, Chapter 3

Important Names

1. John Locke
2. Charles Darwin
3. John B. Watson; B. F. Skinner
4. Jean Piaget
5. Lawrence Kohlberg
6. John Bowlby
7. Sigmund Freud
8. Erik Erikson

Vocabulary and Details

1. developmental psychology
2. biological factors (nature); environmental events (nurture)
3. continuous; stages

INTERACTION BETWEEN NATURE AND . . .

1. maturation

STAGES OF DEVELOPMENT

1. dominant theme; qualitatively different; in the same order
2. critical periods
3. sensitive periods

COGNITIVE DEVELOPMENT IN CHILDHOOD

1. schemata (schema)
2. assimilation; accommodation
3. 2; sensorimotor stage
4. object permanence; mental representation
5. 2; 7; preoperational stage
6. operations
7. conservation
8. moral realism
9. concrete operational stage; 7; 12
10. formal operational stage; 11 or 12; symbolic

PERSONALITY AND SOCIAL DEVELOPMENT

1. temperaments
2. stranger anxiety
3. attachment
4. Strange Situation
5. gender identity
6. sex typing
7. gender constancy
8. gender schema

DEVELOPMENT AFTER CHILDHOOD

1. psychosocial stages
2. adolescence
3. puberty
4. adolescent growth spurt; secondary sex characteristics
5. menarche; late
6. identity crisis
7. generativity

Sample Quiz 3.1

1. b, 71
2. c, 72
3. d, 79
4. b, 81
5. b, 92
6. c, 92
7. a, 96
8. d, 104
9. b, 106
10. d, 105

Sample Quiz 3.2

1. a, 70
2. a, 70
3. c, 73-75
4. a, 84
5. b, 87
6. c, 89
7. c, 91
8. d, 93
9. a, 95
10. b, 107

Psychological Development   49

Sensory Processes

Learning Objectives

1. Be familiar with the procedures for measuring absolute thresholds and difference thresholds. Know what is meant by the terms psychometric function, just noticeable difference (jnd), Weber's law, and Fechner's law.

2. Be able to discuss the process of sensory coding, including what single–cell recording experiments tell us about how sensory systems code the intensity and the quality of a stimulus.

3. Be able to describe the stimulus for vision. Know the main parts of the visual system, the sequence by which light passes through them, and the functions of the two types of receptor cells in the retina.

4. Understand the phenomena of color appearance, color mixing, and color deficiency. Be able to discuss these phenomena from the perspective of trichromatic theory, opponent–color theory, and two–stage color theory.

5. Be able to describe the physical aspects of a sound wave. Know the main parts of the auditory system and the sequence by which sound passes through them and is transduced into an electrical impulse.

6. Be prepared to describe temporal (frequency) and place theories of pitch perception. Be familiar with the problems encountered by each.

7. Understand the evolutionary significance of smell and its function as a primitive means of communication. Know the stimulus for smell, the parts of the olfactory system, and how the system codes the quality of an odor.

8. Be familiar with the stimulus for taste, the nature of taste receptors, and how the gustatory system codes taste.

9. Be able to describe the pressure and temperature senses in terms of the class of stimuli to which each responds and the receptors involved.

10. Understand the pain system in terms of stimuli and two kinds of pain. Be familiar with the gate control theory of pain and how it accounts for several of the phenomena of pain.

Important Names

1. The German physiologist _____ first determined the psychophysical law that the greater the intensity of a stimulus the larger the change in the stimulus that is necessary for a change to be noticed. (117)

2. Assuming this law to be true, later the German physicist _____ proposed also that, for a given stimulus, every just noticeable difference is perceptually equal to every other one. (118)

3. _____ proposed that the stimuli reaching our sense organs produce different types of sensations in different nerves, the idea of "specific nerve energies." (120)

4. The trichromatic or Young–Helmholtz theory of color vision was developed and quantified by _____ in the 1850s based upon an earlier theory. (130)

5. Limitations of the trichromatic theory led _____ to develop the opponent–color theory a little later in the nineteenth century. (132)

Vocabulary and Details

1. At the psychological level, the experiences elicited by simple stimuli (such as a flashing red light) are termed _____, while those that are integrations of sensations (such as a fire engine) are called _____. (115)

2. At the biological level, _____ processes are associated with the sense organs and connecting neural pathways, while _____ processes are associated with the higher levels of the nervous system. (115)

3. Individual senses are also called _____. (115)

COMMON PROPERTIES OF SENSORY MODALITIES

1. The weakest magnitude of a stimulus that can be reliably discriminated is called the _____, defined as the value of the stimulus at which it is detected _____ percent of the time. (116)

2. The procedures used to determine thresholds of stimuli are called _____. (116)

3. A graph of the data obtained in a psychophysical experiment that relates stimulus magnitude to subject reports is called a _____. (116)

4. The smallest difference in stimulus magnitude necessary to tell two stimuli apart _____ percent of the time is called the _____ or _____ (_____). (117)

5. The translation of physical energy into electrochemical energy in the nervous system is called _____. (119)

6. Cells specialized for transduction are located in the sense organs and are called _____. (119)

7. In essence, a receptor is a specialized nerve cell or _____. (119)

8. Experiments designed to determine which specific neurons are activated by a given stimulus use a procedure called _____. (119)

9. In the absence of a stimulus, the usual single–cell recording will depict a slow rate of _____, in the form of vertical spikes on an oscilloscope; by contrast, when a stimulus is presented, the rate of spike activity will be _____ (fast/slow). (120)

10. Müller's notion that different sensory modalities are represented by different sensory nerves to the brain is called the doctrine of _____. (120-121)

VISUAL SENSE

1. Light is energy produced by the oscillation of electrically charged matter; this energy (like X rays, infrared rays, or television waves), is called _____ radiation and is measured in _____. (121)

2. Actually, only the small portion of such radiation visible to humans, that is, _____, is that in the wavelength range of _____ to _____ nanometers. (124)

3. Radiation within the visible range is called _____. (124)

4. The image–forming system of the eye consists of the _____, _____, and _____. (124)

5. When the lens of the eye does not flatten enough to bring far objects into focus, but does focus on near objects, a person is said to be _____ or _____. (124)

6. Conversely, when the lens of the eye does not become spherical enough to focus on near objects, but does focus on far objects, a person is said to be _____ (or _____). (124)

7. The image in the eye is formed on a thin layer at the back of the eyeball, the _____, where transduction occurs. (125)

8. In the retina, there are two types of cells: a) _____, elongated cells that are specialized for responding to light at low intensities (at night, for example); and b) _____, specialized for light at high intensity and in color (especially in daylight). (125)

9. Rods and cones contain chemicals that absorb light called _____ which start the process of nerve impulses. (125)

10. The rods and cones function to enable us to respond to a light's intensity, that is to have visual _____; the ability to see *details* of light is visual _____. (125-126)

11. The phenomenon of _____ refers to the fact that the sensitivity of the visual system changes as a person's visual system adjusts to the prevailing level of illumination. (127)

12. Experientially, a colored light may be characterized along three dimensions, the first of which is _____, its perceived whiteness. (128)

13. The second dimension of color is _____, which refers to its quality (e.g., red or greenish–yellow). (128)

14. The third dimension of color is _____, its purity or "colorfulness," where a color that appears pale is said to be _____ and a color that appears to contain no white is said to be _____. (128)

15. When we mix lights of different colors we obtain an _____ mixture; whereas when we mix colored paints or pigments we obtain a _____ mixture. (129)

16. Three wavelengths of light, drawn from the long–, middle–, and short–wave portions of the spectrum, can be combined to match almost any color of light, a phenomenon termed the _____. (129)

17. Most people have the ability to match a wide range of colors with _____ (how many?) colored lights in a way that resembles the matching of most other people. (130)

18. People who match colors using two wavelengths are called _____ and have _____ color vision, while those who match colors using only the intensity of a single wavelength are called _____ and are said to be truly _____. (130)

19. According to the Young–Helmholtz, or _____ theory of color vision, there are _____ (how many?) types of cone receptors for color vision that act jointly. (130)

20. Alternatively, according to the _____ theory of color vision devised by Hering, there are _____ (how many?) types of color–sensitive units, one responding to either red or green and the other to either blue or yellow. (132-133)

AUDITORY SENSE

1. A _____ is a wave of pressure changes that is transmitted through the air when an object moves or vibrates. (134)

2. The waveform of any sound may be decomposed into some number of simpler wave forms described mathematically as _____ and perceived as _____. (134)

3. Pure tones vary in terms of (a) _____, perceived as pitch; (b) _____, perceived as loudness; and (c) the time at which they start. (134)

4. Frequency of sound waves is measured in _____ (_____); intensity is measured in terms of the pressure difference between peak and trough of the sound wave, usually specified in _____. (134)

5. The _____ system of the ear functions to amplify and transmit sounds. Anatomically, this system consists of the _____, including the _____ and _____. (136)

6. Additionally, the transmission system includes the _____, consisting of the _____ and a chain of _____. (136).

7. The _____ system of the ear functions to transduce sound into neural impulses. This system is housed in the _____ (or _____), a coiled tube of bone which contains the sound receptors. (136)

8. The sound receptors are called _____ because they resemble tiny hairs that extend into fluids in the inner ear. (136)

9. Because a sound provides slightly different intensity at each of our two ears, termed the _____ difference, we can determine the direction of its source; that is, we can _____ sound. (138)

10. Also contributing to the ability to localize sound, sound waves arrive slightly later at one ear than the other, the _____ difference. (138)

11. The prime *quality* of sound is _____, which _____ (increases/decreases) as frequency increases. (138)

12. The _____ (or _____) theory of pitch perception holds that the basilar membrane vibrates at the same frequency as a sound wave, thus allowing us to hear different sound frequencies. (139)

13. The _____ theory of pitch perception proposed by Helmholtz maintains that it is the place on the basilar membrane that vibrates the most that determines what neural fibers are activated, thus enabling us to distinguish pitches. (139)

OTHER SENSES

1. The sense with the most direct neural route to the brain, is _____ (_____). (142)

2. Chemicals secreted by insects and some animals that may be smelled and that communicate various forms of information are called _____. (142)

3. Taste or _____ begins in taste receptors located in bumps on the tongue and around the mouth called _____. (144)

4. The stimulus for passively sensed pressure is _____ on the skin. (145)

5. Temperature is sensed by _____ and _____ that respond to temperature decreases and increases, respectively, during transduction. (145)

6. According to the _____ theory of pain, a neural "gate" in the spinal cord may block transmission from pain receptors to the brain. (147)

7. The neural gate appears to involve a region of the _____ called the _____ or (_____). (147)

8. In the phenomenon called _____, stimulation of the PAG acts like an anesthetic (pain reducer). (147)

9. A Chinese healing procedure that involves inserting needles into the skin to reduce pain is _____. (147)

Ideas and Concepts

1. In what respects is the biological distinction between sensation and perception "somewhat arbitrary"? (115)

COMMON PROPERTIES OF SENSORY MODALITIES

* 1. What is the most noticeable thing about the minimum stimulus in various sense modalities? Cite some data to show the sensitivity of human vision. (115-116)

* 2. a) What is the most common way to determine the sensitivity of a sensory modality? (116)

   b) Cite an example of one commonly used psychophysical method. (116)

   c) Be able to interpret a psychometric function, such as that in Figure 4-1. (116)

* 3. a) There must be a minimum amount of energy of a stimulus that can be perceived. What other aspect must there be before we can distinguish between two stimuli? (117)

   b) Outline an experiment to find a just noticeable difference (jnd) and the results that enable determination of its actual size. (117)

* 4. a) State *Weber's law* in your own words and indicate in the following equation what each term represents. (117)

$$\frac{\Delta I}{I} = k$$

   b) Be able to interpret the data displayed in Figure 4–2 in terms of Weber's law. (117-118)

* 5. a) Similarly, state *Fechner's law* in your own words and indicate in the following equation what each term represents. (118)

$$P = c \, \log I$$

   b) What additional assumption did Fechner make as he generalized Weber's law? (118)

   c) To show Fechner's law in operation, use specific values to demonstrate that the intensity of, say, a light bulb might not appreciably affect its perceived magnitude (P). What happens to perceived changes in magnitude as the physical intensity of a stimulus increases from low levels to high levels? (118)

* 6. a) What formidable problem is faced by the brain in sensing the world and how does it solve this difficulty? (119)

   b) Using the modality of vision, illustrate the process of transduction. (119)

*Basic ideas and concepts

7. a) Trace the progress of an electrical signal once a receptor is activated. (119)

* b) Where is the experience of sensation actually located? Then how do our sensory systems accurately relate external events to conscious sensory experience? (119)

* 8. a) What two sensory experiences are coded for every modality of stimulus? Cite examples. (119)

b) What is the usual way to study coding processes? Describe a single–cell recording experiment, noting especially how the signals are displayed and how they appear. (119-120)

* 9. a) What is the primary means for coding the intensity of a stimulus, as revealed by the single–cell recording method? (120)

* b) Describe another means by which the intensity of a stimulus can be coded. Note especially the relationship between intensity and regularity of neural firing. (120)

* c) Discuss the coding of distinctive qualities *between* sense modalities, as formulated by Müller. (120-121)

* d) In what two ways are distinctive qualities of a stimulus coded *within* a sense modality? Use examples and the terms *specificity* and *pattern* in your answer. (121)

VISUAL SENSE

1. Which of the body's "six" senses obtain information that is at a distance? (121)

* 2. a) Be able to list the three main components of the human visual system and the two systems within the eye itself. (124)

* b) Using the information in Figure 4-6 and the letters in the diagram below, enter the letter that corresponds to the location of each part of the eye in the corresponding cell of the table provided for item 2c). (124)

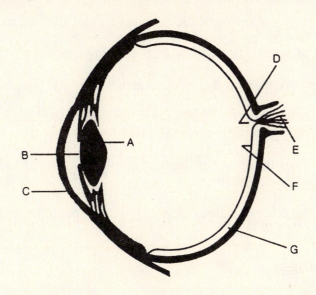

*   c) In the table below, where possible describe and indicate the functions of the various parts of the eye. (124-126)

Part of the Eye   Location   Description (if possible)   Function (if possible)

cornea			
lens			
pupil			
retina			
fovea			
optic nerve			
blind spot			

*   3. In terms of the distribution of receptors in the eye, why do we move our eyes in order to assure that a visual stimulus projects onto the center of the retina? (125)

    4. Trace the course of a nerve impulse in the retina using the terms *bipolar cells* and *ganglion cells*. (125)

*   5. a) In detail, what two features of the eye determine our sensitivity to a light's intensity or brightness? (125)

*   b) What is one consequence of the difference in location of rods and cones? Be able to describe how cones and rods connect to ganglion cells using the term *convergence of neural activation* (see also Figure 4-10). (125-126)

*   c) What is the price paid for this advantage in sensitivity? Explain. (126-127)

*   d) What is another consequence of the difference in location of rods and cones? How may this difference be measured? (127)

*   6. In detail, why does the course of light adaptation illustrated in Figure 4-11 show essentially two different patterns? (127)

    7. a) Indicate what color corresponds to each of the spectrums of light below. (See also Figure 4-12.) (127-128)

    —short wavelengths:

58   Chapter 4

—medium wavelengths:

—long wavelengths:

*   b) What determines color perception when a color sensation is due to light reflected from an object rather than to emission of light by the stimulus itself? What is another factor that may then modify the color sensation? (127-128)

* 8. a) In your own words, what is meant by the term *color solid*, devised by Albert Munsell? (128)

     b) How many different colors can people discriminate and how many actually can be named? (129)

* 9. a) Why are the rules for additive mixtures of color different from those of subtractive mixtures? (129)

*   b) Be sure to note how many different wavelengths of light are necessary to match any color. Also, what must characterize the relative differences in wavelengths of colors that are used to match other colors? (That is, should they be very different or very similar?) (129-130)

     c) Discuss a practical application of the rule expressed in 9b). (130)

 10. Indicate the origin of most color deficiencies. Why do they occur more in males than females? (130)

* 11. a) Outline the Young–Helmholtz theory of color vision. Use the terms *short, medium,* and *long receptor*. (130-131)

*   b) How is quality of color (hue) coded in this theory? (131-132)

*   c) Indicate how the trichromatic theory explains these facts of color vision: (132)

—discrimination of different wavelengths:

—the law of three primaries:

—color deficiencies:

* 12. a) Summarize the observations that led Ewald Hering to postulate the opponent–color theory of color vision. Use the term *opponent pair*. (132)

*   b) Discuss Hering's opponent–color theory in detail, indicating some of the limitations on color vision explained by the theory and how it accounts for the experience of hues. (132-133)

*   c) Indicate from Hering's theory why it is that when we stare at a color for a while and then look at a neutral surface, we see the complementary color. (133)

* 13. a) Indicate a theoretical resolution to the problem faced by proponents of the trichromatic theory and opponent–color theory, namely that neither approach could explain all of the facts of color vision. (133-134)

*   b) Outline how the discovery of *color opponent neurons* in the brain relates to this resolution of the two theories of color vision. (134)

    c) In what respects does research in the area of color vision exemplify your authors' contention throughout this text that psychological and biological approaches interact with and complement one another? (134)

AUDITORY SENSE

  1. a) Why are pure tones important in the analysis of audition? (134)

     b) Characterize the power of some sounds in terms of decibels and note the mathematical relationship between sound power and decibels. (134-135)

* 2. a) Using the information in Figure 4-22 and the letters in the diagram below, enter the letter that corresponds to the location of each part of the ear in the corresponding cell of the table provided for item 2b). (136)

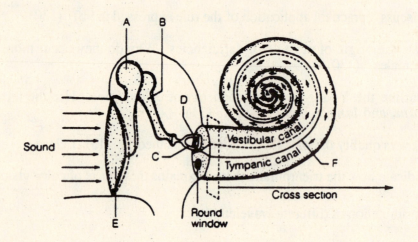

*   b) In the table below, where possible describe and indicate the functions of the various parts of the ear. (136-137)

Part of the ear   Location   Description (if possible)   Function (if possible)

Part of the ear	Location	Description (if possible)	Function (if possible)
eardrum			
malleus			
incus			
stapes			
oval window			
basilar membrane			

*   c) Trace the course of sound transduction in the inner ear from the basilar membrane to the auditory neurons. To what side(s) of the brain is sound information transmitted? (136-137)

d) Can you indicate what the relative number of neurons in the ear and the eye says about the relative sensitivity of each of these receptor organs? (137)

*   3. a) How does reception of sound resemble that of light? Therefore, in what relative frequency range is hearing best, low, middle, or high? (See also Figure 4-24.) (137)

*   b) Describe the two kinds of hearing loss. Which would be more typical of rock musicians? Use the terms *conduction loss* and *sensory–neural loss* in your answer. (137-138)

*   c) Discuss the phenomenon of "sound shadow." Is this interaural intensity difference a limitation on our hearing? Explain. (138)

*   4. Are the sensations when sound is mixed the same as when color is mixed? Explain and indicate the implications of the differences for theories of sound reception. (138-139)

*   5. a) Outline two important features of Rutherford's temporal theory of pitch perception. (139)

*   b) What major problem did this theory encounter and how did Weaver propose to resolve it? (139)

c) Indicate the research support that this theoretical resolution received. (139)

*   d) What problem is faced by even the modified temporal theory, and what answer was proposed by the anatomist, Duverney? In what respect is this *resonance* notion essentially correct? (139)

*   6. a) Does Helmholtz's later place theory of pitch perception hold that we hear with our basilar membrane? Explain. (139)

     b) What observations did von Békésy make that validate the place theory? (139)

*   7. What major problem is encountered by the place theory and what is a tentative solution to this difficulty as well as to the difficulty encountered by temporal theory? (140-141)

OTHER SENSES

1. Why have vision and hearing been called the "higher senses" and how do other senses differ? (142)

*   2. a) What anatomical information tells us that olfaction is more important in many species than it is in humans? Cite an example to show the utility of this fact. (142)

     b) Describe examples of the power of pheromones in the love life and death of certain species. (142-143)

     c) Discuss two kinds of data indicating that humans have retained at least some remnants of an effective olfactory communication system. (143)

*   3. a) Trace the transduction pathway of olfaction from molecule to *cilia*, to *olfactory bulb*, and to *olfactory cortex*. (143)

     b) Why should a distinctive smell be a powerful aid in retrieving an old memory?

*   4. a) About how much *less* sensitive is a human's ability to smell than a dog's? Is this because our receptors are less sensitive? Explain. (143-144)

     b) Generally, what evidence indicates that people are nevertheless able to sense many different qualities of odor? (144)

*   c) Describe the apparent mechanism for the coding of odors by the olfactory system. (144)

5. a) List three factors that determine taste. Cite examples. (144)

*   b) Describe the gustatory system, including the nature of the stimulus for taste and the transduction process. (144)

     c) Be able to identify the locations of the four different kinds of taste buds on the tongue. (See Figure 4-26.) (144)

*   6. a) Given the choice, how many basic tastes do people use to describe substances and what are they? (145)

*   b) Describe the neural coding system that underlies the classification of tastes indicated in 6a). (145)

* 7. What are the three senses of the skin? (145)

* 8. a) What is the stimulus for sensed pressure? Does this mean that any steady pressure will be sensed? Explain. (145)

        b) Where are we the most sensitive to variations in pressure? (145)

*   c) What do your authors mean when they say that pressure sensing "shows profound adaptation"? (Can you see how this characteristic of pressure sensing relates to your answer to 8a?) (145)

    9. Distinguish between *active* and *passive touching*. (145)

* 10. a) How are the qualities of temperatures coded and what are the limits of this system? Explain how we sense very hot objects. (145-146)

*   b) Why is it important that we are so sensitive to temperature changes at the skin? (146)

        c) Describe the process of adaptation of skin temperature and illustrate with an everyday example. (146)

* 11. a) Why would we be at risk if we had no pain sensation? (146)

        b) In general, what is the stimulus for pain? Describe the process of pain sensing in the skin. (146)

*   c) Distinguish in detail between *phasic pain* and *tonic pain*. (146)

*   d) List some of the factors that may modify pain sensations. Cite one astonishing demonstration of the psychological aspects of pain control. (146-147)

* 12. a) In the gate control analysis of pain sensation, how can mental states alter the experiencing of pain? (147)

*   b) Discuss the role of PAG neurons in gating action. (146)

*   c) Describe the following kinds of evidence consistent with gate control theory. (147-148)

—effects of morphine and endorphins:

—stimulation–produced analgesia:

—acupuncture:

Sample Quiz 4.1

1. The attribute of an event that *must* be coded in a sensory system is: a) duration; b) quality; c) intensity; d) both b and c.

2. The individual known for the doctrine of "specific nerve energies" was: a) Johannes Müller; b) Ernst Weber; c) Hermann von Helmholtz; d) Gustav Fechner.

3. The fact that more rods connect to a ganglion cell than cones explains why: a) vision is more sensitive when based on rods than on cones; b) rod–based vision is more acute than cone–based vision; c) we are better able to detect a dim light that falls on the fovea; d) both a and b.

4. Lights of different colors are to additive mixture as colored paints are to: a) additive mixture; b) subtractive mixture; c) divisive mixture; d) multiplicative mixture.

5. Ewald Hering's opponent–color theory maintained that there are: a) three types of cone receptors; b) differing numbers of cone receptors depending upon a person's acuity; c) two types of color–sensitive units; d) color–opponent neurons in the thalamus.

6. When hearing loss occurs largely at higher frequencies (as in older people), we speak of: a) conduction loss; b) sensory–neural loss; c) a sound shadow; d) acuity loss.

7. The sense with the most direct neural route to the brain is: a) sight; b) sound; c) pressure; d) smell.

8. Which of the following best describes the transduction pathway for olfaction? a) olfactory bulb to cilia to olfactory cortex; b) olfactory cortex to cilia to olfactory bulb; c) cilia to olfactory bulb to olfactory cortex; d) cilia to olfactory cortex to olfactory bulb.

9. Relative to other species, lack of sensitivity in humans to intensity of smells is due to: a) less sensitive olfactory receptors; b) location of smell receptors so far above the ground; c) fewer olfactory receptors; d) deficient speed of cortical processing.

10. Indicate the item with respect to pain that does *not* belong with the other three: a) stimulation of the PAG; b) morphine; c) opening of the neural gate; d) ability to participate in an Indian hook swinging ceremony.

Sample Quiz 4.2

1. The retina: a) is where transduction of light energy occurs; b) contains rod and cone cells; c) is the location for photopigments; d) all of the above.

2. That three wavelengths of light can be combined to match almost any color of light is a finding referred to as the: a) color–solid principle; b) color–saturation hypothesis; c) three primaries law; d) trichromatic theory of color vision.

3. Monochromats are: a) people who match colors using two wavelengths; b) people who match colors using the intensity of a single wavelength; c) people who are color deficient but not completely color blind; d) both b and c.

4. We would expect that a long wavelength receptor would be most sensitive to colors in the portion of the spectrum we label: a) red; b) green; c) yellow; d) blue.

5. The resolution of the differences between the color vision theories of Helmholtz and Hering: a) maintains that there are just two types of color receptors in the retina; b) argues that color–opponent units are located at a higher level in the nervous system than the receptors in the eye; c) rejects all aspects of Hering's opponent–color model; d) none of the above; no resolution of these theories has been proposed to date.

6. With respect to sound waves, cycles per second is to frequency as _____ is to pressure differences between peak and trough. a) hertz; b) nanometers; c) decibels; d) molecules per second.

7. Sight and hearing are termed the "higher senses" because they are: a) richer in patterning and organization; b) represented at higher levels of the cortex; c) mainly found in the higher species; d) more difficult to study in the laboratory.

8. Olfaction is apparently more important in other species than in man based on: a) the fact that it plays no role in human survival; b) the finding that larger areas of the cortex are devoted to smell in other species; c) anatomical differences showing more direct neurons to the brain in other species than in man; d) none of the above; researchers have found that olfaction is more important in man than in other species.

9. Which of the following is *not* mentioned in your text as one of the factors that may influence pain perception? a) the immediate stimulus; b) culture; c) previous experience; d) speed of neural transmission along an established pain pathway.

10. Which of the following lines of evidence appears to fit with the gate control theory of pain? a) effects of morphine and endorphins; b) stimulation–produced analgesia; c) acupuncture; d) all of the above.

Important Names

1. Ernst Weber
2. Gustav Fechner
3. Johannes Müller
4. Hermann von Helmholtz
5. Ewald Hering

Vocabulary and Details

1. sensations; perceptions
2. sensory; perceptual
3. sensory modalities

COMMON PROPERTIES OF . . .

1. absolute threshold; 50
2. psychophysical methods
3. psychometric function
4. 50; difference threshold; just noticeable difference (jnd)
5. transduction
6. receptors
7. neuron
8. single–cell recording
9. spontaneous activity; fast
10. specific nerve energies

VISUAL SENSE

1. electromagnetic; wavelengths
2. visible energy; 400; 700
3. light
4. cornea; pupil; lens
5. myopic (nearsighted)
6. hyperopic (farsighted)
7. retina
8. rods; cones
9. photopigments
10. acuity; sensitivity
11. light adaptation
12. lightness
13. hue
14. saturation; unsaturated; saturated
15. additive; subtractive
16. three primaries law
17. three
18. dichromats; deficient; monochromats; color blind
19. trichromatic; three
20. opponent–color; two

AUDITORY SENSE

1. sound wave
2. sine waves; pure tones
3. frequency; intensity
4. cycles per second (hertz); decibels
5. transmission; outer ear; external ear (pinna); auditory canal
6. middle ear; eardrum; three bones
7. transduction; cochlea (inner ear)
8. hair cells
9. interaural intensity; localize
10. interaural time
11. pitch; increases
12. temporal (frequency)
13. place

OTHER SENSES

1. smell (olfaction)
2. pheromones
3. gustation; taste buds
4. physical pressure
5. cold receptors; warm receptors
6. gate control
7. midbrain; periaqueductal gray; PAG
8. stimulation–produced analgesia
9. acupuncture

Sample Quiz 4.1

1. d, 119
2. a, 120
3. a, 126-127
4. b, 129
5. c, 132
6. a, 137-138
7. d, 142
8. c, 143
9. c, 143-144
10. c, 147

Sample Quiz 4.2

1. d, 125
2. c, 129
3. b, 130
4. a, 131
5. b, 133-134
6. c, 134
7. a, 142
8. b, 142
9. d, 146
10. d, 147

Perception

Learning Objectives

1. Be familiar with the two major functions of the perceptual system and the division of labor in the visual cortex that underlies these functions.

2. Be prepared to discuss the processes by which we segregate objects, including figure–ground organization and the Gestalt principles of grouping.

3. Be able to list and describe the various monocular and binocular cues that determine perceived distance (depth). Understand the difference between Helmholtz's notion of unconscious inference and Gibson's direct perception as explanations of distance perception.

4. Understand the phenomena of stroboscopic motion and induced motion. Be able to present evidence that the perception of real motion depends on the activation of specific cells in the visual cortex as well as on information from the motor system about eye movements.

5. Be able to discuss the role of feature detectors in the early stages of object recognition and to cite the behavioral evidence for primitive features.

6. Know how connectionist models explain the process of matching an object's description with shape descriptions stored in memory.

7. Be able to describe, with examples, how top–down processes and context influence our perception of objects.

8. Be able to describe the process of selective attention (both visual and auditory) and know the separate brain systems that appear to mediate selection.

9. Be able to show, with examples, how each of the five perceptual constancies contributes to our perception of stable wholes.

10. Understand how perceived distance contributes to size constancy and how the size–distance principle explains some perceptual illusions.

11. Be prepared to discuss the contemporary view of perception as it relates to traditional views of nature and nurture, presenting relevant evidence from research on the perceptual capacities of infants and the rearing of animals under conditions of controlled stimulation.

Important Names

1. The founder of Gestalt psychology and the psychologist who first noted the determinants of grouping (as well as many other perceptual phenomena) was _____. (155)

Vocabulary and Details

1. A _____ is the outcome of a perceptual process. (152)

2. The study of perception is the study of how we integrate _____ into _____ of the objects of our world and the use of the latter in getting around the world. (152)

3. In vision, determining *what* objects are is referred to as _____(or _____). (152)

4. Also in vision, determining *where* objects are is called _____ (or _____). (152)

5. In addition to localizing and recognizing objects, our perceptual systems also function to keep the appearance of objects constant in the phenomenon called _____. (152)

DIVISION OF LABOR IN THE BRAIN

1. The method of positive emission tomography, abbreviated _____, is a method of scanning the brain by way of radioactive molecules injected into the bloodstream. (153)

2. The division of labor in the visual cortex appears to be specialized for many particular recognition tasks by way of numerous _____. (154)

LOCALIZATION

1. Localization in a three–dimensional world is made possible by three perceptual abilities: (a) _____ (separating) objects from one another and from their background; (b) determining the _____ of objects from us; and (c) determining the _____ patterns of objects. (154)

2. An early twentieth century German approach to psychology that studied how we organize objects and stressed the importance of perceiving *whole* objects or forms was called _____. (154)

3. In a stimulus that contains two or more distinct regions, we usually see part of the stimulus as a _____ containing objects of interest and the rest as _____. (154)

4. When objects cluster into pairs or sets of some kind, we speak of the perceptual phenomenon called _____. (155)

5. Among the determinants of grouping objects are: (a) _____, the tendency to group elements that are near to one another; (b) _____, the tendency to group elements to complete figures with gaps; and (c) _____, the tendency to group similar objects. (155-156)

6. _____ are two–dimensional cues that a perceiver uses to infer distance in a three–dimensional world; if these involve one eye they are said to be _____, and if they involve both eyes they are said to be _____. (156)

7. Five of the monocular distance cues that artists use to create depth on a two–dimensional surface include _____, _____, _____, _____, and _____. (156-157)

8. A _____ is a device that displays a different image to each eye and creates the illusion of depth through binocular distance cues, including _____ and _____. (157).

9. One of the "invariant" cues in perception discussed by Gibson is the fact that when a textured surface is viewed in perspective, its elements appear to be packed more closely together as the surface recedes; this phenomenon is termed the _____. (158)

10. In darkness, when a light is flashed followed by another light spatially close to it, it appears that the light has moved from the one position to the other in the perceptual event called _____. (158)

11. A second motion phenomenon, called _____, occurs when a large object surrounding a smaller one moves, causing the smaller one to appear that it is moving. (158-159)

12. Of course, we also perceive _____, caused by real movement across the retina. We appear to be more sensitive to _____ (an object is seen against a structured background) than we are to _____ (the background is dark or neutral and only the moving object can be seen). (159)

13. A loss of sensitivity to motion in a specific direction that occurs when we continuously view that motion is one form of _____. (160)

14. One effect of selective adaptation is apparent motion in the opposite direction of that which has just been viewed, termed _____. (160)

RECOGNITION

1. The region of the retina that is associated with a specific neuron in the visual cortex is that neuron's _____; when a stimulus appears anywhere in the field, the associated neuron fires. (162)

2. Single–cell recordings in the visual cortex by Hubel and Wiesel identified three types of cells that can be distinguished by the features to which they respond; these are called _____, _____, and _____ cells. (162)

3. Collectively, the cells described in item 2 are referred to as _____ and may be called the "building blocks of perception" because the features they respond to approximate numerous shapes. (162)

4. A model of recognition—matching features with shape descriptions stored in memory—that incorporates a network of nodes with excitatory and inhibitory *connections* is called a _____, a model bridging psychology and biology. (163-164)

5. In storing shape descriptions of letters, at the neural level hypothetical connections may be either (a) _____, if a feature is activated then activation spreads to a letter, or (b) _____, if a feature is activated then activation of the letter decreases. (164)

6. Perceptual processes that are _____ are those driven solely by the input; by contrast, _____ processes are those driven by a person's knowledge and expectations. (167)

7. The effect of context is extremely important to perception when a figure is _____, that is, when it can be perceived in more than one way. (167)

ATTENTION

1. The process by which we select stimuli for awareness is termed _____. (170)

2. In "selective looking," the eyes are engaged in noncontinuous motion, or _____; the periods during which the eyes are still are called _____. (170)

3. In _____, we can selectively ignore something _____ (before/after) we know what it means; in _____, we can ignore something _____ only (before/after) we know its meaning. (172)

4. One system in the brain that mediates the selection of inputs in attention is geared to _____; it is referred to as the _____ because the structures are located in the back of the brain. (173)

5. Another system in the front of the brain, referred to as the _____, is geared to attributes of an object other than location, such as _____. (173)

PERCEPTUAL CONSTANCIES

1. The tendency to perceive an object as the same regardless of changes in, say, lighting, position, or distance is called _____. (174)

2. The _____ principle states that perceived size is a product of retinal size multiplied by perceived distance. (176)

3. An _____ is a percept that is false or distorted when evaluated by means of physical measurement. (176)

PERCEPTUAL DEVELOPMENT

1. An infant's tendency to look at some objects more than others is studied through the _____ method. (178)

2. Another method, called the _____, takes advantage of the fact that infants tire of looking at familiar objects; so objects perceived as different (novel) should be stared at more. (178)

3. To be able to discriminate one part of an object from another when perceiving forms is called _____. (179)

4. Closely related, the ability to discriminate between dark and light stripes is called _____. (179)

5. In the _____ method for the study of depth perception, an infant or animal is placed on a transparent surface and observed for its movement over a "shallow" or "deep" checkerboard pattern. (180)

6. A stage in development during which the organism is optimally ready to acquire certain abilities is called a _____. (181)

Ideas and Concepts

* 1. According to the text, what two basic questions (problems) must our perceptual system answer? (152)

2. Indicate the survival functions of pattern recognition and spatial location. (152)

DIVISION OF LABOR IN THE BRAIN

* 1. a) Why can we assume that the perceptual functions, recognition and localization, are qualitatively different processes? Discuss a related study. (152-153)

* b) Describe the methods of a study using more recent PET brain scanning to document object and location systems in the brain. (153)

* c) Indicate the major results of this study. (153)

2. What other kinds of information appear to be processed in different regions or by different cells in the cortex? Discuss the results of related single-cell recording studies on nonhuman primates. (153-154)

LOCALIZATION

* 1. What kind of organization was of the greatest concern to Gestalt psychologists and is considered to be the most elementary form of perceptual organization? (154)

* 2. a) How do we know that figure-ground organization is not in the physical stimulus but rather in the perceptual system? (154-155)

b) Give some instances of figure-ground relationships in other sense modalities. (155)

* 3. Be sure you can recognize the determinants of grouping operating in Figure 5-5. (155-156)

4. a) What was Wertheimer's contribution to the study of grouping? (155)

* b) What has been the purpose of modern studies of grouping? Give an example of the kind of results that have been obtained and provide an explanation for these results. (155-156)

5. Cite some examples of perceptual grouping in modalities other than vision. (156)

*Basic ideas and concepts

6. a) Why has the idea of distance cues arisen in the context of perceiving depth? (156)

b) In what respect does seeing with both eyes have an advantage in depth perception? (157)

* c) In the tables below, provide definitions in your own words and indicate the way in which each of the types of depth cues function in depth perception. (Also, be able to recognize the operation of these cues in the related figures in your text.) (156-157)

Monocular Cues	Definition and Function
relative size	
superposition	
relative height	
linear perspective	
motion (motion parallax)	

Binocular Cues	Definition and Function
binocular parallax	
binocular disparity	

* 7. a) Explain in your own words what is meant by the term, *unconscious inference* in connection with Helmholtz's view of the nature of perception. (157-158)

* b) By contrast discuss Gibson's more recent notion that we use *invariant* cues in perception. Use an example to illustrate this important theoretical position in the context of perceiving depth. (158)

* 8. Distinguish among the three forms of motion perception by describing how each is produced: (158-160)

—stroboscopic motion:

72   Chapter 5

—induced motion:

—real motion:

9. What are the limits of stroboscopic motion? Cite a real–life example of what happens when the time interval is too long and how this problem is addressed. (158)

* 10. In Gibson's view, why is it easier to distinguish relative than absolute motion? (160)

* 11. In what sense is selective adaptation "selective"? Cite an example and indicate what it is that we usually notice in this process. (172)

* 12. a) Discuss the animal studies that demonstrate the neural bases for some aspects of real movement. What are two kinds of movement cells that have been found? (160)

    b) In similar physiological terms, why does selective adaptation apparently occur? (172)

*   c) However, cite the evidence that motion perception involves more than single cell activity. What sources of information does the visual system apparently combine in such cases? (160)

13. a) Describe Michotte's demonstration of motion and causality. What are the limits of this phenomenon? (160)

    b) Is the perception of causality mediated by unconscious inferences? Why or why not? (160-161)

RECOGNITION

* 1. a) Describe two kinds of recognition. What does recognition allow us to infer? (161)

*   b) List some of the attributes we may use for recognition of objects. Which attribute seems to play a critical role? Therefore, what is the critical question with regard to the perceptual function of recognition? (161)

2. Describe the two stages of recognition. (161)

* 3. a) What procedure was used by Hubel and Wiesel to study feature detectors in animals? (161-162)

*   b) Indicate the features to which each of the kinds of cells identified by Hubel and Wiesel respond. (Are these the only kind of cells there are?) (162)

—*simple cells:*

—*complex cells:*

—*hypercomplex cells:*

* 4. a) Describe and illustrate the behavioral procedure used by Treisman and colleagues to study feature detection. (162-163)

* b) What type of examination should an observer be able to use in a search for a target with primitive features and what should be the effect of changing the number of nontargets in the display? Use the terms *parallel* and *pop–out effect* in your answer. (163)

* c) List three types of features identified by Treisman with this technique. (163)

d) Do results suggest that all primitive features relate to shape? (163)

* 5. a) Be able to discuss in your own words the application of a connectionist model to the recognition of letters in a *simple network*, such as that in Figure 5–14. Use the term *network node* in your answer. (163-164)

* b) Why is this model considered to be too simple to account for all aspects of recognition? What is needed? (164)

* c) What does the term *augmented network* mean and how does this concept address the problem outlined in 5b) above? (See also Figure 5-15.) (164)

* d) Indicate the two fundamental entities in the networks described in 5a) and 5c). What two types of processing are possible in this theoretical approach to recognition? (164-165)

e) What is the basic idea behind this theoretical model? (165)

* 6. a) Even with the added features of the augmented network, what problem arises in trying to account for the perception of letters? (165)

* b) Discuss the two solutions to this problem outlined in your text and in Figure 5-17. Use the term *feedback*. Therefore, in your own words, why is it easier to recognize a letter in a word than when it is presented alone? (165-166)

* 7. a) What two criteria have guided the search for object features that are used in the recognition of natural objects? (166)

* b) Outline one proposal for what constitutes the features of objects. Use the term *geons* in your answer. (166)

c) Discuss the research designed to show that geons are features of objects. (See Figure 5-19.) (166-167)

d) Discuss the matching process that takes place between a description of an external object and its representation in memory. (167)

* 8. Using examples, be sure you are able to explain bottom–up and top–down processes. Also use the term *context* in your answer. (167)

* 9. a) Describe the effects of *ambiguity* and *temporal context* and be able to recognize them in the related figures, 5-20 and 5–21. (167-169)

74   Chapter 5

b) Give an example to show that a stimulus object does not have to be ambiguous for there to be context effects. (168)

c) What is another influence of top–down processing on our perceptions? (168-169)

10. Discuss the role of top–down processing in reading and the role of familiarity of the material being read. (170)

* 11. a) When does top–down processing occur even in the absence of context? Give an example. (170)

b) Why is the processing in this example top–down and what relevance does this have for everyday life? (170)

ATTENTION

1. a) Provide an example of selectivity in an everyday activity. (170)

b) Describe the television technique for studying selective looking. (170-171)

* c) In terms of the structure of the eye, what function does scanning a picture serve? (171)

d) Do we always have to move our eyes to obtain selectivity? Give an example. (171)

* 2. a) In what respect is selective listening like selective looking? Under what conditions does this mechanism show limited utility? Use the term *cocktail party phenomenon* in your answer. (171)

b) Indicate several cues that enable us to select a verbal message from a background of conversation. Which can we use even in the absence of the others? (171)

* 3. a) Discuss a common experimental procedure in which a subject is asked to *shadow* a message. (171)

* b) What outcomes are obtained with this technique? (171)

* c) Does current evidence support the idea that we completely select out information that is not shadowed? Explain and cite an example. (171-172)

4. a) Discuss some evidence for early selection that used the brain waves triggered by auditory stimuli. (172)

b) Similarly, outline one experiment demonstrating the phenomenon of late selection. (172-173)

* 5. a) What two major questions have been addressed in research on the neural basis of attention? (173)

b) Cite several lines of evidence to support the involvement of the posterior system in attention to locational aspects of objects. Is there also evidence for the role of the anterior system in nonlocational features? (173)

c) Turning to the second question in 5a), discuss the evidence that suggests that brain regions relevant to attributes being attended to are amplified in activity? (173-174)

PERCEPTUAL CONSTANCIES

*   1.   In the table below, be sure you can define each of the terms and provide at least one example. (174-176)

Perceptual Phenomenon   Definition and Example

Perceptual Phenomenon	Definition and Example
lightness constancy	
color constancy	
shape constancy	
location constancy	
size constancy	

*   2.   a)   Outline a perceptual demonstration of the phenomenon of lightness constancy and a procedure that will alter the apparent lightness of the object. (174)

*   b)   What does this demonstration tell us about the process that underlies lightness constancy? (174)

*   3.   What procedure can eliminate color constancy, and again, as in the case of lightness constancy, what does this tell us about the basis for the phenomenon? (174-175)

      4.   In the case of location constancy, what two sources of cues must the perceptual system take into account? (175)

      5.   Discuss the relationship between shape and location constancy and the phenomena you studied earlier in this chapter, localization and recognition. (175)

*   6.   a)   What are the two major variables in the determination of size constancy? Cite a demonstration of the way in which they interact. (176)

*   b)   How does the size–distance invariance principle explain size constancy? Be able to interpret an example. (176)

76   Chapter 5

* 7. Apply the size–distance principle to the problem of the *moon illusion*. (176)

* 8. In detail, what is the *Ames room* illusion? (177).

9. a) What other kinds of perceptual constancies are possible? (177)

b) On what do all constancies depend? (177)

PERCEPTUAL DEVELOPMENT

* 1. a) What is the view of contemporary psychologists with regard to the role of heredity and learning in perceptual phenomena? (178)

* b) List three major questions guiding modern research in perception on issues related to the role of heredity and learning that, in turn, provide an outline for this section of your text. (178)

2. a) Since research on perceptual capacities in infants often is aimed at the question of what processes are inborn, why has it not been restricted to newborns? (178)

* b) Describe in detail the "preferential looking" method, including how the experimenter may conclude that the infant is showing a lack of discrimination. (178)

* c) Similarly, detail the habituation method in the study of infant perception and the ways an experimenter determines whether objects are similar to or different from others. (178-179)

* 3. a) Describe the method typically used in the study of perceiving forms and one main result of this procedure. (179)

* b) Answer the question in your text, "What do these studies tell us about the infant's perceptual world?" by completing the following table. (Be sure to note when an infant can discriminate facial expressions.) (179-180)

Age of Infant	Ability to Discriminate
1 month	
3 months	

4. What is the evidence regarding other forms of object discrimination besides dark and light edges? In particular, what shapes do young infants find more interesting and why? (180)

* 5. a) At what age does depth perception begin to appear in infants and at what point is it fully developed? (180)

*   b) At what age do infants begin to use monocular cues to infer depth and what procedures reflect this use? (180)

* 6. Describe a study in infants using teddy bears indicating the results that established the presence of size constancy. (180-181)

* 7. a) What was the purpose and method of the earliest experiments on controlled stimulation? (181)

*   b) Indicate the idea behind these studies and the principal results. (181)

*   c) Discuss the difficulty with the dark–rearing procedure that argues for caution in interpreting these data. (181)

* 8. a) Indicate the relationship between the duration of light deprivation and effects on visual perception. (181)

*   b) What results suggest that there is a critical period in visual development during early life? (181)

* 9. a) What has become the preferred method in the study of the effects of controlled stimulation of perceptual development? (181)

*   b) In this method, describe the effects of deprivation of horizontal or vertical stripes. (181)

        c) What happens to cells in the visual cortex as a result of these procedures? (181)

* 10. a) What condition provides information about visual deprivation in humans? Discuss its effects upon visual development. (181)

*   b) Indicate the conclusion to be drawn from these observations, noting a probable critical period in humans for visual development. (181)

  11. Do the effects of controlling stimulation on perceptual development favor a learning interpretation of the origins of perception? Explain and cite a related example. (181-182)

* 12. a) Discuss evidence obtained with kittens showing the importance of self–produced movements in response to stimulation in perceptual motor coordination. (182)

*   b) Cite the results obtained with humans that show similar effects for self–produced movement. (182)

* 13. Overall, based on the evidence presented in this section, what is your authors' conclusion with respect to whether perception is innate or learned? (182)

Sample Quiz 5.1

1. The outcome of a perceptual process is a(n): a) idea; b) sensation; c) percept; d) firing of a receptor cell.

2. Segregating objects one from another and determining movement pattern and distance of objects are processes in the phenomenon of: a) localization; b) stroboscopic motion; c) scanning; d) selective adaptation.

3. Apparent motion in the opposite direction of that which has just been viewed is the phenomenon called: a) induced motion; b) opposition action motion; c) motion aftereffect; d) absolute motion.

4. All connectionist models are restricted to: a) inhibitory connections; b) nodes; c) connections; d) both b and c.

5. The search for object features used in the recognition of natural objects (e.g., animals, plants, people) has been guided by the criterion that: a) shape features must be able to be constructed from more primitive features (such as lines and curves); b) shape features must not be combinable to form just any shape, but only specific ones; c) the features of organic objects are different from those of inorganic objects; d) both a and b.

6. Which of the following is *true*? a) When material being read is unfamiliar, there is a great deal of top–down processing. b) A stimulus object has to be ambiguous in order for there to be context effects in object perception. c) Top–down processing occurs if the input is sufficiently degraded even without context. d) Context effects appear to have only a minimal role in the processing of letters and words during reading.

7. Research showing reduced amplitude of brain waves in the auditory cortex in a task demanding divided attention provided evidence in support of: a) selection during early stages of recognition; b) color constancy; c) depth perception in infants; d) effects of rearing with limited stimulation.

8. A variable that determines size constancy is: a) retinal size of an object; b) perceived distance of an object; c) actual distance of an object; d) both a and b.

9. Contrast sensitivity is: a) the ability to discriminate dark and light stripes; b) the tendency to perceive an object regardless of changes in contrast; c) the process by which we select stimuli for awareness; d) the phenomenon in the dark in which two lights flashed in succession appear as a moving light.

10. In a study cited in your text using the habituation method to determine which of two teddy bears infants would look at, the critical variable was: a) softness; b) color; c) size constancy; d) face contour.

Sample Quiz 5.2

1. Which of the following is *not* included in your text as one of the functions of the perceptual system? a) localizing objects; b) transducing stimulus input; c) keeping the appearance of objects constant; d) recognizing objects.

2. Using a PET scanner, it was found that localization and recognition correspond to: a) blood flow in different areas of the brain; b) differing electrical potentials recorded at the surface of the brain; c) electrical activity in subcortical brain structures; d) none of the above; the PET scanner has not shown differential responsiveness of brain locations in perception.

3. The texture gradient: a) is one of the five monocular distance cues; b) is one of Gibson's "invariant" cues in perception; c) was an item of considerable interest to early Gestalt psychologists; d) is among the determinants of grouping.

4. In storing shape descriptions of letters, we speak of _____ if activation of a feature results in a decrease in activation of a letter. a) inhibitory connections; b) habituated connections; c) excitatory connections; d) hypercomplex connections.

5. That a letter is more perceptible when presented briefly in a word than when presented alone demonstrates: a) preferential looking; b) feedback connections in networks; c) receptive fields; d) bottom-up processing.

6. Perceptual processes that are driven by a person's knowledge are termed: a) top-down; b) bottom-up; c) knowledge-determined; d) input-oriented.

7. A system in the brain that mediates the selection of inputs relative to location is located: a) in the front of the brain; b) in the back of the brain; c) in the middle of the brain; d) in the brain stem.

8. If we removed an object from its background, we would: a) eliminate color constancy; b) eliminate lightness constancy; c) maximize perceptual constancy of any kind; d) both a and b.

9. The method for studying perceptual development that takes advantage of the tendency for infants to tire of staring at objects is the: a) preferential looking method; b) visual cliff method; c) contrast sensitivity method; d) habituation method.

10. Which of the following is *false*? a) The results of studies on rearing in the absence of stimulation point to a critical period beyond which the visual system is impaired. b) The earliest experiments on controlled stimulation attempted to determine the effects of rearing an animal without any visual stimulation. c) One of the difficulties in perceptual development studies of chimpanzees raised in darkness was that receptor and brain cells atrophied. d) The preferred method in studying effects of controlled stimulation is to raise animals without light from any source.

Answer Key, Chapter 5

Important Names

1. Max Wertheimer

Vocabulary and Details

1. percept
2. sensory information; percepts
3. pattern recognition; recognition
4. spatial localization; localization
5. perceptual constancy

DIVISION OF LABOR IN THE BRAIN

1. PET
2. processing modules

LOCALIZATION

1. segregating; distance; movement
2. Gestalt psychology
3. figure; ground
4. grouping
5. proximity; closure; similarity
6. distance (or depth) cues; monocular; binocular
7. relative size; superposition; relative height; linear perspective; motion
8. stereoscope; binocular parallax; binocular disparity
9. texture gradient
10. stroboscopic motion
11. induced motion
12. real motion; relative motion; absolute motion
13. selective adaptation
14. motion aftereffect

RECOGNITION

1. receptive field
2. simple; complex; hypercomplex
3. feature detectors
4. connectionist model
5. excitatory; inhibitory
6. bottom–up; top–down
7. ambiguous

ATTENTION

1. selective attention
2. scanning; fixations
3. early selection; before; late selection; after
4. locations; posterior system
5. anterior system; shape or color

PERCEPTUAL CONSTANCIES

1. perceptual constancy
2. size–distance invariance
3. illusion

PERCEPTUAL DEVELOPMENT

1. preferential looking
2. habituation method
3. visual acuity
4. contrast sensitivity
5. visual cliff
6. critical period

Sample Quiz 5.1

1. c, 152
2. a, 154
3. c, 160
4. d, 165
5. a, 166
6. c, 170
7. a, 172
8. d, 176
9. a, 179
10. c, 180-181

Sample Quiz 5.2

1. b, 152
2. a, 153
3. b, 158
4. a, 164
5. b, 165
6. b, 167
7. b, 173
8. d, 174
9. d, 178
10. d, 181

Consciousness and Its Altered States

Learning Objectives

1. Be familiar with the history of the study of consciousness. Be able to define consciousness in terms of its function in monitoring information and controlling our actions.

2. Know what is meant by the terms subconscious processes, preconscious memories, and the unconscious. Be familiar with the phenomenon of dissociation as illustrated by dissociate identity disorder.

3. Be able to discuss in some detail sleep schedules, stages of sleep, REM and NREM sleep, and sleep disorders.

4. Be familiar with Freud's theory of dreams and with the theories proposed by Evans and by Crick and Mitchison. Know the answers to the questions about dreams discussed in the text.

5. Know what is meant by the term psychoactive drug. Be able to characterize drug dependence and drug abuse.

6. Be able to give examples of each of the subcategories of psychoactive drugs discussed in the text. Be familiar with typical patterns of use of these drugs.

7. Be able to define meditation and describe the various techniques used to induce a meditative state. Be familiar with the research findings on meditation.

8. Be able to describe the procedure and typical effects of a hypnosis session. Be familiar with the phenomena of posthypnotic amnesia and other posthypnotic suggestions; understand the questions of conscious control that these phenomena raise.

9. Be able to define the phenomena included under the term psi. Be familiar with the ganzfeld procedure, the results obtained, and the issues involved in evaluating these results.

Important Names

1. In the view of _____, the father of behaviorism, the data of psychology must be objective and measurable, thus limiting study to public events and substituting verbal reports for "consciousness." (187)

2. At the other end of the spectrum, according to the psychoanalytic theory of _____, some memories, impulses, and desires that are of great importance are in the unconscious and cannot enter consciousness. (189)

3. The French psychiatrist _____ is credited with the concept of dissociation. (190)

Vocabulary and Details

1. Whenever there is a change from an ordinary pattern of mental functioning to a state that *seems* different to the person experiencing the change, psychologists speak of an _____. Such states are personal and _____. (187)

ASPECTS OF CONSCIOUSNESS

1. Early psychologists defined psychology as the study of _____ and used the method of _____. (187)

2. Later, behaviorists reserved the term _____ events for those observable only to the experiencing person (such as those in consciousness), and restricted the term _____ events to actual behavior (such as verbal reports of consciousness). (187)

3. In the current definition, the term *consciousness* involves two processes: (a) _____ ourselves and our environment so that our awareness of events is accurate; and (b) _____ ourselves and our environment so that we can initiate and terminate behavior and cognitions. (188)

4. Stimuli may be registered and evaluated without conscious perception; in this case, the stimuli are said to influence us _____. (189)

5. Memories that are not part of consciousness at a given moment but are accessible if you wish to retrieve them are termed _____. (189)

6. In Freud's psychoanalytic view, some emotionally painful memories, wishes, and impulses are _____, that is, assigned to the _____, where they may continue to influence behavior even though we are not aware of them. (189)

7. One example of the influence of the unconscious upon behavior is an unintentional remark that is assumed to reveal hidden impulses; this remark is termed a _____. (189)

DISSOCIATION

1. When certain skills become so well–learned that they no longer require attention, they are termed _____. (190)

2. One interpretation of automatic processing is that the control is still there (we can focus on the automatic process if we wish to), but that it has been severed or _____ from consciousness. (190)

3. In Janet's concept of _____, under certain conditions some thoughts and actions become split off (dissociated) from consciousness and function outside of awareness. (190)

4. _____, also called _____, is the existence of two or more integrated and well–developed personalities within the same individual. (191)

SLEEP AND DREAMS

1. The graphic recording of electrical changes on the scalp associated with brain activity, or brain waves, is termed an _____ or _____. (193)

2. During periods of relaxation with eyes closed, such as prior to sleep, the brain may show a regular pattern of slow waves, termed _____. (193)

3. _____ sleep are periods of sleep detected with electrodes showing rapid eye movements, characteristically active EEG patterns, and dreaming; these periods occur repeatedly in alternation with the other four stages of sleep, termed _____ sleep. (194)

4. REM sleep is characterized by a brain that is _____ in a virtually _____ body; NREM sleep by an _____ brain in a very _____ body. (195)

5. A _____ exists whenever the inability to sleep well produces impaired daytime functioning or excessive sleepiness. (195)

6. When a person complains about dissatisfaction with amount or quality of his or her sleep, we speak of the sleep disorder _____. (196)

7. A very rare sleep disorder, _____, is characterized by recurring, irresistible attacks of drowsiness and the tendency to fall asleep at inappropriate times, for periods ranging from _____ to _____ . (196)

8. A third sleep disorder is the condition called _____, in which the individual stops breathing from _____ to _____ (how many?) times while asleep. (196-197)

9. _____ is an altered state of consciousness in which remembered images and fantasies temporarily are confused with external reality. (197)

10. In a _____, events seem so normal, without the illogical character of most dreams, that dreamers feel they are awake and conscious. (197)

11. In Freud's view, the _____ content of a dream consists of the symbolic representation of the repressed (unconscious) wishes that underlie it; the _____ content of a dream consists of the characters and events that make up the actual dream narrative. The transformation of the former into the latter is done by _____. (198)

PSYCHOACTIVE DRUGS

1. Drugs that affect behavior, consciousness, and mood are called _____. (199)

2. Through repeated use, a person can become dependent on a drug, a phenomenon called _____ dependence, or _____. Drug dependence is characterized by a) _____, that is, a need for more of the drug to achieve the same effect, b) _____, unpleasant physical and psychological reactions if the drug is discontinued, and c) _____, taking more of a drug than intended, inability to control its use, and spending time trying to obtain it. (200-201)

3. By contrast, when a person is not dependent on a drug but continues to use it despite the consequences, we speak of _____. (201)

4. A drug that depresses the central nervous system is called a _____; this class includes _____, _____, _____, and the most commonly used member of the group, _____. (201-202)

5. Maternal drinking may cause _____, a condition of the child characterized by mental retardation and multiple deformities of the face and mouth. (203)

6. Another group of drugs that diminish physical sensation and the capacity to respond to stimuli by depressing the central nervous system are known collectively as _____; these drugs include the substance from the poppy plant _____ and its derivatives _____ and _____, as well as the powerful derivative of morphine, _____. (203-204)

7. A group of neurotransmitters, called _____, resemble the opiates in molecular shape and produce sensations of pleasure and reduced discomfort through binding to _____. (205)

8. Drug abuse medications fall into two categories, (a) _____, those that modulate the opioid receptors by binding to them, and (b) _____, those that lock onto the opioid receptors and that serve to "block" them so that the opiates cannot gain access. (205)

9. One example of an agonist that is used for suppressing the craving for heroin and preventing withdrawal is _____. (205)

10. An example of an antagonist that blocks heroin action because it has a greater affinity for an opioid receptor site than heroin itself is _____. (205)

11. By contrast with depressants and opiates, drugs that *increase* arousal are called _____, for example, _____ and _____. (205-206)

12. Long-term stimulant use may cause _____, the false belief that people are out to get you (sometimes accompanied by violent behavior), or experiences in the absence of stimulus input, that is, _____, in visual, auditory, and (in the case of cocaine) sensory forms. (206-207)

13. Psychoactive drugs whose main effect is to change perceptual experience are called _____, including the natural substances from cactus and mushrooms, _____ and _____, respectively, and the laboratory produced drugs, _____ and _____. (207-208)

14. The plant _____ yields the substance _____ from its leaves and flowers and _____ from a solidified resin; the active ingredient is _____. (208)

MEDITATION

1. In _____, a person achieves an altered state of consciousness by performing certain rituals and exercises, including controlling and regulating _____, restricting _____, assuming _____, and forming _____. (209)

2. Traditional forms of meditation follow either the religious practices of _____, from Hinduism, or _____, from Buddhism—including so–called _____ in which the subject clears the mind for receiving new experiences, and so–called _____ in which there is active attention to some object, word, or idea. (210)

3. The recent, secularized form of meditation, called _____ or _____, involves the repeated saying of a sound termed a _____ while sitting quietly and in relaxing conditions. (210)

HYPNOSIS

1. In _____, a cooperative subject relinquishes some control over his or her behavior to the hypnotist (becomes more suggestible) and accepts some reality distortion. (212)

2. Subjects who have been brought out of hypnosis may respond with movement to a prearranged signal in the phenomenon called _____. (213)

3. At the suggestion of the hypnotist, events occurring during hypnosis may be forgotten until a signal enables the subject to recall them, a phenomenon called _____. (213)

4. In _____ during hypnosis, some individuals are able to relive episodes from earlier periods of life. (214)

5. During hypnosis, a subject may see an object or hear a voice that is not actually present in the phenomenon of _____; conversely, the subject may also *not* perceive something that is present in the phenomenon called _____. (215)

PSI PHENOMENA

1. The term _____ refers to information and/or energy exchanges not currently explicable in terms of known physical mechanisms. These phenomena are the subject matter of _____. (216)

2. One class of such psi phenomena is _____, a response to external stimuli without known sensory contact. (216)

3. Three examples of ESP are (a) _____, thought transference between two people without known sensory communication; (b) _____, perception of objects or events that do not provide a physical stimulus; and (c) _____, perception of a future event without the use of known inferential processes. (216)

4. Another class of psi phenomena is _____, mental influence over physical events without the intervention of a known physical force. (216)

5. The term _____, as applied to research in parapsychology and other fields, is a statistical technique that treats accumulated studies as a single grand experiment and each individual study as a single observation. (218)

Ideas and Concepts

ASPECTS OF CONSCIOUSNESS

* 1. a) Discuss the changing views of consciousness from early definitions through the views of behaviorism. (187-188)

   b) Did behaviorism require a radical change in its views of private events? Explain, using the term **verbal responses** in your answer. (187)

   c) What difficulty with the behaviorist position espoused by John Watson did many psychologists see and what was said to be neglected in this view? (187-188)

* d) Indicate the view of consciousness that became prominent in psychology beginning in the 1960s. (188)

2. a) Why can we not attend to all of the stimuli that impinge on us? (188)

* b) In what sense is attention "selective" and what determines priority of selectiveness? (188)

* 3. a) List the three aspects of the controlling function of consciousness. What special function of consciousness can occur in planning? (188)

   b) Are all actions and problem solving guided by conscious experience? Explain. (188)

4. From the text and your own experience, give some examples of the following. (189)

   —subconscious phenomena:

   —preconscious memories:

* 5. a) List several ways in which unconscious thoughts and impulses can appear. (189)

   b) In Freud's view, what is the cause of most mental illness and what is the goal of psychoanalysis with respect to material in the unconscious and in consciousness? (189)

* c) In what respects would many psychologists accept and challenge Freud's view of the unconscious? Provide an example where possible. (189)

   d) Why do some psychologists speak of a **nonconscious-unconscious** continuum? (190)

*Basic ideas and concepts

88   Chapter 6

DISSOCIATION

1. a) Cite some examples of automatic processes from the text and your own experience. (190)

* b) What is the apparent function of automatic processes? Cite an instance in which they may have negative consequences. (190)

* 2. a) In what respect does Janet's concept of dissociation differ from Freud's notion of repression? (190)

b) Give some examples of mild forms of dissociation. (190)

* 3. a) Discuss some of the characteristics of dissociative identity disorder. On what dimensions may the primary and alternate identities within the same individual differ? (191)

* b) Is the primary identity usually aware of the other identities? What can be a clue to the presence of dissociative identity disorder? (191)

* 4. a) What is a frequent report of persons with dissociative identity disorder and why is the accuracy of such a report controversial? (192)

* b) Indicate the nature of the initial dissociation and outline the mechanism by which the dissociation process may work. (Relatedly, why are many cases of multiple personality female?) (192)

c) Discuss another factor in the development of dissociative identity disorder. (192)

d) What may happen when an individual discovers that an alternate personality developed through self–hypnosis relieves emotional pain? (192)

5. How common is dissociative identity disorder and what are the opposing positions as to its prevalence? (192)

SLEEP AND DREAMS

* 1. List four ways in which sleep and wakefulness are alike. (192-193)

* 2. Characterize the stages of sleep listed below in terms of their respective EEG patterns and, where possible, other features. Use the terms *spindles, delta waves,* and *non–REM sleep* in your answer. (193)

—Stage 1:

—Stage 2:

—Stages 3 and 4:

3. a) Describe the typical alternation of the various stages of sleep throughout the night, noting the common pattern of REM sleep. (194)

Consciousness and Its Altered States   89

b) Is the pattern of sleep cycles consistent across age? Explain. (194-195)

* 4. Discuss the evidence concerning the state of the brain and body in REM sleep. (195)

* 5. a) What are the data with regard to the incidence of dreaming in REM and NREM sleep? (195)

   b) Therefore, in what two respects is mental activity different in REM and NREM periods? (195)

6. Cite the statistics on normal sleep patterns. What happens if the usual requirement is not met? (195)

* 7. Why do your authors say that having insomnia is always a "subjective decision"? That is, is insomnia always accompanied by abnormal sleep patterns? Cite the evidence. (196)

8. a) Describe the intrusion of REM states in narcolepsy. (196)

   b) What evidence suggests that narcolepsy is genetic? (196)

* 9. a) Discuss two mechanisms for apnea attacks. (197)

   b) Why does the sleeper awaken during an apnea? (197)

   c) Who is especially afflicted by sleep apnea? Are sleeping pills a good remedy? Why or why not? (197)

* 10. a) Does everyone dream? Indicate the most widely accepted hypothesis concerning dream recall. 197)

   b) How long do dreams last? Cite the evidence relating the length of incidents in dreams versus real life. (197)

*   c) Do people know when they are dreaming? Be familiar with some of the "experiments" that have been conducted by individuals experiencing lucid dreams. (197-198)

*   d) Can people control the content of their dreams? Describe how this control is made possible by citing examples of *implicit predream suggestion, overt predream suggestion,* and *posthypnotic suggestion.* (198)

* 11. Outline Freud's theory of dreams, using the terms *wish fulfillment* and *censor* in your answer. (198)

* 12. a) Discuss Evan's theory of dream sleep in terms of the nature of the process that is ongoing during sleep and what actually forms the content of a dream. (198-199)

   b) Why is the value of a dream in understanding the underlying process somewhat limited by this view? (199)

* 13. a) By contrast, what are the essential ideas of the Crick and Mitchison theory of dreams. Use the term *neural networks* in your answer. (199)

90   Chapter 6

b) What is the specific role of REM sleep in this view? Relatedly, is it a good idea to try to remember one's dreams? Why or why not? (199)

* 14. Compare the Evans and the Crick and Mitchison theories of dreams from the standpoint of the following: (199)

—Two differences:

—Two similarities:

PSYCHOACTIVE DRUGS

* 1. a) Discuss the shift of this society in drug use over the past 40 years. (200)

* b) Indicate a reason for the apparent decline in drug use among young people and note the most recent trend. (200)

2. a) Give an example of a drug that may produce rapid tolerance and one that seems to produce little. (201)

b) Similarly, indicate the patterns of withdrawal for a number of commonly abused drugs. (201)

3. a) List some common inhalants. (202)

* b) Why are inhalants a source of concern? (202)

* 4. a) What is the most commonly abused depressant? (201-202)

b) List some of the effects of the following *blood alcohol concentrations*: (202)

—.03 to .05 percent:

—.10 percent:

—.20 percent:

—.40 percent:

c) Can we state how much a person can drink without becoming legally intoxicated? Explain. (202)

* 5. a) Indicate some of the positive and negative effects of alcohol consumption among college students including effects on physical health. What is the most serious problem? (202)

* b) Cite some of the physical effects of regular use of substantial amounts of alcohol. (202)

* 6. a) Discuss some of the recent trends in the use of alcohol among young people. What is particularly disturbing about *binge drinking*? (202-203)

  b) What are some of the steps being taken to deal with this problem? (203)

  c) How much alcohol is needed to cause fetal alcohol syndrome in babies? (203)

7. What is the common name for the "opiates" and why is it not a very accurate term? (203)

8. a) In what ways can heroin be taken into the body? Describe some of the cognitive and behavioral influences of the drug. (204)

* b) What effects of heroin apparently induce people to *start* its use? Outline the course of events that may lead to other methods of heroin ingestion, including "mainlining." (204)

* c) Then what seems to underlie the tendency to *continue* use of heroin? Use the terms withdrawal and addiction in your answer. (204)

* d) Indicate three other hazards of heroin use. (204)

* 9. a) What major breakthrough was made in the 1970s in understanding opiate addiction? (204-205)

* b) Discuss the mechanism by which morphine and heroin relieve pain and the relationship of this process to the endorphins. In this analysis, why does discontinuation of heroin use lead to withdrawal? (205)

* c) Describe some treatment advances that have resulted from increasing knowledge of the mechanism of opiate action at the receptors, using the terms agonists and antagonists. (205)

  d) What are some of the advantages and disadvantages of the drugs methadone and naltrexone in dealing with drug abuse? (205)

10. a) Cite some of the trade names and colloquial terms for amphetamines. (205)

* b) What are two immediate effects of amphetamine consumption? List some other psychological and behavioral effects of their use. (205-206)

  c) Describe the likely sequence that leads to overuse and the development of tolerance for amphetamines. What happens when oral ingestion is no longer effective and what is a common result? (Use the term *crash* in your answer.) (206)

* d) Discuss the effects of long–term amphetamine use. In what three respects do the behaviors of "speed freaks" resemble those of acute schizophrenics? (206)

* 11. a) List some of the psychological effects of cocaine. (206)

  b) In what forms can cocaine be taken into the body? (Use the term *crack*.) (206)

92   Chapter 6

*   c) What characteristic of cocaine did Freud discover under unfortunate circumstances and what current form of coke listed in b) above renders this effect even more serious? (206-207)

   12. a) Identify the abnormal symptoms of heavy cocaine use, including the terms *snow lights* and *cocaine bugs* in your answer. (207)

*   b) Outline the effects of maternal use of cocaine and the mechanism that renders this particularly dangerous for a fetus. (207)

   c) Indicate the connection between the use of coke and AIDS. (207)

* 13. a) Outline some of the effects of the hallucinogens in terms of perceptions and hallucinations. (207)

*   b) Indicate four adverse reactions to LSD. (208)

   c) Why has the use of LSD *generally* declined? (208)

* 14. a) Why is PCP a widely used drug and why is it technically classified as a "dissociative anesthetic"? (208)

   b) Why was PCP first made and what caused the discontinuation of its legal manufacture? (208)

   c) What are some typical effects of PCP at low doses and at high doses? (208)

* 15. a) Describe typical effects of THC, including the stages of reactions that occur and sensory and perceptual changes that have been reported. (208)

   b) Are all marijuana experiences pleasant? Cite the data. (208)

   c) Describe the experiences of regular users of marijuana. (208-209)

*   d) Discuss the effects of marijuana use upon performance on complex tasks and some of the implications of these findings for common activities, such as driving and flying aircraft. In what respect do such effects persist? (209)

   e) Indicate two clear effects of marijuana on memory. (209)

MEDITATION

* 1. a) Indicate several results of meditative exercises. (209)

   b) Cite some perceptual effects of concentrative meditation. (210)

   2. Be familiar with Benson's five steps for a *relaxation response* through meditation. What effects can this procedure produce? (210-211))

* 3. a) List the physiological effects of meditation that indicate its effectiveness as a relaxation technique. (211)

   b) Discuss some of the uses for meditation in the context of sports psychology, including for stress reduction and mental image formation. (211)

Consciousness and Its Altered States   93

* 4. What is your authors' conclusion with regard to the evidence on meditation? (211)

HYPNOSIS

* 1. a) Describe three of the methods used in inducing a hypnotic condition, including one other than relaxation. (212)

  b) Does modern hypnosis use authoritarian commands? Explain, indicating when subjects enter the hypnotic state. (212)

* c) Summarize six changes to be expected in a subject when hypnotized. (212)

  2. a) Is everyone equally susceptible to hypnosis? Cite the evidence. (212-213)

  b) Is a very hypnotizable subject also highly suggestible in social settings? Then what is a good predictor of responsiveness to hypnosis? (213)

* 3. Describe the effects of hypnotic suggestions on each of the following aspects of behaviors and experiences citing examples and the results of related studies, where possible. (213-216)

  —control of movement (use the term *posthypnotic response*):

  —posthypnotic amnesia:

  —age regression:

  —positive and negative hallucinations (be sure to note the uses of hallucinations in pain control):

PSI PHENOMENA

* 1. Discuss the current attitudes of some scientists on parapsychology. In your authors' view, what is the real question to be answered? (216)

  2. a) Describe the method of parapsychology termed the *ganzfeld procedure*. (216)

  b) What results have been obtained with this method and what is the likelihood of such results that lead your authors to state that this is the "most promising" of the methods of parapsychology? (217)

* 3. As an exercise in scientific methods, summarize the debate over evidence obtained from the ganzfeld studies in terms of:

  a) *Problems of replication.* How replicable is the phenomenon when meta–analysis is employed? What role does the strength of effect and number of observations play in this issue? (217-218)

  b) *Problems of inadequate controls.* By contrast with the typical history of parapsychology insofar as proper controls are concerned, how has meta–analysis been applied to the ganzfeld studies to deal with this issue and what have been the results? Use the term *sensory leakage* in your answer. (218)

c) *The file–drawer problem.* What is the file–drawer problem in the context of the ganzfeld studies? How has meta–analysis been used to address this issue? (218-219)

4. Discuss the three types of problems that emerge in the analysis of anecdotal evidence. Use the example of *precognitive dreams* to illustrate one of these problems. (219)

* 5. Discuss why there is such a level of continuing skepticism regarding psi phenomena in terms of:

a) *Extraordinary claims.* In the view of scientists, what do extraordinary claims demand and on what does extraordinariness depend? (220)

b) *The views of psychologists.* List three reasons why psychologists are so skeptical of the claims of parapsychology. In your authors' view, is all of this skepticism well–founded? Why or why not? (220-221)

Sample Quiz 6.1

1. The term consciousness involves: a) monitoring ourselves; b) initiating our own behavior; c) controlling our environment so as to initiate behavior; d) all of the above.

2. Which of the following is characteristic of both sleep and wakefulness? a) planfulness; b) sensitivity to the environment; c) ability to form memories; d) all of the above.

3. The latent content of a dream consists of: a) the symbolic representation of unconscious wishes; b) the characters in a dream narrative; c) the actual sequence of events within a dream; d) the material that is reorganized in Evans's theory of dreaming.

4. Your authors attribute a decline in drug use among young people during the 1980s especially to: a) tougher law enforcement; b) stricter penalties; c) education about hazards; d) stronger family units.

5. Long–term use of stimulants may cause: a) depression of the central nervous system; b) persecutory delusions; c) hallucinations; d) both b and c.

6. With respect to the drug PCP, which of the following is *false*? a) It is classified as a dissociative anesthetic. b) The substance is widely used. c) In low doses its effects are unpleasant and remain in memory for long periods. d) It is easy to manufacture.

7. A method in which a person relinquishes some control over their behavior to another person and accepts some reality distortion is: a) meditation; b) clairvoyance; c) hypnosis; d) narcolepsy.

8. Failing to perceive something in the environment that is present is termed a: a) Freudian slip; b) negative hallucination; c) posthypnotic response; d) positive hallucination.

9. The ganzfeld procedure is: a) a statistical procedure; b) a means for achieving an altered state of consciousness by controlling breathing, movement, and images; c) a procedure for inducing hallucinations during hypnosis; d) testing for telepathic communication between a sender and receiver who are isolated from one another in rooms that create a totally restricted field.

10. The difficulty in obtaining the same results in psi experiments both within a laboratory and between laboratories is the problem of: a) inadequate controls; b) replication; c) overreliance on meta–analysis; d) sensory leakage.

Sample Quiz 6.2

1. In the development of the concept of consciousness in psychology, at the earliest stage: a) it was held that the field could only study public events; b) verbal responses were observed as a substitute for introspection; c) consciousness was equated with mind; d) neurological methods were already available to enable direct measurement of mental events.

2. Processes that apparently function to free up consciousness for other tasks are termed: a) precognitive processes; b) psi phenomena; c) opening–up processes; d) automatic processes.

3. The graphic recording of brain waves is called an: a) EMG; b) EEG; c) EGG; d) EOG.

4. A point of *difference* between the Evans and the Crick and Mitchison models of dreaming is: a) the view of the function of REM sleep as a period of reorganization or a means for eliminating useless information; b) the notion that REM sleep plays a role in memory storage; c) the degree to which each assigns symbolism and concealed meaning to dreams; d) both b and c.

5. A condition in newborns characterized by mental retardation and multiple deformities of the face has been related to the mother's abuse of: a) alcohol; b) marijuana; c) amphetamines; d) naltrexone.

6. Which of the following is *true* of meditation? a) In the concentrative method, the individual clears the mind for receiving new experiences. b) In Benson's procedure for attaining relaxation, it is important to make efforts to force out distracting thoughts whenever they occur. c) Research on effects of meditation is of high quality and strongly supports the value of the method. d) None of the above.

7. The posthypnotic response refers to: a) movements in response to a signal made after hypnosis as a result of a suggestion previously made by the hypnotist; b) forgetting the events that took place during hypnosis; c) the ability to relive episodes from earlier in life; d) convincing perceptual distortions of the world after hypnosis.

8. Precognition is defined in your text as: a) mental influence over physical events without the intervention of a physical force; b) thought transference between two people without known sensory communication; c) perception of a future event without the use of known inferential processes; d) perception of objects that do not provide a physical stimulus.

9. A statistical technique that treats individual experiments as single observations is termed: a) meta–analysis; b) correlational analysis; c) single–subject design; d) the ganzfeld method.

10. The most skeptical group with respect to the phenomena of parapsychology is: a) professors in the arts and humanities; b) psychologists; c) the common public; d) physicists and natural scientists.

Important Names

1. John Watson
2. Sigmund Freud
3. Pierre Janet

Vocabulary and Details

1. altered state of consciousness; subjective

ASPECTS OF CONSCIOUSNESS

1. mind and consciousness; introspection
2. private events; public events
3. monitoring; controlling
4. subconsciously
5. preconscious memories
6. repressed; unconscious
7. Freudian slip

DISSOCIATION

1. automatic processes
2. dissociated
3. dissociation
4. dissociative identity disorder; multiple personality

SLEEP AND DREAMS

1. electroencephalogram; EEG
2. alpha waves
3. REM; NREM
4. wide awake (or active); paralyzed; idle; relaxed
1. sleep disorder
2. insomnia
3. narcolepsy; a few seconds; 15–30 minutes
4. sleep apnea; a few; several hundred
5. dreaming
6. lucid dream
7. latent; manifest; dreamwork

PSYCHOACTIVE DRUGS

1. psychoactive
2. drug dependence; addiction; tolerance; withdrawal; compulsive use
3. drug abuse
4. depressant; tranquilizers; barbiturates; inhalants; ethyl alcohol
5. fetal alcohol syndrome
6. opiates; opium; morphine; codeine; heroin
7. endorphins; opioid receptors
8. agonist; antagonist
9. methadone
10. naltrexone
11. stimulants; amphetamines; cocaine
12. persecutory delusions; hallucinations
13. hallucinogens; mescaline; psilocybin; LSD (or lysergic acid diethylamide); PCP (or phencyclidine)
14. cannabis; marijuana; hashish; THC (or tetrahydrocannabinol)

MEDITATION

1. meditation; breathing; attention; yogic positions; mental images
2. yoga; Zen; opening–up meditation; concentrative meditation
3. transcendental meditation; TM; mantra

HYPNOSIS

1. hypnosis
2. posthypnotic response
3. posthypnotic amnesia
4. age regression
5. positive hallucination; negative hallucination

PSI PHENOMENA

1. psi phenomena; parapsychology
2. extrasensory perception (or ESP)
3. telepathy; clairvoyance; precognition
4. psychokinesis (or PK)
5. meta–analysis

Sample Quiz 6.1   Sample Quiz 6.2

Sample Quiz 6.1	Sample Quiz 6.2
1. d, 188	1. c, 187
2. d, 192-193	2. d, 190
3. a, 198	3. b, 193
4. c, 200	4. a, 199
5. d, 206	5. a, 203
6. c, 208	6. d, 210-211
7. c, 212	7. a, 213
8. b, 215	8. c, 216
9. d, 216	9. a, 218
10. b, 217-218	10. b, 220

Learning and Conditioning

Learning Objectives

1. Be able to explain what is meant by the term associative learning. Know the distinction between the two forms of associative learning—namely, classical conditioning and operant conditioning.

2. Be familiar with Pavlov's experiments. Be able to define and to differentiate between the CR, UCR, the CS, and the UCS. Know how these are related during both the acquisition and extinction of a classically conditioned response.

3. Know how generalization and discrimination function in classical conditioning. Be able to give examples of each in human learning. Be familiar with the role of temporal contiguity and predictability in establishing a conditioned response.

4. Be familiar with the ethologists' objections to a strictly behavioristic approach to learning and their notion of behavioral constraints. Know why experiments on taste aversion are critical to an ethological analysis of behavior.

5. Understand some of the neural bases for classical conditioning in terms of the structural changes that appear to be involved and the mechanisms for habituation.

6. Be prepared to discuss the law of effect in relation to operant conditioning. Be familiar with the "Skinner box" and be able to define extinction and discrimination for operant conditioning in this apparatus.

7. Know how behavior can be shaped and why shaping is an important advantage of operant conditioning over classical conditioning.

8. Be able to define conditioned reinforcement, schedules of reinforcement, and partial reinforcement; show, by examples, how each increases the generality of operant conditioning in everyday life.

9. Understand the nature of aversive conditioning, its several forms, and applications to behavior in everyday situations.

10. Know what is meant by the term mental representation and the role it plays in a cognitive analysis of learning via cognitive maps and insight.

11. Understand what the study of learning in situations with less than perfect associations indicates about the role of cognitive processes. Know what the term spurious associations means in these experiments.

Important Names

1. The Nobel prize–winning Russian physiologist who pioneered research on classical conditioning in dogs was _____. (228)

2. The study of a form of operant conditioning began at the turn of the century with a series of experiments on problem solving in cats by _____, who became known for his related formulation of the law of effect. (239)

3. A more recent and influential psychologist who has reconceptualized the study of operant conditioning is _____. (239)

4. An early advocate of a cognitive view of learning was _____, who studied the behavior of rats in mazes and other tasks demanding complex solutions. (249)

5. The study of "insight" in chimpanzees and other primates in the 1920s was pioneered by the researcher _____. (250)

Vocabulary and Details

1. A relatively permanent change in behavior that results from practice is termed _____. (227)

2. In the simplest of four different kinds of learning, we learn to ignore a stimulus that has become familiar and has no serious consequences, a form of learning called _____. (227)

3. Learning that certain events go together is called forming _____. (227)

4. In one form of associative learning, termed _____, an organism learns that one event follows another; in the other form of associative learning, termed _____, an organism learns that a particular consequence will follow a response event. (227)

5. The fourth form of learning, what your authors call _____, involves something more than forming associations, for example, applying a cognitive strategy or using a mental map. (227)

CLASSICAL CONDITIONING

1. Prior to classical conditioning, a stimulus, termed the _____ (_____), evokes a response, termed the _____ (_____). (228)

2. During classical conditioning, a second stimulus, termed the _____ (_____), is presented regularly with the UCS; as a result, a response to the second stimulus, termed the _____ (_____) comes to be evoked. (228)

3. After classical conditioning, we say that the organism has been taught, or _____, to associate the CS (for example, a light) with the UCS (for example, food) such that it responds similarly (for example, salivates) to both. (228)

4. Each time a CS is paired with a UCS, we speak of a _____. (228)

5. During the _____ stage of conditioning, pairings of the UCS with the CS are said to strengthen or _____ the association between them, as measured by the strength of the CR. (228)

6. Conversely, in the process called _____, the CS is presented alone repeatedly and there is no reinforcer (UCS); as a result, the strength of the association gradually diminishes, as measured by the CR. (228)

7. Recovery of a CR that has undergone extinction, for example by moving an organism to a new context, is termed _____. (229)

8. In _____, a stimulus (say, a light) that has become a CS during previous conditioning may act as a "UCS" (say, like food) in a new conditioning relationship; that is, the light may now be used to condition a CR to a new stimulus (say, a tone) by pairing the two stimuli. (230)

9. When a CR has been associated with a particular CS, other stimuli will tend to evoke the CR to the extent that they are similar to the CS, in the process called _____. (230)

10. Conversely, when a CR occurs to a CS but not to other stimuli that deliberately have not been reinforced with the UCS (or that are dissimilar to the CS), we speak of _____. (230)

11. To produce conditioned discrimination, we selectively may reinforce one conditioned stimulus, CS_1, and not reinforce another stimulus, CS_2, in the procedure called _____; as a result the strength of the CR to CS_1 will _____ (increase/decrease) and to CS_2 will _____ (increase/decrease). (230-231)

12. In _____, an organism is conditioned to be fearful in the presence of a CS due to its repeated pairings with a powerful and negative UCS. (231)

13. Pavlov maintained that the critical factor in classical conditioning was _____ of the CS and UCS. (232)

14. More recent theorists, such as Rescorla, have maintained that the critical event in classical conditioning is that the CS be a _____ of the UCS. (232)

15. In the _____ phenomenon first demonstrated by Kamin, the learning of one association may "block" the learning of a second association to the extent that the second association is _____, that is, provides information an organism already has (and fails to render the UCS any more predictable). (233)

16. Biologists and psychologists who study animal behavior in the natural environment are called _____. (235)

17. In the phenomenon of _____, an animal learns to avoid a given taste because it has been associated with poison and sickness in a classical conditioning relationship. (235)

18. Indirect support for the possibility that there are structural neural changes in learning comes from the phenomenon called _____, that is, increases in rate of activity of electrically stimulated neurons that were previously stimulated. (237)

1. In _____, responses are learned because they _____ on (or affect) the environment. (238)

2. The likelihood that an operant response will be repeated depends upon the nature of its environmental _____. (238)

3. The _____ states that when a reward immediately follows a behavior the learning of the action is strengthened. (239)

4. In a "Skinner box" an operant response such as pressing a bar may be followed by food (the "reinforcer") which is said to _____ bar pressing and _____ (increase/decrease) the rate of pressing. (239-240)

5. The conditioned response in an operant conditioning setting is termed simply the _____. (240)

6. If an operant is not reinforced, it will undergo _____, that is, its rate will _____(increase/decrease). (240)

7. If an operant response is selectively reinforced (say, with food) only in the presence of a given stimulus (say, a light), the response will come under the control of what we now term the _____ (that is, the light in this example). (240)

8. A useful measure of the strength of an operant is its _____, that is, its frequency in a given time interval. (240-241)

9. In the technique called _____, only those variations in response that deviate in the direction desired by the experimenter are reinforced. (242)

10. Some reinforcers, such as food, are called _____ because they satisfy basic bodily needs. (242)

11. Most reinforcers, however, such as money or praise, are called _____ or _____ reinforcers because they are stimuli that acquire their value through association with a primary reinforcer. (242)

12. Reinforcing a response only some of the time it occurs is termed _____. (244)

13. The _____ refers to the fact that extinction following partial reinforcement is slower than extinction following reinforcement of every response (that is, continuous reinforcement). (244)

14. The particular basis on which reinforcement is provided or "scheduled" is called a _____. (244)

15. When an aversive event is used in an effort to weaken a response or teach a new response we speak of _____. (245)

16. Technically, when an operant response is followed by an aversive event in an effort to weaken or suppress the behavior, we speak of _____. (245)

17. In another form of aversive conditioning, called _____, an organism may learn to make a response to terminate an ongoing aversive event; relatedly, if a response prevents an aversive event from even starting, the procedure is called _____. (246)

18. In a cognitive approach, we can say that operant conditioning occurs only when the organism *perceives* a _____ between its responses and reinforcement. (247)

COMPLEX LEARNING

1. Also in the _____ approach to intelligence and problems of learning, the organism is understood to "operate" on _____ of the world rather than on the world itself. (248)

2. In Tolman's cognitive approach to learning, he maintained that rats may develop a mental representation of the layout of mazes (and other spatial relationships), termed a _____. (249)

3. In studies of associative learning in humans, it appears that subjects may have _____ about relations to be learned that may determine what is learned. (251-252)

4. Nonexistent but plausible relations between events, called _____, are one kind of prior belief that may influence behavior. (252)

5. When a prior belief about, say, an associative relation is combined with objective input about that relation to yield an estimate of the strength of the relation, we may speak of _____. (252)

Ideas and Concepts

1. Distinguish classical from operant conditioning by example. (227)

PERSPECTIVES ON LEARNING

* 1. a) What perspective in psychology dominated early work in the field of learning and upon what was its focus? (227)

* b) Outline several assumptions of the traditional behavioristic approach to learning. (227)

 c) To what did these assumptions lead? (227)

2. In your authors' view, what are three reasons why the behaviorist's assumptions have to be modified? (227-228)

*Basic ideas and concepts

CLASSICAL CONDITIONING

* 1. Outline Pavlov's basic classical conditioning experiments by filling in the blanks in the diagram below. Use the technical terms and abbreviations for each of the stimuli and responses and be sure you can cite a real example for each event from Pavlov's research. (See also Figure 7-1.) (228-229)

BEFORE CONDITIONING

DURING CONDITIONING

AFTER CONDITIONING

* 2. a) Using examples, outline the procedures and outcomes of acquisition and extinction. (Be sure to note the course of acquisition and extinction in Figure 7-2.) (228-229)

* b) Why can extinction not involve true unlearning of a response? Then what view do modern researchers subscribe to in interpreting this phenomenon? (228-229)

c) Describe the processes of classical conditioning in more intuitive terms, such as "prediction" and "success." (229)

* 3. To illustrate classical conditioning in different species, for both of the examples described in your text, be able to indicate the UCS, UCR, CS, and CR: (229-230)

—conditioning in flatworms:

—conditioning of nausea during chemotherapy in humans:

* 4. a) Can you describe the process of second–order conditioning in the following situation? During World War II, a child participating in a school program hears a musical passage from one of Wagner's operas playing in the background during the unfurling of a flag bearing a swastika emblem. The child is excited by the stirring music. Later, the flag is seen during speeches by a number of Hitler's followers, exciting the child's earlier emotions in the course of the speeches. (230)

b) By extension from the example in your text, what do you think would happen if the flag were never again paired with the music. (230)

*   c) What is the importance of second–order conditioning in understanding human behavior? Cite an example. (230)

* 5. a) Use the example of a classically conditioned *galvanic skin response (GSR)* to demonstrate the process of generalization. (230)

*   b) What do your authors mean when they say that "Whereas generalization is a reaction to similarities, discrimination is a reaction to differences"? (230)

    c) Cite an everyday example of generalization and of discrimination. Can you think of other examples? (231)

* 6. a) Indicate how classical conditioning plays a role in conditioning negative emotional reactions, most notably, fear. (231)

    b) What evidence reinforces the notion that fear may be learned in childhood? (231)

* 7. a) Does the CR always resemble the UCR? Explain using an example. (231-232)

    b) How does this phenomenon relate to the development of *drug tolerance*? (232)

* 8. a) In your own words, state Rescorla's view regarding the importance of predictability in classical conditioning by contrast with Pavlov's position. (232)

*   b) Outline the procedures of Rescorla's important experiment with dogs demonstrating the role of predictability in conditioning. (232)

*   c) What were the results of this study and what conclusion may be drawn relative to the issue of contiguity versus predictability? (232)

* 9. a) Outline the procedures and results of Kamin's important blocking experiment. (233)

*   b) In terms of the predictability concept, why did the earlier light–shock association apparently block the learning of the new association? (233-234)

* 10. Discuss some ways in which predictability and lack of predictability may play a part in emotional reactions and cite examples. (234)

* 11. Discuss the main features of each of the cognitive models of classical conditioning in the following table and be able to apply them to Kamin's blocking phenomenon. (234-235)

Theorists	Main Features of Theory	Application to Blocking
Rescorla & Wagner		
Wagner	Use the term *short-term memory*	
Holyoak et al.	Use the terms *generation and testing of rules*	

* 12. a) Discuss two major areas of difference between the approaches of the ethologists and behaviorists. To what assumptions may these differences lead in the area of learning? (235)

   b) What is a **behavioral blueprint**? How does this concept relate to issues in the field of learning? (235)

* 13. a) Discuss how we know that an important event in the taste aversion studies is the particular CS that is chosen for study. Outline the procedures and relevant results of the classic taste aversion experiment by Garcia and Koelling. (235-236)

*   b) Why does **selectivity of association** in the area of classical conditioning fit so well with the ethological approach but not with a more traditional view of the nature of learning? (Be sure to note in particular why taste should be a particularly good CS under some conditions whereas a visual CS may be effective under others.) (236)

   c) How does evolution (that is, the species of the animal) enter into the issue of selectivity of association in the taste aversion paradigm? (236)

*   d) Indicate your authors' conclusion with regard to this line of classical conditioning research. (236)

   14. Cite a practical application of the findings of the taste aversion research. (236-237)

* 15. a) Discuss two possible structural views of learning that will not work and the reasons why. (237)

*   b) Then what neurological approach to learning will work? Outline the key ideas of this approach using the term **synapse** in your answer. (237)

   c) How might we obtain evidence for such an idea and what is a problem and one solution for this approach in terms of long-term potentiation? (237)

16. a) What are some of the possibilities for structural changes that could affect synaptic efficiency in learning? (237-238)

* b) Outline research on each of the following phenomena showing that it is amount of a neurotransmitter secreted by a sending neuron (rather than other changes at the synapse) that is the critical mediator. (Be certain you can also define these terms as used in this context.) (238)

—*habituation*:

—*sensitization*:

OPERANT CONDITIONING

* 1. a) Describe the nature of the response in classical conditioning. What kind of behavior cannot be learned through these types of procedures? (238)

   b) Cite examples of operant conditioning in humans and animals. What are the "goals" of the behavior in each example? (238)

* 2. a) Outline Thorndike's problem–solving procedures used in his classic studies with cats. Describe a typical pattern of behavior exhibited by an animal in the experimental cage. (239)

* b) Did Thorndike argue that the cats demonstrated "intelligence" or "insight" in this situation? Explain, using the term *trial–and–error* to describe the cats' behavior. (239)

* c) How does the law of effect apply to problem solving behavior such as this? (239)

   d) What does it mean to say that the law of effect "promotes the survival of the fittest response"? (239)

* 3. a) Describe in detail the *Skinner box* procedure for the study of operant conditioning using the terms *baseline level*, *reinforcement*, and *extinction*. (239-240)

* b) How would the experimenter set up a *discrimination* procedure in this setting? What would serve as the discriminative stimulus? (240)

4. Describe an application of operant conditioning principles in the case of young boy with temper tantrums. (241)

* 5. In what respect are the temporal relations between events in operant conditioning important? Discuss the impact of delay of reinforcement upon operant conditioning in general and in a specific example. (241-242)

* 6. a) A psychologist has a dog that presses a button with its paw to sound a buzzer whenever it wants to go outside. Using the shaping example in your book, how would you have accomplished this training? (242)

* 7. a) Why would operant conditioning be an uncommon event in our lives if only primary reinforcers were effective? Therefore, what extends the range of operant conditioning possibilities for us? (242)

b) Describe a demonstration of conditioned reinforcement in an animal experiment. (242-243)

* c) Why is money such an effective conditioned reinforcer? Why do you think that praise is so powerful? (243)

* 8. Provide illustrations of the phenomena of *generalization* and *discrimination training* in the case of operant behavior. When will a discriminative stimulus be useful? (243-244)

9. a) Cite an example of partial reinforcement in an animal experiment. (244)

* b) Why does the partial reinforcement effect make intuitive sense? (244)

* 10. For each of the following schedules of reinforcement, provide an abbreviation, a definition that is helpful for you, and cite an example. (244-245)

Schedule	Abbrev.	Definition	Example
fixed ratio			
variable ratio			
fixed interval			
variable interval			

11. a) Cite a human and an animal example of punishment. (245)

* b) Discuss three disadvantages of the use of punishment to control operant behavior. (245)

* c) Do these disadvantages mean that punishment should never be used? Discuss the conditions under which punishment may be useful when dealing with "undesirable" behaviors. (245-246)

12. a) Cite some human and animal examples of escape and avoidance learning. (246)

* b) Discuss one of the puzzles about avoidance learning that arises from an intuitive approach. What is one theoretical solution to this problem that emphasizes two traditional behavioral principles of learning? (246)

108   Chapter 7

*   b) Discuss one of the puzzles about avoidance learning that arises from an intuitive approach. What is one theoretical solution to this problem that emphasizes two traditional behavioral principles of learning? (246)

      c) Outline an alternative cognitive (*expectancy*) solution to the nature of avoidance learning. What important fact about avoidance responses is explained easily by this approach? (246)

* 13. a) Contrast two possibilities for what serves as the critical factor in operant conditioning. (247)

      b) Outline the procedures of the Maier and Seligman study of learned helplessness in dogs. (247)

*   c) What results were obtained in the Maier and Seligman study and which of the two alternative views of the operant conditioning process outlined in 13a) was favored by this research? Explain. (247)

* 14. a) What do your authors mean when they say that in "operant conditioning, what the organism seems to learn is a contingency between two events" just as in classical conditioning? Use the Maier and Seligman study to illustrate your point. (247-248)

      b) Give another example of contingency learning in human infants. (248)

* 15. Discuss the constraints on reward and escape learning that have been demonstrated in pigeons. In what respect do these results appear to make sense from an ethological point of view? (248)

COMPLEX LEARNING

* 1. a) What is the "crux of learning" from the cognitive perspective? (248)

      b) Indicate some of the cases in which the mental representations and the operations performed on them seem too complex to be mere associative processes. (248-249)

* 2. a) How did Tolman interpret his findings regarding learning of mazes by rats? (249)

*   b) Describe a more recent maze learning problem and results that favor the concept of cognitive maps. Do rats favor the strategy that humans might in analogous situations? What does this imply the rats are learning? (249)

* 3. Describe in detail Premack's demonstrations of even more sophisticated learning of "abstract" linguistic concepts in chimpanzees. List three such abstractions that chimps appear able to learn. (249-250)

* 4. a) How did Köhler allow for the occurrence of *insight* in his chimpanzees? (250)

      b) Describe some of the typical results obtained using the multiple–stick problem in one of Köhler's studies. (250)

Sample Quiz 7.2

1. The phenomenon of spontaneous recovery: a) shows that extinction involves true learning; b) is regarded by modern researchers as due to the loss of inhibitory effects of a CS through a change in context; c) refers to a decrease in strength of a previously extinguished CR; d) all of the above.

2. If we selectively reinforce CS1 and not reinforce CS2, the strength of a CR to CS1 will _____ and to CS2 will _____. a) increase, increase; b) decrease, decrease; c) increase, decrease; d) decrease, increase.

3. Blocking occurs when information that is available to an organism is: a) unique; b) simple; c) negative; d) redundant.

4. Long–term potentiation provides evidence for: a) classical conditioning; b) generalization; c) second–order conditioning; d) structural neural changes in learning.

5. Sensitization has been shown to be mediated by: a) an increase in amount of neurotransmitter in the sending neuron; b) a decrease in amount of neurotransmitter in the sending neuron; c) activity in a "learning center" in the brain; d) the number of neurons leading from a particular receptor.

6. Which of the following is *true*? a) Operant conditioning would be an uncommon event if only primary reinforcers were effective. b) Secondary reinforcers extend the range of operant conditioning. c) Praise and money are powerful primary reinforcers. d) Both a and b.

7. Cognitive mapping, mental trial–and–error, and the use of strategies exemplify: a) complex learning; b) operant conditioning; c) aversive conditioning; d) outcomes of differential reinforcement.

8. Which of the following is one of the abstractions that Premack's chimpanzees appeared to be capable of learning? a) causal relations; b) abstract concepts, like "sameness"; c) references between objects that bear no physical resemblance; d) all of the above.

9. The researcher who is known for his study of the phenomenon of "insight" was: a) Wolfgang Köhler; b) Edward Tolman; c) E. L. Thorndike; d) Ivan Pavlov.

10. Top–down processing in learning refers to: a) learning first about relations between stimuli, then about relations between responses and stimuli; b) development of a mental representation regarding the layout of a maze; c) a combination of a prior belief with objective input to yield an estimate; d) none of the above.

Answer Key, Chapter 7

Important Names

1. Ivan Pavlov
2. E. L. Thorndike
3. B. F. Skinner
4. Edward Tolman
5. Wolfgang Köhler

Vocabulary and Details

1. learning
2. habituation
3. associations
4. classical conditioning; operant conditioning
5. complex learning

CLASSICAL CONDITIONING

1. unconditioned stimulus; UCS; unconditioned response; UCR
2. conditioned stimulus; CS; conditioned response; CR
3. conditioned
4. trial
5. acquisition; reinforce
6. extinction
7. spontaneous recovery
8. second–order conditioning
9. generalization
10. discrimination
11. differential reinforcement; increase; decrease
12. conditioned fear
13. temporal contiguity
14. reliable predictor
15. blocking; redundant
16. ethologists
17. taste aversion
18. long–term potentiation

OPERANT CONDITIONING

1. operant conditioning; operate
2. consequences
3. law of effect
4. reinforce; increase
5. operant
6. extinction; decrease
7. discriminative stimulus
8. rate of response
9. shaping
10. primary reinforcers
11. secondary; conditioned
12. partial reinforcement
13. partial reinforcement effect
14. schedule of reinforcement
15. aversive conditioning

16. punishment training
17. escape learning; avoidance learning
18. contingency

COMPLEX LEARNING

1. cognitive; mental representations
2. cognitive map
3. prior beliefs
4. spurious associations
5. top–down processing in learning

Sample Quiz 7.1

1. b, 227
2. d, 234-235
3. c, 237
4. a, 238
5. b, 242
6. c, 245
7. c, 247
8. a, 248
9. a, 250-251
10. b, 252

Sample Quiz 7.2

1. b, 228-229
2. c, 230-231
3. d, 233
4. d, 237
5. a, 238
6. d, 242-243
7. a, 248-249
8. d, 250
9. a, 250
10. c, 252

Memory

Learning Objectives

1. Understand the distinctions between the three stages and the two types of memory described in the text. Be able to relate these distinctions to the role of the hippocampus and frontal cortex in memory processes.

2. Know the difference between acoustic encoding and visual encoding in short–term memory.

3. Be able to discuss the limits of short–term storage represented by the number seven plus or minus two (7 ± 2). Explain how this concept is related to memory span, displacement, decay, and rehearsal. Be familiar with research on the time required to retrieve information from short–term memory.

4. Be able to describe how chunking uses information stored in long–term memory to increase the capacity of short–term memory. Understand the role that short–term memory plays in problem solving, language comprehension, and higher mental processes such as reading.

5. Be prepared to describe the transfer of material from short–term to long–term memory and show how free–recall evidence supports it.

6. Understand the concept of encoding for meaning in long–term memory and how elaboration can improve memory.

7. Be able to discuss forgetting in terms of storage versus retrieval failure, citing the relevant evidence. Be familiar with research on interference, the importance of organization in encoding, and the effect of context on recall.

8. Be familiar with the various ways that emotion can affect memory.

9. Be able to differentiate between retrograde amnesia and anterograde amnesia. Be familiar with the evidence indicating that there may be different kinds of memories.

10. Be able to describe the various methods for improving both short–term and long–term memory. Be able to explain the mnemonic systems called the "method of loci" and the "key word method." Be familiar with the PQRST method.

11. Know what is meant by constructive memory. Be able to show how inferences, stereotypes, and schemata each contribute to constructive memory processes.

115

Important Names

1. The experimental study of memory was begun in the late 1800s by the famous psychologist _____. (262)

Vocabulary and Details

DISTINCTIONS ABOUT MEMORY AND THEIR BIOLOGICAL BASES

1. In the three stages of memory, the first is _____, which refers to transforming information (such as visual or verbal) into a code that memory accepts. (257)

2. In the second stage of memory, _____, the information is retained or stored. (257)

3. In the third stage of memory, _____, information is recovered from storage. (257)

4. The concept _____ refers to the fact that information may be stored in memory for relatively short periods, say, a few seconds; whereas _____ refers to storage for longer intervals, from minutes to years. (258)

5. A brain structure located beneath the cortex and near the middle of the brain, in the _____ lobe area, is called the _____; this structure is important in _____ (long–term/short–term) memory. (258)

6. Owing to its location, damage to the hippocampus causing severe difficulty in remembering material for _____ (long/short) intervals is called _____. (258)

SHORT–TERM MEMORY

1. _____ of material in short–term memory means to repeat material over and over to keep it active. (260)

2. A rare phenomenon, but one more likely in children, is the ability to recall photographically detailed information about previously viewed visual material, termed _____. (260)

3. It appears that short–term memory has a capacity limited to _____ items, a constancy referred to by George Miller as the _____. (261-262)

4. The maximum amount of material that a subject can recall in a short–term memory task is called the subject's _____. (262)

5. Larger, meaningful units of material in short–term memory are called _____. Based on the information in item 3 directly above, we would expect a person to be able to remember about _____ (how many?) units when "chunking" information. (262)

6. Forgetting of items in short–term memory may be due to _____ with time or to _____ by newer items. (262)

116   Chapter 8

7. In the _____ method for assessment of memory, a number of items are provided one at a time for a subject to remember and then the subject is asked to recall them in any order. (265)

LONG–TERM MEMORY

1. A _____ is anything that helps us to retrieve a memory; the better these cues are, the _____ (better/worse) our memory. (268)

2. In a _____ test of memory, we are asked if we have seen a particular item before; on the other hand, in a _____ test, we have to produce the memorized material with minimal retrieval cues. (268)

3. An important factor that can impair retrieval from long–term memory is _____; that is, when we try to use a retrieval cue, other items associated with that cue may become active and interfere with the item we are trying to retrieve. (268-269)

4. In _____, an electric current is applied to the brain producing a brief seizure and momentary unconsciousness followed by some memory loss. (270-271)

5. When memory is partly dependent upon the internal conditions that prevailed during learning, we speak of _____. (273)

6. A vivid and permanent record of the circumstances surrounding a significant, emotionally charged event is called a _____. (274)

7. In Freud's analysis of memory, traumatic experiences may be blocked actively from consciousness; this view is called the _____. (276)

IMPLICIT MEMORY

1. In distinguishing between kinds of memories, memory of a personal *fact,* or _____, is often a conscious recollection of something in the past. (276)

2. In contrast, it appears that perceptual or cognitive *skills* often are learned without conscious recollection of the experiences during learning, a kind of memory called _____. (276-277)

3. A partial or total loss of memory is called _____. (277)

4. In one form of amnesia, the primary symptom is a serious inability to acquire new factual information or to remember everyday events; this loss is termed _____. (277)

5. In another form of amnesia, there is an inability to remember events that occurred prior to the event causing the memory loss; this loss is termed _____. (277)

IMPROVING MEMORY

1. A system that aids memory is called a _____. (283)

2. One mnemonic, connecting items of information to an ordered sequence of imaginal locations, is termed the _____. (283)

3. Another mnemonic involves finding a part of a term to be remembered, such as part of a foreign word, that sounds like some object that can be imagined; this technique is called the _____. (284)

4. Another technique for improving long–term memory is the PQRST method, in which the letters stand for _____, _____, _____, _____, and _____. (287)

CONSTRUCTIVE MEMORY

1. We tend to use our general knowledge of the world to build a more complete memory of complex, meaningful events; that is, memory may be _____. (288)

2. In one form of construction, when we fill in material based on available facts, we are making use of _____. (288)

3. In another form of construction, the use of social _____, we may rely on inferences about the psychological or physical traits of a class of people. (289)

4. In general, mental representations of a class of people, objects, events, or situations, including the use of stereotypes, are called _____ (singular: _____). (289)

Ideas and Concepts

* 1. Indicate a primary reason why we must give a central place to the concept of memory in the understanding of human psychology. (257)

DISTINCTIONS ABOUT MEMORY AND THEIR BIOLOGICAL BASES

* 1. Cite examples of encoding, storage, and retrieval of a memory. At what stage can memory fail? (257)

2. a) Discuss the two parts of the PET experiments designed to investigate the biological bases of memory. (257-258)

* b) What is the most striking finding obtained in such studies and what does this suggest regarding the distinction between encoding and retrieval? (258)

3. a) Give an example to illustrate the difference between short–term and long–term memory. (258)

b) Distinguish between short–term and long–term memory in terms of ease of retrieval. (258)

4. a) Describe the research procedures with nonhuman species designed to show the different functions of the frontal cortex and hippocampus in memory. (258)

* b) Indicate the results of this research and their implications for short– and long–term memory. (258)

*Basic ideas and concepts

118   Chapter 8

*   c) Outline an "experiment of nature" and its implications for long-term memory at the human level. (258-259)

*   d) Conversely, what problem indicates organic difficulties in regions other than the medial temporal lobe in humans? What memory system is apparently involved? (259)

*   5. a) What has been the assumption of psychologists about memory until recently? What different kinds of long–term memories may there be for different kinds of information? (259)

       b) What kind of memory forms the basis for this chapter and why? (259)

SHORT–TERM MEMORY

*   1. What is first necessary in order to encode information into short–term memory? Therefore, when we have "memory problems," does it necessarily mean that our memory is not functioning properly? Explain. (259-260)

*   2. a) In what three forms may material be encoded in short–term memory? What form do we seem to favor, at least unless verbal rehearsal is employed? (260)

*   b) Cite some evidence that demonstrates this tendency to code acoustically. (260)

*   3. a) What is the evidence on the duration of visual versus acoustical codes? (260)

       b) Under what conditions is visual coding more important than acoustic coding? Illustrate with an example of eidetic imaging. (260)

*   c) How common is eidetic imagery in actuality? What indicates that the visual coding in short–term memory is via something shorter than a paragraph? (260-261)

*   4. a) To what model of short–term memory have researchers been led owing to evidence on acoustic and visual coding? Use the terms *acoustic buffer* and *visual buffer* in your answer. (261)

*   b) Discuss the PET scanning evidence supporting the possibility that different brain structures underlie short–term memory buffers. Where are these two buffers apparently located? (261)

*   5. Describe a procedure for demonstrating Miller's "magic number seven." (262)

    6. a) Cite a demonstration of chunking and indicate how this phenomenon demonstrates so well the interaction between short–term and long–term memory. (262)

*   b) Use some additional examples to illustrate the principle that we can facilitate short–term memory through chunking, using units that already exist in long–term memory. (262)

*   7. a) Discuss a line of evidence that favors the decay view of forgetting of material in short–term memory. (262)

b) As an aside, linguists have long noted that there is a tendency in human language gradually to adopt abbreviated versions of words across time, such as "TV" for "television" and "car" for "automobile." Using the information in 7a), can you speculate as to why this might be the case? (262)

8. a) In what respect does the notion of forgetting through displacement accord with what we know about short–term memory? (262)

b) Discuss the *activation* view of short–term memory as it applies to these displacement demonstrations of its fixed capacity. (262)

* 9. a) Intuitively, why should retrieval of information in short–term memory *not* depend on the number of items being remembered at one time? Is this assumption correct? (263)

* b) Describe an experiment in detail that demonstrates clearly that retrieval times are directly proportional to the number of items in short–term memory. Use the terms *memory list* and *decision time*. (263)

* c) What is so remarkable about the relationship obtained in the experiment outlined in 9b) and how much time is required for a decision whether or not an item is present in short–term memory? Is this function dependent upon the type of material that is remembered or the type of subject that is employed? (263)

10. Contrast the view of retrieval as a *serial search* with the *activation model* approach. (263)

* 11. a) Illustrate that short–term memory plays an important role in conscious thought. Why is the term *working memory* applied to the functions of short–term memory? (263-264)

b) What is the apparent relationship between solving complex problems and the size of working memory? (264)

* c) How do we know that this same working memory function does not apply to understanding simple sentences? Discuss the evidence showing the existence of a special memory for language. (264)

* d) On the other hand, what happens as we progress to memory for relatively complex sentences? (264-265)

e) Discuss additional evidence to show the role of short–term memory in helping us to relate material in conversation or reading to previously known material. (265)

* 12. Summarize the two known functions and one additional possible function of short–term memory. (265)

* 13. a) Describe in detail a basic free–recall procedure to demonstrate the idea that short–term memory may be a way–station to long–term memory. (265)

b) Why would we expect retrieval to be better for both the last few items and the first few items in a list of memorized words? (265-266)

120   Chapter 8

LONG–TERM MEMORY

1. Indicate two complications in the study of long–term memory from the standpoint of encoding, storage, and retrieval processes. (266)

* 2. a) What is the major form of information representation in long–term memory? Give some examples to support this observation. (266)

* b) List some other forms of information representation in long–term memory. (266)

* 3. a) How can we improve long–term memory for material that has no inherent meaning? Try to think of an example other than the one in your text. (266-267)

* b) What is one of the best ways to add connections to material during memorization? Cite an example and a related experiment. (Can you see the relationship between the outcome of this experiment and the benefits of using this *Study Guide*?) (267)

* 4. a) Contrast the nature of forgetting in the case of long–term memory to that of short–term memory. (267)

* b) Describe several types of everyday experiences, including some that may happen during psychotherapy, indicating that apparent forgetting may at times be a failure of retrieval. Use the term **tip–of–the–tongue** phenomenon. (268)

c) Discuss the "banker–lawyer" experiment to show the powerful role that retrieval cues play in helping us to remember. (268)

d) From the information in your text, why would we expect the multiple choice sample quizzes at the end of this section of the *Study Guide* to show better memory performance than questions that called for short answers or essays? (268)

* 5. a) Cite an everyday example of interference. (269)

* b) Similarly, describe an experimental demonstration of interference. Indicate the related results of such studies. (269)

c) Therefore, why does forgetting increase with time from this perspective? (269)

* 6. a) Why may recognition have been slower for one set of facts than the other set in the banker–lawyer experiment, and what does this suggest regarding the nature of the process of retrieval from long–term memory? Be sure to use the term **search process** in your answer. (269-270)

b) Discuss yet another model of the retrieval process that could be applied to this experiment. (270)

* 7. a) Are retrieval failures the only cause for forgetting? Indicate a procedure that appears to cause actual loss of storage in long–term memory. How do we know? (270-271)

*   b) In your own words, what do your authors mean when they say that the shock in electroconvulsive therapy disrupts the process of *consolidation*? (271)

c) Indicate the brain structures that play a role in consolidation; cite some observations about the relative importance of these structures. (271)

*   d) Outline the methods and results of a recent study with monkeys that further establishes the role of the hippocampus in memory storage. Do these results also indicate that long–term memory storage is in the hippocampus? Explain. (271)

* 8. a) Indicate two encoding factors that increase the chances of successful retrieval (in addition to ones you learned earlier). (271)

b) Cite an everyday example of the role of organization in improving memory. (271)

* 9. a) In terms of retrieval cues, how important is the context in which you acquired a memory? Can you think of an example in your own life? (271-272)

*   b) Must contextual cues always be external to the memorizer? Again, give an example. (272-273)

* 10. Emotions can influence memory in five distinct ways. Using the items in the left–hand column of the following table as a cue, describe or explain each of these ways in your own words and cite an example. (274-276)

	Description or Explanation	Example
rehearsal and organization		
flashbulb memories		
anxiety		
context effects		
repression		

IMPLICIT MEMORY

* 1. Describe some of the specific causes and consequences of amnesia. Aside from anterograde and retrograde memory losses, how would the typical amnesia be characterized in terms of intellectual functioning? (277)

* 2. a) What features of amnesia indicate that there are different types of memory skills? (277)

*   b) Describe an experiment demonstrating the aspects of cognitive skill learning that apparently are affected and those that are not influenced by amnesia. Use the term *priming* in your answer and relate the results to the concepts of implicit and explicit memory. (277-278)

* 3. a) Describe a proposed classification of different memory systems using the information in your text and in Figure 8-10. Note why it is that a distinction is made between storage systems for skills and priming. (279-280)

*   b) Distinguish between *episodic* and *semantic memory* as these terms appear in Figure 8-10 and be able to cite examples. (280)

    c) How does data obtained with amnesiacs support the distinction made in 3b)? (280)

*   d) Outline Roediger's retrieval notion offered in criticism of the idea that different kinds of materials are stored in different memories. (280)

* 4. Which alternative, Roediger's or the idea of two memory stores, is favored by the data? Relate to the view that there are two forms of knowledge, "knowing how," and "knowing that." (280-281)

5. a) Discuss a study with normal subjects performed by Tulving et al. that also indicates that we all may have a "split memory system." (281)

    b) Similarly, discuss two other studies that manipulated independent variables to affect different memories supporting the idea of two memory systems. (281)

6. a) Detail the procedures of PET brain scanning experiments aimed at demonstrating biological evidence for the distinction between explicit and implicit memory. (281)

*   b) Indicate the results of these PET studies showing different effects for the explicit–memory task and the implicit–memory condition. (281-282)

IMPROVING MEMORY

* 1. a) In terms of chunks, what can we do to enlarge the capacity of short–term memory? (282)

    b) What do your authors mean by "general–purpose recoding system"? Give one example. (282)

2. a) How can we improve the recall of unrelated items and what is particularly useful for this purpose? (283)

*   b) For both of the following mnemonics, provide an example from the text or from your own experience. (283-284)

—*method of loci*:

—*key–word method*: (Also, be sure to note for what kind of learning this method is especially useful.)

*   c) Why does *elaboration* improve recall? Be able to provide an example. (284)

*   d) Illustrate how we might recreate *context* both in physical terms and by mental methods. (284-285)

* 3. Demonstrate for yourself the power of *organization* for improving memory: Develop a scheme for organizing all of the methods discussed in this section on improving memory, including *retrieval* and the *PQRST* method (see items 4 and 5, below), using all of the italicized terms in items 2 and 3 or the section subheadings. (285)

   4. a) Describe the best way to be sure you can retrieve information efficiently for a class assignment. (285-286)

     b) Describe another form of retrieval practice for a case of implicit memory. What effects may this have on performance? (286)

* 5. a) Be sure you understand what each step means in the PQRST method. (287)

     b) Upon what three principles for improving long–term memory does the PQRST method mainly depend? (287)

CONSTRUCTIVE MEMORY

   1. a) Relate the notions of *top–down processes* and *bottom–up processes* to the general outline of the material in this chapter. (287-288)

     b) According to your authors, why do we engage in construction when remembering? (288)

* 2. a) Provide examples of the use of simple inferences in memory for stories and for visual scenes. In the latter, what compelling evidence was obtained for constructive memory? (288)

     b) At what stage does the constructive process appear to take place, in the forming of the memory or in the process of remembering? (288)

     c) For what area of human affairs might constructive memories have particularly important implications and why? (289)

* 3. Give an example for how a racial stereotype may impact on memory. (289)

* 4. a) Provide some illustrations of schemata. For what two purposes can schemata be used? (289-290)

     b) What does the use of schemata in perceiving and thinking permit and what price do we pay for their use? (290)

*   c) What was the psychologist Bartlett's suggestion regarding the use of schemata in recalling stories and how has this possibility been confirmed? (290-291)

   5. What two stages of memory are aided by schemata? Cite an example. (291)

124   Chapter 8

Sample Quiz 8.1

1. Experiments with both human and nonhuman species indicate that damage in areas other than the middle of the temporal lobe would be more likely to impair: a) short-term memory; b) long–term memory; c) episodic memory; d) semantic memory.

2. It appears that when people "chunk" information in short–term memory, they have the capacity to remember: a) about 3 chunks; b) about 7 chunks; c) a number of chunks determined by the length of the material; d) a number of chunks determined by the complexity of the material.

3. When we try to use a retrieval cue, other items associated with that cue may impair retrieval in the process termed: a) decay; b) displacement; c) interference; d) repression.

4. Which of the following is *true*? a) Freud's view, that traumatic memories may be actively blocked from consciousness, is termed the interference hypothesis. b) A serious inability to acquire new factual information is termed anterograde amnesia. c) State–dependent learning refers to a tendency for vivid recall of emotionally charged material. d) Amnesia refers only to a total loss of memory.

5. When remembering, we may tend to fill in material based on available facts. This is a process: a) of constructive memory; b) termed simple inference; c) that appears to apply to verbal but not visual material; d) both a and b.

6. The experimental study of memory was begun in the 1800s by: a) Sigmund Freud; b) Wolfgang Köhler; c) Hermann Ebbinghaus; d) Richard Atkinson.

7. You volunteer to participate in a psychology experiment in which you are given a list of words one at a time to remember (such as, "moon, road, cat, and computer"), then asked to recall them in any order. The experimental procedure being used is the: a) free–recall method; b) recognition method; c) delayed–response method; d) PQRST method.

8. The experiment in your text regarding the banker and the lawyer, in which three associations were learned in the former case and two in the latter case, demonstrated that: a) retrieval is not a function of number of facts associated with an item; b) the search process is more difficult the more facts are associated with a retrieval cue; c) repressive processes owing to negative associations with lawyers interfere with retrieval; d) stereotyping is an effective aid to retrieval.

9. Recent PET brain scanning research has shown that: a) most brain activity during long–term retrieval is in the right hemisphere of the brain; b) the hippocampus is involved in short–term memory; c) in an implicit memory task, increases in activation occur in the right hemisphere and frontal region of the brain; d) all of the above.

10. The PQRST method appears to depend upon all *except* which method for improving long–term memory: a) organizing the material; b) practicing retrieval; c) associating material with images of specific locations d) elaborating the material.

Sample Quiz 8.2

1. The hippocampus: a) is a structure near the middle of the brain in the temporal lobe area; b) is important in short–term memory; c) when damaged, may result in difficulty remembering material for short periods; d) all of the above.

2. In order to encode information into short–term memory we must first: a) retrieve it; b) link it to meaningful information already in memory; c) attend to it; d) determine whether it is to be assigned to implicit or explicit storage systems.

3. It appears that many instances of forgetting from long–term memory owe to: a) decay processes; b) effects due to displacement; c) a failure to have stored the material in long–term memory in the first place; d) a loss of access to information (retrieval failure).

4. In the application of electroconvulsive therapy, we might expect: a) momentary unconsciousness; b) a brief seizure; c) some memory loss; d) all of the above.

5. Successful retrieval is aided by: a) elaboration; b) organization; c) context; d) all of the above.

6. Which of the following assertions regarding the influence of emotions on memory is *false*? a) Retrieval is best when the context evokes emotions like those at the time of encoding. b) Evidence shows that there is no forgetting at all in the case of flashbulb memories. c) In a sense, repression is the ultimate form of retrieval failure in that access to a memory is actively blocked. d) Anxiety may impair memory retrieval because it tends to cause interference through extraneous thoughts.

7. Remembering how to ski from one year to the next is an example of: a) explicit memory; b) episodic memory; c) implicit memory; d) flashbulb memory.

8. Indicate which types of memory system are included in a classification system for implicit memory: a) semantic, episodic, skills; b) semantic, nonassociative, conditioning; c) conditioning, priming, nonassociative; d) episodic, skills, priming.

9. We can increase the capacity of short–term memory by increasing: a) the size of each chunk; b) the number of chunks remembered; c) the number of items to be remembered; d) the duration of presentation of material to be remembered.

10. Mental representations of a class of, say, people or events, are termed: a) schemata; b) simple inferences; c) mnemonics; d) chunks.

Answer Key, Chapter 8

Important Names

1. Hermann Ebbinghaus

Vocabulary and Details

DISTINCTIONS ABOUT MEMORY . . .

1. encoding
2. storage
3. retrieval
4. short–term memory; long–term memory
5. temporal; hippocampus; long–term
6. long; medial–temporal–lobe amnesia

SHORT–TERM MEMORY

1. rehearsal
2. eidetic imagery
3. 7 ± 2; "magic number seven"
4. memory span
5. chunks; 7 ± 2
6. decay; displacement
7. free–recall

LONG–TERM MEMORY

1. retrieval cue; better
2. recognition; recall
3. interference
4. electroconvulsive therapy
5. state–dependent learning
6. flashbulb memory
7. repression hypothesis

IMPLICIT MEMORY

1. explicit memory
2. implicit memory
3. amnesia
4. anterograde amnesia
5. retrograde amnesia

IMPROVING MEMORY

1. mnemonic
2. method of loci
3. key word method
4. preview; question; read; self–recitation; test

CONSTRUCTIVE MEMORY

1. constructive
2. simple inference
3. stereotypes
4. schemata (schema)

Sample Quiz 8.1

1. a, 258-259
2. b, 262
3. c, 268-269
4. b, 277
5. d, 288
6. c, 262
7. a, 265
8. b, 269-270
9. a, 281
10. c, 287

Sample Quiz 8.2

1. a, 258-259
2. c, 259
3. d, 267
4. d, 270-271
5. d, 271
6. b, 273-276
7. c, 276-277
8. c, 280
9. a, 282
10. a, 289

9

Thought and Language

Learning Objectives

1. Be able to define three modes of thought. Understand the distinction between the prototype and the core of a concept, including the role these properties play in well–defined and fuzzy concepts and the way we use them to acquire concepts.

2. Know how concepts are organized into hierarchies based on levels of abstraction and be able to describe the use and neural bases of exemplar and hypothesis–testing strategies in acquiring concepts.

3. Be able to distinguish between deductive and inductive reasoning; know the rule we use in evaluating both types of arguments and the biases that influence our judgments.

4. Be prepared to describe the three levels of language in both production and comprehension, including the units (phonemes, morphemes, and sentences) involved at each level. Explain the differences between comprehension and production and the effects of context on each.

5. Be familiar with children's development of language at all three levels.

6. Explain why imitation and conditioning are not likely to be the principle means by which children learn to produce and understand sentences. Describe the operating principles children use in forming hypotheses about language.

7. Be familiar with the evidence suggesting that humans have some innate knowledge of language and with the controversy over whether other species similarly are endowed.

8. Be able to explain what is meant by visual thinking, how it has been studied experimentally to determine its relationship to perception, and how it may be involved in creative thought.

9. Describe three problem–solving strategies that can be used to decompose a goal into subgoals.

10. Describe the basic ways in which expert problem solvers differ from novices.

11. Be able to state why it is believed that computers can be used to simulate human problem solving and to note some answers to related criticism.

Vocabulary and Details

1. One mode of thought, called _____, corresponds to the stream of sentences expressing propositions that we seem to "hear in our minds." (296)

2. Another mode of thought, termed _____, involves images (usually visual) that we "see in our minds." (296)

3. Yet a third mode of thought, called _____, corresponds to sequences of movements we make in our minds. (296)

CONCEPTS AND CATEGORIZATION

1. A _____ is a statement that expresses a factual claim. (296)

2. A component of a proposition is called a _____; it is the set of properties we associate with (or use to represent) an entire class. (296)

3. Assigning an object to a concept is referred to as _____. (297)

4. Properties associated with a concept seem to fall into two sets: First, every concept has a _____ that contains the salient properties that describe the *best examples* of a concept. (297)

5. Second, every concept contains a _____, the properties that are *most important* for being a member of the concept. Such properties are diagnostic of concept membership. (297)

6. With concepts that are _____, the core or defining properties are as salient as are the prototype properties, so we can be sure of our classification of the concept. (297-298)

7. In contrast, with concepts that are _____, the core is less salient or hidden, so we mainly depend upon prototypical properties for classification and we lack a true definition. (298)

8. When concepts are grouped on levels, in what is called a _____, two types of knowledge are represented: _____ of concepts and _____ between concepts. (298)

9. In the simple strategy for learning of concepts, termed the _____, children store a representation (that is, _____) of the concept and then note similarities to it. (300)

10. As we grow older, we tend to use another strategy, termed _____, which involves conjecturing whether an item belongs to a concept, analyzing an instance, and determining the correctness of our categorization. (300)

REASONING

1. The term _____ refers to a sequence of thoughts, often in the form of an argument leading to a _____, and propositions that are reasons, or _____, for the conclusion. (304)

2. The strongest arguments are said to be _____, meaning that it is not possible for the conclusion to be false if the premises are true using rules that are _____. (304)

3. To solve problems using deductive reasoning, besides logical rules people may use _____, that is, rules that are less abstract and more relevant to everyday problems. (305)

4. In addition to rules, people may sometimes solve problems by way of a concrete representation of the problem situation, that is, use a _____. (305)

5. By contrast with deductive reasoning, in _____ it is *improbable* (rather than certain) that the conclusion of an argument is false if the premises are true. (305)

6. In inductive reasoning, the use of short–cut procedures that are applied easily and that often (but not always) yield the correct answer is called the use of a _____. (306)

7. In violation of the rules of probability theory, people may use one form of heuristic called the _____ in which they use estimates of similarity to come to inductive conclusions. (306)

8. Yet another heuristic that we employ to estimate probabilities when inducing conclusions is the _____, an estimate of the probability of causal connections between events. (307)

LANGUAGE AND COMMUNICATION

1. In the _____ of language, we start with a propositional thought, translate it into a sentence, and express the sentence with speech sounds. (308)

2. In the _____ of language, we start by hearing sounds, attach meanings (words) to the sounds, combine the words to form a sentence, and extract a proposition. (308)

3. A small discrete speech category based on *sound* is called a _____. (308)

4. A small linguistic unit that carries *meaning* is termed a _____. (309)

5. Words that are _____ name more than one concept. (309)

6. A _____ unit includes sentences and phrases. (310)

7. Analyzing a sentence into noun and verb phrases and smaller units is called _____. (310)

8. The relations between words in phrases and sentences (or the *structure* of language) is termed _____. (310)

DEVELOPMENT OF LANGUAGE

1. One way in which the specifics of language may be learned is through _____, simply copying what is heard; another way is through _____, being rewarded for specific structures and contents of speech. (314)

2. A third way in which language may be learned is through _____ about language rules; that is, a child may form a notion about a rule of language, test it, and if it works, retain it. (314)

IMAGINAL THOUGHT

1. Thinking using visual images is termed _____. (320)

THOUGHT IN ACTION: PROBLEM SOLVING

1. In _____ we are striving for a goal but have no ready means of obtaining it. (323)

2. One strategy in problem solving is to reduce the difference between our _____ and our _____ in the process called _____. (324)

3. A second strategy in the solving of problems is to compare our current state to the goal state in order to find the most important difference between them; this process is termed _____. (324)

4. A third problem–solving strategy is _____, that is, reasoning from the goal to a subgoal, and on backward to a subgoal that is obtainable. (324)

5. Using verbal reports obtained from people during problem solving, researchers may program a computer to solve the problem and then match the results of the program to those obtained by the people; this method is called _____. (327)

Ideas and Concepts

CONCEPTS AND CATEGORIZATION

1. a) Give some examples to show the use of concepts. (296)

* b) Discuss each of the following functions of concepts using examples. (296-297)

—cognitive economy:

—predicting information (use the term *categorization)*:

—communication (also indicate the nature of widely used concepts):

—facilitating planning (use the term *goal–driven concepts*):

* 2. a) Using the concepts for "bachelor" and "bird," distinguish between prototype and core properties. Based upon this distinction, differentiate between well–defined and fuzzy concepts using specific examples. (297-298)

b) How do we decide if an object fits in a well–defined concept? in a fuzzy concept? (298)

*Basic ideas and concepts

132   Chapter 9

* 3. What happens as the number of prototype properties of an instance increases? Discuss and exemplify the effects of the *typicality* of a concept upon (a) categorization and (b) what we think of when given the name of a concept. (298)

4. a) What does a hierarchy allow us to infer? Illustrate using the concepts "apple" and "pear." (See also Figure 9-1.) (298)

b) If it is not known whether a concept has a particular property, how does one proceed using a hierarchy? What is implied about how long that will take and what is the related evidence? (298)

* c) What does evidence suggest regarding how we tend to categorize objects in hierarchies? What determines the "basic level" and why do we apparently categorize the world first at this level? Again, be able to use the "apple" and "pear" examples to illustrate. (298-299)

5. a) Indicate the two main origins of concepts. (299)

* b) In what two ways may concepts be learned? How do these ways relate to whether we are learning cores or prototypes? Use an example. (299)

* c) What must children learn about the relative importance of cores and prototypes, and at what age is this type of learning apparently easier? (299)

* 6. a) Preview this section and list three different ways in which a person can learn a concept through experience with its instances. (300)

b) Illustrate a strategy that young children use to learn a concept. (300)

* c) With what kinds of instances is the exemplar strategy best? Explain why, using an example. (300)

* d) For what concepts is the hypothesis testing strategy appropriate and why? (300)

* 7. a) Define and contrast the notions of *bottom–up* and *top–down* strategies in this context. Which term best applies to our use of exemplar and hypothesis–testing strategies? Why? (300)

b) Outline an experiment to illustrate the use of top–down concept learning, including methods and major outcomes. (300-301)

c) What conclusions may be drawn from this study? (301)

8. Outline the procedures and results of two studies with brain–damaged patients identifying the role of different parts of the brain in the two bottom–up strategies of concept acquisition. (301-303)

—exemplar strategy:

—hypothesis–testing:

REASONING

*   1.   Indicate two ways by which thoughts are organized. (303-304)

      2.   a)   Give an example of a deductively valid argument. How might people decide if this were a valid argument? (304)

*   b)   Is the application of rules of logic to determine validity a conscious or an unconscious process? When does it become more conscious? (304)

*   c)   Cite one piece of evidence to suggest that people do use logical rules in determining validity. (304)

*   3.   a)   Point out two bases on which we may evaluate a deductive argument. (304)

*   b)   Describe some evidence to show *content* effects in deductive reasoning. In what respect is this an example of the use of pragmatic rules? (304-305)

      c)   What is meant by the term *permission rule*? (305)

    4.   a)   Give an example of the use of a mental model. (305)

*   b)   What do pragmatic rules and constructing mental models have in common and how does this affect our logically intuitive reasoning process? (305)

*   5.   a)   Give an example of an inductively strong argument. How is inductive strength expressed? (305)

*   b)   Distinguish by definition and by example between two of the rules of probability used by logicians. (305-306)

      —*base–rate rule:*

      —*conjunction rule:*

    6.   a)   Do people use such probability rules in everyday reasoning? Describe a study by Tversky and Kahneman to show a violation of the base–rate rule. (306)

      b)   Similarly, using an experiment, illustrate a violation of the conjunction rule. (306)

*   c)   Describe the applications of the similarity heuristic in the two studies discussed in 6a) and 6b) and another common reasoning situation in which the similarity heuristic may appear. (306-307)

*   d)   Illustrate a use of a causality heuristic in inductive reasoning. (307)

*   7.   Restate your authors' conclusion regarding the use of rational rules for inductive reasoning in everyday situations. Citing several reasons, why do they maintain that we "should not be too pessimistic about our level of rationality"? (307)

LANGUAGE AND COMMUNICATION

* 1. a) Using the terms in Figure 914, what do your authors mean when they say that "language is a multilevel system"? (308)

* b) Indicate two of the basic properties of language. What is the function of linguistic *rules*? (308)

2. a) About how many different phonemes are in the English language? Are we good at discriminating phonemes under all conditions? Explain. (308-309)

* b) What is one reason why learning a foreign language may be difficult? Give some examples. (309)

* c) Provide some illustrations of the assertion, "we conform to rules we cannot verbalize," with respect to combining phonemes. (309)

* 3. a) Distinguish between *three* types of morphemes. (309)

* b) Be sure you know the meaning of the term *grammatical morpheme* and can cite examples. (309)

c) What is the evidence that we consider multiple meanings of a word when it is ambiguous in meaning? (309)

* 4. a) What is an important property of sentence units and what does this property allow? (310)

* b) What do people do when reading or listening to a sentence? Give an example using the terms *noun phrase* and *verb phrase*. (310)

c) Cite some evidence obtained from linguistics and from memory experiments for the practice outlined in 4b). (310)

d) Cite an example of what happens when normally unconscious syntactic analysis of language fails. Why might this happen? (310-311)

* 5. a) What does Figure 9-6 and your text suggest about producing and about understanding sentences? (311)

* b) In what respect is this analysis of comprehension and production oversimplified? Use the term *context*, and cite an illustration. (311)

* c) Discuss the most salient part of context in terms of an example using the term *intention* in your answer. (311-312)

DEVELOPMENT OF LANGUAGE

1. What must all children master, and what is a wonder about this process? (312)

* 2. a) At the level of development of phonemes, what remarkable ability do infants demonstrate at birth, and by what experimental procedure did this become known? (312)

*   b) In the table below, for each level of language development, characterize the changes that take place at the ages indicated. (312-313)

Level of Language	Age	Description of Development and Examples
Phonemes	0–1 year 4 years	
Words and concepts	1 year 1–2 years 2 1/2 years	Use the term *overextend*
Sentence units (syntax)	1 1/2–2 1/2 years 6 years	Characterize changes in vocabulary

3. Describe the child's progress from two–word utterances to more complex and compound sentences. What characterizes this sequence across children? (313-314)

*   4. What observations suggest that both learning and innate factors play a role in language development? (314)

5. a) Give an example of imitation and indicate three reasons why it cannot be the primary way in which language is acquired. (314)

b) Similarly, what may be limits on the possibility that conditioning experiences account for language development? (314)

*   c) What do your authors consider to be a central problem with imitation and conditioning and how might more general aspects of language learning come about? (314)

*   6. a) Cite an example of the learning of linguistic rules through hypothesis testing. (314)

b) List six *operating principles* used by young children to form hypotheses about language. (See also Table 9-1.) (314-315)

*   c) What challenge recently has been made to the notion that language learning is a process of learning rules through hypothesis testing? Use an example. (314-315)

d) Conversely, cite a study that supports rule learning in this context. (315)

136   Chapter 9

* 7. a) What is the first of the three questions posed by your text regarding the role of innate factors in language development? (Note: We will return to the other two questions below.) (315)

* b) Relative to the first question, cite one observation to suggest that there are innate constraints on syntax across human languages. (315)

c) Discuss a study to further support the richness of our innate knowledge of language. (315-316)

* 8. a) What is the second question that is raised regarding innate factors in language? Cite some examples to show that there are critical periods in the development of phonemes. (315, 316)

b) Discuss recent work that also shows a critical period in learning syntax using the term *American Sign Language (ASL)* in your answer. (316)

* 9. a) State the third question raised in your text regarding innate factors in language. What answer is given by some experts? (315, 317)

* b) In what four respects is the communication system of chimpanzees more limited than that of humans? (317)

* 10. a) Describe both of the following attempts to teach chimpanzees to communicate including what was taught and what results were obtained. (317)

—training in American Sign Language:

—manual communication:

* b) In general, from these studies what does it appear that chimpanzees *can* learn? By contrast, in what areas of language learning is the evidence considerably less definitive, especially in the case of the chimp Washoe? (317-318)

c) Discuss another very recent attempt to train a chimpanzee to communicate. In what respects does this research differ from earlier studies and what cautions are in order? (318-320)

IMAGINAL THOUGHT

* 1. Give some illustrations of the use of images in thinking. What aspects of imaginal thought suggests that we rely upon perceptual processes in forming the images? (320)

* 2. a) Cite evidence from studies of *visual neglect* that imagery may be mediated by the same brain areas as perception. (320-321)

b) Discuss additional evidence from a brain scanning study of blood flow in the cortex indicating the specific parts of the brain that may be involved in imaginal thought. Where in the brain is this activity? (321)

*   c) Outline yet another experiment that used PET techniques to study both perception and imagery. What conclusion can be drawn regarding what imagery is like in terms of cortical processing? (321-322)

* 3. Describe the results obtained in each line of experimentation below to support the view that imaginal operations are similar to perceptual operations. (322-323)

—rotation:

—scanning:

—grain size:

4. Illustrate the use of imaginal thought in creativity with the two examples from your text. Can you think of one of your own? (323)

THOUGHT IN ACTION: PROBLEM SOLVING

* 1. What is necessary in order to solve a problem? Illustrate. (323-324)

2. a) What is Newell and Simon's typical method for studying problem–solving strategies? (324)

*   b) Give an example of the difference reduction strategy for problem solving. What is the critical element of this approach? (324)

*   c) Similarly, provide an example of means–end analysis. Why is this strategy considered to be more "sophisticated" than difference reduction? (324)

    d) Be able to cite an illustration of the third problem–solving strategy, working backward. (324-325)

* 3. Give another term for the three problem–solving strategies discussed in item 2, and indicate when people may rely especially on these methods and when they may develop more powerful procedures. (325)

* 4. a) Besides a strategy, upon what else does solving a problem depend? (325)

*   b) Distinguish between a propositional mode and a visual mode of representation and show by example that visual images may be the most efficient method for some problems. Are some problems solvable by either method? (325)

    c) Show that, besides the mode of representation, problem solving can also depend upon *what* gets represented. (326)

* 5. a) Discuss and exemplify differences between experts and novices in a field along the following dimensions. (326-327)

—representations:

—strategies:

138   Chapter 9

b) Therefore, what are some of the domain–specific procedures that may dominate the "weak methods" of problem solving discussed in item 2 above. (327)

* 6. a) What is Simon's answer to why we should use computers to learn about human problem solving? How would we find support for the claim? (327)

b) What is the parallel between the rules we use in problem solving and a computer's program? Find at least one such parallel in the example of solving an equation. (327-328)

* 7. State a criticism of computer simulation and your authors' replies. (328)

Sample Quiz 9.1

1. Which of the following is *true*? a) We tend to categorize objects in hierarchies first by dividing the world into basic–level concepts. b) The most basic level in a hierarchy is the one with the fewest number of distinctive properties. c) The time needed to establish a relation between a concept and a property is unrelated to the distance between them in the hierarchy. d) All of the above.

2. Hypothesis testing: a) involves conjecturing whether an item belongs to a concept; b) is more likely to be used as we grow older; c) involves determining the correctness of our categorization; d) all of the above.

3. When it is not possible for a conclusion to be false if premises are true, we speak of: a) an inductive argument; b) a deductive argument; c) a well–defined argument; d) none of the above; it is always possible for a conclusion to be false even if the premises are true.

4. In your authors' view regarding the use of rational rules for inductive reasoning: a) we probably should be quite pessimistic about how rational we are; b) we rarely use logical rules appropriately; c) similarity and causality heuristics probably lead to correct decisions most of the time; d) both a and b.

5. Children may learn language through: a) conditioning of grammatical sentences; b) imitation of words; c) hypothesis testing about rules; d) all of the above.

6. Which of the following is *true*? a) Brain scanning studies show that imagery is like perception from early stages of cortical processing. b) Imaginal thought results in increased neural activity in the regions of the cortex that receive visual information. c) Studies of patients with visual neglect show that the same brain structures mediate both imagery and perception. d) All of the above.

7. In the form of problem–solving called working backward: a) we attempt to reduce the difference between our current state and our goal state; b) we reason from the goal to a subgoal that is obtainable; c) we compare our current state to our goal state to find the most important difference between them; d) we solve a problem and then reconstruct the steps we used to reach the goal.

8. Propositional modes and visual modes are two: a) problem–solving strategies; b) forms of motoric thought; c) ways in which problems may be represented; d) forms of inductive reasoning.

9. Matching the results of a computer program to those obtained by people during problem solving is called: a) computer matching; b) program matching; c) computer simulation; d) an exemplar strategy.

10. Your authors contend that: a) computers can do only what they have been programmed to do; b) computers and human minds are the most complex information processing systems; c) the mind–computer analogy will continue to grow as we design computers that function more and more like people; d) both b and c.

Sample Quiz 9.2

1. The properties that are most important for being a member of a concept are termed the: a) core; b) prototype; c) hierarchy; d) exemplars.

2. Difficulty in solving a task that involves hypothesis testing would result from damage to the _____ portion of the brain. a) frontal cortex; b) medial–temporal–lobe; c) rear (occipital) lobes; d) brain stem.

3. Using a short–cut, easily applied procedure in inductive reasoning: a) is use of a heuristic; b) always yields the correct answer; c) is never a good way to arrive at a correct answer; d) both a and b.

4. Which of the following is *false*? a) The structure of language is termed syntax. b) A small linguistic unit that carries meaning is termed a phoneme. c) A sentence unit contains both sentences and phrases. d) In the comprehension of language we start by hearing sounds.

5. Words that name more than one concept are said to be: a) fuzzy; b) general; c) ambiguous; d) well-defined.

6. When we use phonemes to construct the morphemes and phrases of a sentence and then extract from these the underlying propositions, we are engaged in the process of: a) understanding a sentence; b) producing a sentence; c) using a sentence to start a conversation; d) using a sentence to ask for something.

7. Which of the following is an instance of a critical period? a) People who are taught to sign with ASL at a very young age are no better in the use of it than those who learn it later in life. b) Children lose the ability to discriminate phonemes of languages other than their own after about 1 year of life. c) Young children are no more likely to speak a second language without an accent than adults. d) After learning a second language, young children are no more able to understand a second language under adverse noise level conditions than are adults.

8. We must break a goal into subgoals in the process of: a) deductive reasoning; b) problem solving; c) imaginal thought; d) comprehension.

9. Comparing our current state to the goal state in order to find the most important difference between them is termed: a) difference reduction; b) problem solving; c) means-end analysis; d) both b and c.

10. Relative to novices, experts are more likely to: a) formulate a plan for attacking a problem; b) work from a solution backward; c) represent a problem in terms of its surface features; d) all of the above.

Vocabulary and Details

1. propositional thought
2. imaginal thought
3. motoric thought

CONCEPTS AND CATEGORIZATION

1. proposition
2. concept
3. categorization
4. prototype
5. core
6. well–defined
7. fuzzy
8. hierarchy; properties; relationships
9. exemplar strategy; exemplar
10. hypothesis testing

REASONING

1. reasoning; conclusion; premises
2. deductively valid; logical
3. pragmatic rules
4. mental model
5. inductive reasoning
6. heuristic
7. similarity heuristic
8. causality heuristic

LANGUAGE AND COMMUNICATION

1. production
2. comprehension
3. phoneme
4. morpheme
5. ambiguous
6. sentence unit
7. syntactic analysis
8. syntax

DEVELOPMENT OF LANGUAGE

1. imitation; conditioning
2. hypothesis testing

IMAGINAL THOUGHT

1. imaginal thought

THOUGHT IN ACTION: PROBLEM SOLVING

1. problem solving
2. current state; goal state; difference reduction
3. means–end analysis

4. working backward
5. computer simulation

Sample Quiz 9.1

1. a, 298
2. d, 300
3. b, 304
4. c, 307
5. d, 314
6. d, 321-322
7. b, 324
8. c, 325
9. c, 327
10. d, 328

Sample Quiz 9.2

1. a, 297
2. a, 301-303
3. a, 306
4. b, 308-309
5. c, 309
6. a, 311-312
7. b, 316
8. b, 323
9. d, 324
10. a, 326

Basic Motives

Learning Objectives

1. Be able to define the psychology of motivation in terms of its fundamental question and to distinguish between drive and incentive theories of motivation.

2. Be familiar with the reward and incentive approaches to motivation, including the role of the mesolimbic dopamine system in the brain and the bases for addictions.

3. Be able to describe homeostatic systems and understand the mechanisms of temperature and thirst regulation, including the functions of the hypothalamus in the former case and intracellular and extracellular reservoirs in the latter case.

4. Be familiar with variables that affect hunger and the homeostatic functions of deficit and satiety detectors. Be able to describe the lateral hypothalamic and ventromedial hypothalamic syndromes.

5. Be familiar with research on obesity, including twin studies, the role of fat cells, and effects of dieting, and with psychological factors in obesity.

6. Be able to discuss various approaches to weight control and the role of genetic factors.

7. Know the characteristics and causes of anorexia and bulimia.

8. Be familiar with research on the role of prenatal hormones, early experience, and cultural factors in shaping sexual development.

9. Be familiar with the major male and female sex hormones and their role in sexual arousal and behavior in adults. Know the role of neural control, early experiences, and cultural variables in adult sexuality.

10. Be prepared to discuss sexual orientation from the standpoint of a large study on homosexual orientation and the role of hormones and genetics.

11. Be able to integrate research findings in the area of homosexual and heterosexual orientation in terms of the "exotic–becomes–erotic" theory of sexual desire.

Vocabulary and Details

1. *Motivation* is a general term referring to the regulation of need–satisfying and goal–seeking behavior. _____ processes determine the _____ and _____ of goal-directed behavior. (335)

2. Psychologists have traditionally distinguished between two types of motivational theories. In the first type, _____ theories, the role of _____ factors in motivation are emphasized. (335)

3. In the second type of motivational theory, termed the _____ theories, the motivational role of _____ or _____ are stressed. (336)

REWARD AND INCENTIVE MOTIVATION

1. *Incentive motivation* is characterized by _____, the experience or production of pleasure or displeasure. (336)

2. Many natural rewards appear to activate the _____ in the brain, within which neurons use the neurotransmitter _____. (337-338)

3. When *compulsive drug taking* or *drug craving* occurs, we speak of an _____. (340)

HOMEOSTASIS AND DRIVES

1. The tendency to maintain a constant environment, such as the body's internal balance, is termed _____. A system that works to maintain homeostasis is a _____. (341)

2. The front (or preoptic) region of the _____ has been identified as an area for neural control of temperature. (341)

3. Water inside the body's cells, which provides a medium for cell contents, is termed the _____; whereas water outside of the individual cells (i.e., in blood and other body fluids) is called the _____. (343)

4. When there is a loss of *extracellular* fluid and a related drop in blood pressure, the hypothalamus is signaled, and, in turn, the pituitary gland releases _____ (abbreviated _____) into the bloodstream causing the kidneys to _____ (retain/release) water. (343)

5. After time without drinking, the kidneys are signaled by the brain to release the hormone _____. This hormone combines with a substance in the blood to produce the hormone _____, which causes a desire to drink. (343)

6. In parallel with the extracellular thirst system, a separate *intracellular* system in the brain works in part through the process of _____, the tendency for water to move from areas of plenty to areas of scarcity. The resulting dehydration of neurons in the hypothalamus results in their activation producing a kind of intracellular or _____. (343)

HUNGER

1. The main "fuel" used by brain neurons is _____, a simple sugar. (345)

2. In the procedure called _____, swallowed food is allowed to exit the stomach before digestion by way of an opening or *fistula*. (346)

3. That at least part of the fullness we feel after a meal is due to having learned the relationship between taste and the effects of food is termed _____. (346)

4. The common experience that food tastes better (especially evident in the palatability of sweet food) when people are hungry is called _____. (346)

5. A hormone called _____ (abbreviated _____) released by the duodenum promotes digestion and travels in the bloodstream to the brain where it causes _____. (347)

6. An apparent lack of hunger owing to destruction of the parts on each side of the hypothalamus is called the _____. (348)

7. By contrast, voracious eating resulting from destruction of the lower and middle portions of the hypothalamus is termed _____. (348)

OBESITY AND ANOREXIA

1. Two major causes of weight gain are (a) _____ (hereditary predispositions to be overweight) and (b) _____ (eating too much). (351)

2. Cells in which body fat is stored are called _____. (352)

3. Extreme self–imposed loss of at least 15% of minimal normal weight is called _____. (356)

4. The eating disorder, _____, is characterized by recurrent episodes of rapid consumption of large amounts of food in a discrete period of time, termed _____, followed by attempts to purge the excess eating by vomiting and laxatives. (359)

EARLY SEXUAL DEVELOPMENT

1. Motives that typically involve another organism are called _____. (360)

2. The degree to which one regards oneself as male or female is termed _____. (360)

3. The critical hormone in genital development is _____. (360)

4. The influence of androgens upon anatomy and brain cells is called _____. (361)

ADULT SEXUALITY

1. Hormonal changes that serve to distinguish between males and females begin during _____, roughly ages _____. (363)

2. The hypothalamus is the first step in the hormonal control of sexual behaviors through its secretion of _____, which, in turn, acts to stimulate the pituitary to produce the hormones called _____. (363)

3. Gonadotropins exert their influence on the _____, that is, the ovaries or testes. (363)

4. Hormones produced by the gonads are called the _____. (363)

5. Two female hormones produced when the ovaries are stimulated by gonadotropins from the pituitary are (a) _____, which affects sexual development and sexual motivation, and (b) _____, which prepares the uterus for implantation of a fertilized egg and possibly affects sexual motivation. (364)

6. In males, the hormones produced by stimulation of the testes due to gonadotropins from the pituitary are called _____, most notably _____, which function in physical development and sexual desire. (364)

7. Removal of the gonads, either the ovaries or testes, is called _____. (364)

8. Removal of the testes, which affects androgen production, is called _____. The same effect may be obtained by _____, using synthetic hormones to block androgen production. (364)

9. Hormones fluctuate cyclically with accompanying changes in fertility in the _____ (or _____) cycle. (365)

10. The degree to which an individual is sexually attracted to persons of the opposite and/or same sex is termed _____. (368)

11. Whereas most people are *heterosexual*, that is, have sexual relations with the opposite sex, some are considered _____ if they are attracted sexually primarily to members of the same sex. Those who have sexual relations with members of both sexes are termed _____. (368)

Ideas and Concepts

* 1. What question defines the psychology of motivation and where are the causes of motivation to be found? (335)

2. a) For basic motivations, what are the main areas of difference between the drive and incentive theories? (335)

*   b) Give some examples of internal drives, and discuss their relationship to physiological need states. (335-336)

*   c) Similarly, provide some examples of incentives. What property do many incentives share? (336)

* 3. a) Be able to distinguish between and provide examples for the terms you learned in Chapter 7, *primary reinforcers* and *secondary reinforcers*. (336)

*Basic ideas and concepts

b) What is the role of learning relative to primary and secondary reinforcers? (336)

c) Is there a conflict between drive and incentive theories of motivation? Explain. (336)

REWARD AND INCENTIVE MOTIVATION

* 1. a) Outline Wundt's ideas regarding the notion of a *hedonic continuum*. (336-337)

* b) What answer do your authors give for the question as to why pleasure and displeasure should be so pervasive? That is, what is the basic psychological role that the hedonic value of incentives may serve? (337)

* 2. a) What appears to be the brain's way of translating the "common currency" of reward? Cite some examples of rewarding stimuli that appear to activate the mesolimbic dopamine system. (337-338)

   b) Discuss some examples to show that the mesolimbic dopamine system seems to *create* the desire for a diverse array of incentives, both natural and artificial. (338-339)

* 3. Discuss in detail the role of the following three factors in the ability of some drugs to produce addiction. (340)

   —overactivation of the mesolimbic dopamine reward system:

   —withdrawal symptoms:

   —neural sensitization:

HOMEOSTASIS AND DRIVES

1. Cite two bodily examples and a familiar household device to illustrate homeostatic control processes. Use the term *set point* in the latter illustration. (Can you guess what the normal set point is in the case of core body temperature?) (340-341)

* 2. a) Discuss in detail the homeostatic processes in body temperature regulation including also the related region of neural control in the brain. (341-342)

* b) What is one way that the brain can be "fooled" into motivating behavior to regulate temperature when no regulation is actually needed? (342)

   c) What is a more "natural" way in which the set point for temperature can be altered? Describe this process. (342)

* 3. a) Discuss in detail the chain of events that takes place when loss of water occurs through, say, water deprivation or exercise, and the volume of extracellular fluid is reduced. Use the terms ADH, renin, and angiotensin defined in the Vocabulary section. (342)

b) How does this mechanism explain why it is that a wounded soldier or injured person may feel intense thirst? (342-343)

* 4. a) Be able to describe the second, osmotic or intracellular thirst system that explains the effects of such activities as eating salty food. (343-344)

b) What is another way in which intracellular thirst can be triggered? (344)

HUNGER

1. a) Why is eating more complex than drinking? What is the role of evolution in this difference by way of food preferences? (344)

* b) Indicate the contributions of each of the following factors in food preferences, citing examples and the evolutionary explanations where appropriate. (344)

—flavor:

—individual and social learning:

c) When are conditioned aversions especially strong and why? (344-345)

2. a) Why do weight watchers exercise? (345)

b) Does exercise of the brain similarly cause a greater utilization of "brain fuel"? Describe what the effects of concentrated thought might cause and where this fuel comes from. (345)

* c) Given the importance of glucose and other body fuel, what would we expect to be the dominant principle operating in the control of hunger? Are there any other factors that are important? (345)

3. a) Describe the procedures of the classic Miller and Kessen experiment with rats designed to show the role of incentives in interaction with the hunger drive. (345)

* b) What were the results of this study, and what implications do they have for our understanding of hunger? (345)

c) Give another illustration, this time at the human level, indicating the importance of incentives to appetite. (346)

* 4. a) Describe the method using sham feeding whereby conditioned satiety has been demonstrated in animals. (346)

* b) Discuss an experiment with humans that essentially demonstrates the same phenomenon as that described in 4a). (346)

c) Outline a method for showing yet another form of interaction between hunger drive and food incentives, alliesthesia. (346)

* 5. a) What was the early notion regarding the role of stomach contractions in hunger, and what are the current facts? Cite one piece of evidence. (346)

b) What kinds of food-related receptors are located in the stomach, and what appears to be their role? (346-347)

* c) Then what is more directly related to the physiological signal for hunger? Discuss this mechanism in detail, indicating a related finding with laboratory animals. (347)

6. a) What do your authors mean when they say that "the control of hunger is therefore the reverse of the control of satiety"? (347)

* b) Describe the following mechanisms for the feelings of satiety after we eat. (347)

—stomach receptors:

—CCK:

—receptors in the liver:

* c) What is the most sensitive signal of nutrient availability, and why does the brain apparently rely on this source? (347)

* 7. a) Discuss the two stages by which signals for hunger and satiety are processed by the brain to produce the motivation to eat. Use the terms *integrated hunger assessment* and *hypothalamus* in your answer. (347-348)

* b) Using the following table, describe the patterns of eating in animals that have had lesions or electrical stimulation in the lateral and ventromedial portions of the hypothalamus. Use the terms lateral hypothalamic syndrome and ventromedial hypothalamic syndrome defined in the Vocabulary section. (348)

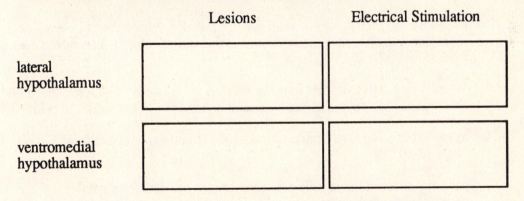

	Lesions	Electrical Stimulation
lateral hypothalamus		
ventromedial hypothalamus		

c) Why might some prescription diet drugs help inhibit appetite? (349)

* 8. a) Why is the notion that there is a "hunger center" and a "satiety center" in the hypothalamus too simplistic? (349)

b) What is one consequence of having multiple neural centers for appetite? Detail two related experiments with laboratory animals (that indicate that lesions in the hypothalamus do not actually destroy hunger) with respect to: (349-350)

Basic Motives   149

—lateral hypothalamic lesions:

—ventromedial hypothalamic lesions:

OBESITY AND ANOREXIA

*   1.   a)   What is the most frequent deviation from homeostatic regulation of eating? Cite some statistics in relation to: (350)

— overall prevalence rates:

—differences between the sexes:

—socioeconomic differences:

b)   In what respects is obesity a major health hazard and social stigma? Is the latter always fair? Explain. (350)

*   c)   Is obesity just one disorder? Explain. (351)

d)   Roughly, what are the two reasons why people become obese? (351)

2.   a)   Indicate some statistics to suggest a biological basis for obesity. (351)

*   b)   Why are studies with identical twins useful in understanding the role of genetics in obesity? Outline the methods of an experiment designed to look at the role of calorie intake and genetics in obesity. (351)

*   c)   Discuss the conclusions that may be drawn from this study. (351)

d)   From this study, why should we not assume that obese people necessarily eat more than nonobese people? What was the apparent factor that differed among the pairs of twins? (351-352)

3.   What is one criticism that may be leveled at the study discussed in 2 above, and how was this addressed in yet another experiment? What were the results? (352)

*   4.   a)   What are the two characteristics of fat cells that contribute to their role in obesity? (352)

b)   Cite some data in relation to numbers of fat cells as one of the genetic determinants of obesity. (352)

*   5.   What are *three* mechanisms by which diet drugs and other drugs might work to cause weight reduction (and, in some cases, subsequent gain)? Discuss the related *set point hypothesis* in detail. (352)

6.   Thus, in overview of this section, what are the various routes by which genes can be responsible for excessive weight gain? (352-353)

150   Chapter 10

* 7. a) Besides the physiological variables reviewed to this point, some psychological factors may induce people to consume too many calories. List these by noting the subheadings for this section below: (353)

—i:

—ii:

—iii:

* b) What two types of people are differentiated by questionnaires concerning diet and weight? Which type of individual eats more like an obese person? (353)

c) Cite the results of one study on differing feeding behaviors of restrained and unrestrained eaters. Give an explanation for these results. (353)

* 8. a) What differences appear in the eating behaviors of obese and normal–weight subjects under conditions of low and high anxiety? (353)

b) Cite some additional findings to implicate emotional arousal in general in the tendency for obese people to overeat. (353)

* 9. a) How do obese people differ from underweight people in their sensitivity to external cues for food? Describe a related study. (353-354)

b) What is *externality*, and is it a perfect indicator of degree of obesity? Explain. (353-354)

* 10. a) Discuss in detail the following two reasons why most dieters are not successful and the related evidence: (354)

—overeating (binge eating):

—lowered metabolic rate:

b) Outline the evolutionary reasons for these powerful responses to food deprivation. (354)

* 11. a) What two things must overweight people do to lose weight and maintain the loss? (354-355)

* b) Describe in detail the results of the Craighead et al. study supporting the conclusion that to control weight an individual must establish new eating and exercise behaviors. (355)

c) What do you think your authors mean when they say that perhaps "self–efficacy" may have been a factor in the behavior modification group? What was yet another possibility? (355-356)

12. a) Why is anorexia, the extreme desire not to gain weight, considered so dangerous? (356)

*   b)   Discuss some of the statistics relevant to anorexia, including the changing incidence data and the demographics of the typical anorexic. (356)

      c)   Describe the focus of anorexics on food and exercise. (356)

13.   a)   Outline some evidence to demonstrate the remarkable distortions in body image that accompany anorexia. (357)

*   b)   Discuss the methods and results of another study to show that such distortions in body image are actually prevalent among college–aged women in general in our society. (357)

*   c)   In the study discussed in 13b), what additional data suggests that college women have a very different view of themselves than do college men? (357-358)

* 14.   Discuss the possible causes of anorexia in terms of each of the following sets of variables. (358-359)

      —personality factors:

      —social factors:

      —biological factors:

15.   a)   What are some of the behavioral and physiological features of bulimia, the other form of expression of the desire not to gain weight? (359)

*   b)   Describe a few of the demographics of the bulimic person, and contrast with those of the anorexic. (359)

* 16.   As you did for anorexia, discuss the possible causes of bulimia in terms of each of the following sets of variables: (359)

      —personality factors:

      —biological factors:

      —social factors:

* 17.   Summarize three qualifications on any interpretation of the causes for anorexia and bulimia. (359-360)

EARLY SEXUAL DEVELOPMENT

*   1.   a)   Indicate some of the important differences between sexual desire and the survival motives, such as thirst and hunger. (360)

*   b) Discuss two critical distinctions with regard to sex: (360)

—adult sexuality vs. sexual development:

—biological vs. experiential factors:

* 2. a) Describe the genital development of the fetus from conception to about three months and the determining genetic factors operating. (360)

*   b) What happens when the testes or ovaries develop? Discuss in detail the role of androgen in combination with the chromosomes during the prenatal stage of development. (360-361)

     c) What structure particularly is involved in the effects of prenatal androgen upon the brains of rats, and why is this significant? (361)

* 3. a) Discuss the effects of *testosterone* (a kind of androgen) when injected into female monkeys. (361)

     b) By contrast, what circumstances may tend to "feminize" male animals? Use the term *maternal stress*. (361)

*   c) Is there any relevance of the results obtained with laboratory animals discussed in 3b) to human behavior? Note some of the differences cited by your text. (361)

* 4. In humans, there have been cases in which the prenatal hormonal environment and the social environment have not been consistent with regard to sexual development. Describe the observations made in each of the following cases, and cite the conclusions to be drawn from each. (361-362)

—females born to mothers exposed to diethylstilbestrol:

—male children raised as females in remote villages of the Dominican Republic (use the term *androgen insensitivity*):

—an identical twin boy who was treated surgically, hormonally, and socially as a girl:

* 5. What conclusion can be drawn about the impact of environment and hormones upon gender identity? (363)

* 1. In the table below, indicate the origin and functions of the hormones involved in sexuality. (See also Figure 10-11.) (363-364)

Hormone	Origin	Function
follicle-stimulating hormone (FSH)		Use the terms follicles, estrogen
luteinizing hormone (LH)		Use the term progesterone
interstitial-cell stimulating hormone (ICSH)		Use the term androgen

* 2. a) What are the effects of castration for animal subjects and for human males? (364)

* b) What is the relationship between hormonal (testosterone) fluctuation and sexual interest in human males? Be sure to distinguish between *copulatory function* and *desire*. (364)

c) What are the major determinants for sexual desire in men (as well as women)? (364)

* 3. a) Contrast the role of hormones in female nonprimates and women, including the effects of menopause in the latter case. (364)

b) Outline the course of the estrous cycle and its effects on sexual motivation in most mammals. (364-365)

* c) By contrast, what is the effect of the fertility cycle upon human female sexual desire and arousal? (365)

* 4. What is your authors' conclusion regarding the role of hormonal control in humans? (365)

* 5. a) What might be considered the "primary sex organ" and why? (365)

* b) Discuss the role of the spinal cord in sexual responses of men and women. (365)

b) Describe some effects of control via the hypothalamus in both lower animals and humans. (365)

6. a) Discuss in detail the influence of early experiences of monkeys on their sexual responses. (365-366)

*   b)   Outline the influence of social deprivation on interpersonal sexual activities in monkeys. What do these findings suggest concerning the determinants of normal heterosexual behavior in primates? (366)

*   c)   What general clinical statements may be made regarding the role of early experience in human sexuality? (366)

7.   a)   Cite and compare some examples of culturally–specific sexual practices in primitive permissive and very restrictive societies. (366-367)

*   b)   Describe the changes that took place in sexual activities in the United States from the 1940s to the 1970s. (See also Figure 10-12.) For which sex were the changes the greatest and during what period? (367, 368)

8.   a)   What appears to be bringing an element of cautiousness to the "sexual revolution"? (367)

*   b)   Indicate the data suggesting that the revolution between the 1940s and 1970s pertained more to behaviors than to feelings. (367-368)

      c)   In the same vein, illustrate differences (and at least one similarity) between men and women with respect to sexual attitudes. (368)

*   9.   Discuss the female–typical and male–typical sex differences that characterize: (368)

—attitudes regarding emotional and sexual infidelity:

—sexual behavior (in heterosexual and homosexual couples):

10.   a)   Describe Kinsey's scaling of people's sexual orientation. (368)

*   b)   Why do your authors say that this way of defining sexual orientation "oversimplifies the situation"? (368-369)

11.   a)   Summarize the data obtained in a national random sample of people in the United States regarding homosexual orientations. (369)

      b)   Why are these data considered to be underestimates? (369)

12.   a)   Is an adult's sexual orientation primarily determined by early life experiences or by innate biological factors? Summarize the findings of the important Bell et al. study conducted on large numbers of homosexual and heterosexual men in the San Francisco area in terms of: (369-370, also Table 10-2)

*   —one major factor that predicted a homosexual orientation:

*   —strength of the data for men and women:

—exceptions in the data:

*   b) Summarize some of the findings of this study that disconfirmed common theories regarding homosexual orientations: (370)

—identification with the opposite–sex parent:

—first sexual encounters:

—time of determination of sexual orientation:

*   c) With respect to the last two sets of findings, what are the crucial antecedents of an adult homosexual orientation, and how does this disconfirm the popular view? (370)

d) Is a person's sexual orientation simply a matter of choice? Explain. (370)

e) Returning to the question raised in 12a), what does appear to be the origin of gender nonconformity and homosexual orientations—nature or nurture? (370-371)

* 13. a) Outline evidence on the role of sex hormones, especially androgens, in terms of differences in gay and heterosexual men. (371)

*   b) If there are few differences in adult humans, what about the effects of sex hormones during prenatal development in both males and females? (371)

c) Why is it difficult to test hypotheses regarding prenatal hormones in humans? Cite some examples. (371)

* 14. a) By contrast with the hormonal data, how certain are the genetic data on sexual orientation? Be able to explain how twin studies contribute to this certainty. (371)

b) Outline two studies that show a genetic component in adult homosexual orientation. (371-372)

* 15. Summarize the attempt by your author, Daryl Bem, to put together all the findings regarding sexual orientation in this chapter in terms of his *exotic–becomes–erotic* theory of sexual orientation as it applies to: (372-373)

—the influence of genetic factors on temperament and personality:

—resulting predispositions to enjoy gender–conforming or –nonconforming activities:

—arousal due to dissimilarity and discomfort (the "exotic"):

—transformation of arousal into sexual attraction (the "exotic becomes erotic"):

—development of comfortable, nonerotic friendships:

—behavior in the Sambian culture:

156   Chapter 10

*   16. a)   Why do your authors contend that the question "what causes homosexuality?" is scientifically misconceived? Then what additional question(s) must be addressed, according to both Freud and your authors? (373)

*   b)   What is your authors' general point regarding the relationship between reproductive advantage and the genetic bases of behavior? Then what *will* ensure that our "species will not perish from the earth"? (373)

Sample Quiz 10.1

1. Motivational processes determine the: a) direction of goal–directed behavior; b) intensity of goal–directed behavior; c) conscious experience of goal–directed behavior; d) both a and b.

2. Which of the following is *not* discussed in your text as a factor in the ability of some drugs to produce addiction? a) overactivation of the mesolimbic dopamine reward system; b) neural sensitization; c) social modeling factors; d) withdrawal symptoms.

3. Which of the following is *true*? a) When there is a loss of extracellular fluid and a related drop in blood pressure, the pituitary gland releases ADH into the bloodstream. b) ADH causes the kidneys to release water. c) After time without drinking, the kidneys are signaled by the brain to release the hormone CCK. d) All of the above.

4. Conditioned satiety refers to: a) learning to associate food with time since eating; b) stopping eating only after one feels full; c) learning to associate hunger and eating; d) the fact that part of the fullness we feel after eating owes to having learned a relationship between taste and the effects of food.

5. Obesity is: a) the most frequent form of deviation from the homeostatic regulation of eating; b) somewhat more common in men than women; c) more prevalent in lower socioeconomic classes in developing countries; d) both a and c.

6. Genetics and calorie intake are two causes for: a) anorexia; b) alliesthesia; c) weight gain; d) androgenization.

7. Nicotine has been reported by some people to be effective in keeping their weight down. In the view of your text, the drug may have this effect by way of: a) suppressing the set point at which body weight is regulated; b) suppressing appetite; c) increasing metabolism in the body's cells; d) reducing the flavorful aspects of food.

8. Gender identity is defined: a) by the biological structures that distinguish males from females; b) as the degree to which one regards oneself as male or female; c) by the degree to which a person is sexually attracted to persons of the opposite and/or same sex; d) as the influence of androgens upon anatomy and brain cells.

9. Hormonal changes that distinguish males and females psychologically and physically begin during: a) the early postnatal period; b) puberty; c) post-puberty; d) early adulthood.

10. Current expert opinion argues that when prenatal hormones and the social environment are in conflict with respect to determining gender: a) the prenatal hormones will dominate; b) the social environment will be the primary determining factor; c) additional hormones will become important that would not otherwise; d) genetic factors become predominant.

Sample Quiz 10.2

1. Drive is to internal factors as incentive is to: a) internal factors; b) external events; c) need states; d) sex and aggression.

2. The "common currency" for the value of many different primary and secondary reinforcers appears to be translated in activity of the: a) hypothalamus; b) brain stem; c) mesolimbic dopamine system; d) cerebral cortex (in conscious processes).

3. Food preferences are a function of: a) individual learning processes; b) social learning mechanisms; c) flavor of a particular food owing to the evolutionary history of the species; d) all of the above.

4. The main "fuel" used by brain neurons is: a) ADH; b) renin; c) glucose; d) angiotensin.

5. Behaviorally, the ventromedial hypothalamic syndrome refers to: a) voracious eating; b) lack of hunger; c) heightened sexual arousal; d) extreme self–imposed weight loss.

6. Which of the following is *true* with respect to psychological factors in overeating? a) Obese as well as normal–weight people eat more in high–anxiety situations. b) The eating behavior of restrained eaters is closer to that of obese people than to that of unrestrained eaters. c) All obese people are overly sensitive to external hunger cues. d) All people with high externality with regard to hunger cues become obese.

7. Bulimia: a) primarily afflicts women; b) is more common than anorexia; c) is not a function of socioeconomic level; d) all of the above.

8. In laboratory animals, maternal stress has been shown to cause: a) androgenization; b) alliesthesia; c) feminizing of later sexual behavior of males; d) birthing of more male animals.

9. Stimulation of the testes due to gonadotropins produces: a) progesterone; b) testosterone; c) cholecystokinen; d) all of the above.

10. Which of the following is *not* a difference that has been found between the sexes? a) Heterosexual men react more strongly to emotional infidelity than to sexual infidelity in their partners. b) Heterosexual women have fewer premarital sexual partners than men. c) Male homosexuals have sex more often than heterosexual couples. d) Heterosexual women react less strongly to sexual infidelity in their partners than to emotional infidelity.

Vocabulary and Details

1. Motivational; direction; intensity
2. drive; internal
3. incentive; external events; objects of desire

REWARD AND INCENTIVE MOTIVATION

1. affect
2. mesolimbic dopamine system; dopamine
3. addiction

HOMEOSTASIS AND DRIVES

1. homeostasis; homeostatic control process
2. hypothalamus
3. intracellular reservoir; extracellular reservoir
4. antidiuretic hormone (ADH); retain
5. renin; angiotensin
6. osmosis; osmotic thirst

HUNGER

1. glucose
2. sham feeding
3. conditioned satiety
4. alliesthesia
5. cholecystokinen (CCK); feelings of satiety
6. lateral hypothalamic syndrome
7. ventromedial hypothalamic syndrome

OBESITY AND ANOREXIA

1. genetics; calorie intake
2. fat cells
3. anorexia (or anorexia nervosa)
4. bulimia; binge eating

EARLY SEXUAL DEVELOPMENT

1. social motives
2. gender identity
3. androgen
4. androgenization

ADULT SEXUALITY

1. puberty; 11 to 14
2. gonadotropin–releasing factors; gonadotropins
3. gonads
4. sexual hormones

5. estrogen; progesterone
6. androgens; testosterone
7. gonadectomy
8. castration; chemical castration
9. estrous (fertility)
10. sexual orientation
11. homosexual; bisexual

Sample Quiz 10.1

1. d, 335
2. c, 340
3. a, 343
4. d, 346
5. a, 350
6. c, 351
7. d, 352
8. b, 360
9. b, 363
10. b, 363

Sample Quiz 10.2

1. b, 335
2. c, 337-338
3. d, 344
4. c, 345
5. a, 348
6. b, 353-354
7. d, 359
8. c, 361
9. b, 364
10. a, 368

Emotions

Learning Objectives

1. Know the distinction between motives and emotions and the six components of an emotion.

2. Understand the role of the sympathetic and the parasympathetic divisions of the autonomic nervous system in emotional arousal.

3. Be able to discuss the research relating physiological arousal to the intensity of an emotion and to the ability to differentiate among emotions. Know the James–Lange theory, Cannon's objections to the theory, and Ekman's relevant findings.

4. Understand the concept of cognitive appraisal and its role in emotional experience. Be familiar with attempts to dimensionalize emotions in terms of primary emotions and dimensions of appraisals.

5. Be able to discuss the research on the experimental manipulation of cognitive appraisal and emotion without cognition.

6. Be familiar with research on facial expressions of emotion, including the communication of emotions and the brain mechanisms involved in the recognition of emotions. Know what is meant by the facial feedback hypothesis.

7. Be able to discuss the general reactions of being in an emotional state, including the relationship between arousal level and performance, attention to events, and the effect of mood on our evaluation of people and events.

8. Be able to discuss the idea of aggression as a drive and the frustration–aggression hypothesis. Be familiar with research on aggression in other species and brain–stimulated aggression in animals.

9. Be able to discuss the social–learning theory of aggression as a learned response. Be familiar with research on imitation and the reinforcement of aggression and the relevance of the research to social–learning theory.

10. Understand the concept of aggression as cathartic and the implications of such a concept.

11. Be able to discuss research concerning the effects of viewing violence on television and to list several reasons why such viewing can lead to aggressive behavior.

Important Names

1. The famous American psychologist _____ is noted for his dictum, "We are afraid because we run," which derives from the James–Lange theory of emotion. (382)

2. The physiologist _____ countered the James–Lange theory with observations that the autonomic nervous system could *not* play the differentiating role in emotion that this theory had suggested. (382)

3. Another historically prominent figure in the field of emotion was _____, who emphasized the importance of innate expressions of emotion in communication and species survival. (390)

Vocabulary and Details

COMPONENTS OF AN EMOTION

1. Intense emotions include six components that come together. These components are (a) the _____ (that is, the feelings associated with the emotion); b) internal _____ (such as rapid heartbeat and trembling), (c) _____ (that is, thoughts and beliefs about the emotion), (d) _____ expressions (such as frowning), (e) _____ to an emotional stimulus, and (f) _____ associated with the emotion. (378)

2. Theorists of emotion are moving toward a _____ perspective, in which these components of a given emotion are seen to have reciprocal effects on one another. (378)

AROUSAL AND EMOTION

1. Most of the physiological changes that occur during emotional arousal stem from activation of the _____ division of the autonomic nervous system, which functions to increase energy output. (380)

2. As an emotion subsides, the _____ division of the autonomic nervous system takes over to conserve energy and return the organism to a state of lower arousal. (380)

3. The _____ theory of emotion holds that activity in the autonomic nervous system and other bodily changes differentiate the emotions. (382)

COGNITION AND EMOTION

1. _____ refers to the process of analysis of a situation in which we interpret events or actions in terms of our personal goals and well–being. (383)

2. The group of theories termed _____ suggest it is people's appraisals of situations that lead to the subjective experience of emotion and associated physiological reactions. (388)

3. A small mass of tissue located in the lower brain called the _____ has been shown to have various roles in registering emotional reactions. (390)

4. One possibility supported by recent research is that the amygdala responds to alarming situations before the cortex, giving rise to _____. (390)

EXPRESSION AND EMOTION

1. Facial expression has been shown to play an important role in the _____ of emotions. (390)

2. Each culture has a set of rules called _____ that specify the types of emotions and related behavior people should have in certain situations. (392)

3. The interpretation of emotional expressions appears to be localized largely in the _____ of the brain. (393)

4. A person who has difficulty recognizing familiar faces because of damage to his cortex is termed a _____. (393)

5. Besides communication, facial expression might contribute to our _____ of emotions, a notion termed the _____. (393)

GENERAL REACTIONS TO BEING IN AN EMOTIONAL STATE

1. In the classic function relating performance to levels of emotional arousal, efficiency of performance is highest when arousal is _____ (low, moderate, high) and lowest when arousal is _____ (low, moderate, high). (395 and Figure 11-5)

AGGRESSION AS AN EMOTIONAL REACTION

1. An emotional reaction in anger is _____, that is, behavior *intended* to injure or destroy. (397)

2. According to Freud's _____ theory, aggressive behaviors stem from an underlying instinctual _____. (397)

3. A related notion is that whenever goal–directed activities are blocked, an aggressive drive motivates attack behavior; this view is termed the _____. (398)

4. The approach that focuses on the role of (a) environmental contingencies and (b) cognitive processes in human social behavior is termed _____. (399-400)

5. Social–learning theory also emphasizes the importance of learning by observation, or _____, and the role of _____ in transmitting specific behaviors and emotional responses in this form of learning. (400)

6. The discharge or purging of an emotion by experiencing it intensely is called _____. (402)

Ideas and Concepts

* 1. Compare the concepts of *emotions* and *motives*. Are these distinctions absolute? (378)

   —two similarities:

   —two differences:

COMPONENTS OF AN EMOTION

   1. a) Cite examples of the six components of emotions. (378)

      —subjective experiences:

      —internal bodily responses:

      —cognitions:

      —facial expression:

      —global reactions:

      —action tendencies:

* b) Is any one of the components of emotion discussed in 1a) an emotion by itself? Explain. (378)

* 2. Discuss the two sets of questions regarding the issues below that have guided research in the field of emotion: (378-379)

      —intensity of emotions:

      —differentiation of emotions:

AROUSAL AND EMOTION

* 1. List some of the changes during emotional arousal that result from activation of the sympathetic nervous system. (380)

   2. a) Outline the role of the *hypothalamus* and the *limbic system* in emotional arousal. (380)

      b) Of what emotions in particular is emotional arousal characteristic and why? (380-381)

*Basic ideas and concepts

164   Chapter 11

* 3. a) Outline the study by Hohmann relating the role of the sympathetic system in emotional intensity through observations of spinal cord injury victims. Note which emotions were assessed. (381)

* b) What is the significance of the response of Hohmann's subjects cited in your text, that "it's a mental kind of" emotion that they experienced? (381-382)

c) Cite a second more objective experiment that yielded similar results. (382)

* 4. a) Discuss Lange's contribution to the James–Lange theory of emotion through restatement of James's theory in terms of autonomic arousal. (382)

* b) Discuss three of Walter Cannon's criticisms of the James–Lange theory. (382)

* c) What evidence was obtained recently in studies by Ekman and his colleagues that provides support for the James–Lange theory? (383)

* d) Give three reasons why your authors contend that results like Ekman's do not "provide unequivocal evidence" for the view that autonomic arousal differentiates the emotions. Therefore, what is the view of most psychologists on this issue? (383)

COGNITION AND EMOTION

1. a) Cite two instances of the impact of "cognitive appraisal" (a concept developed by Lazarus and his colleagues) on emotional experience. (383, 386)

* b) Provide three arguments why cognitive appraisal might help in differentiating the emotions. (386)

* 2. a) Describe the procedures of the classic Schacter and Singer experiment, being sure to distinguish clearly between the *informed* and *misinformed* conditions. (386)

* b) What were the results of these manipulations? (386-387)

c) Indicate several reasons why the considerable influence of the Schacter and Singer experiment may not have been justified. (387)

* d) Describe some follow–up experiments to the Schacter and Singer study, noting in particular how the results of these studies contrasted with those of the original experiment. (387)

* e) Discuss in detail your authors' conclusions regarding the role of both cognitions and autonomic arousal in the experience of emotion. (387)

* 3. a) Be able to fill in the blanks on the following page corresponding to the relationships between the components of emotion in the two major theories of emotion discussed to this point in your text. (387-388, Figure 11-4)

James–Lange Theory:

_____ -----> _____ -----> _____

Schacter–Singer Theory:

_____ -----> _____ -----> _____ -----> _____

b) In what respects have the two theories outlined in 3a) "oversimplified the emotion process," in your authors' view? (387)

4. a) What is the distinguishing feature of the appraisal theories shown in the third level of Figure 11-4? That is, what is appraised in this approach? (388)

* b) Indicate the two major classes of appraisal theories. (388)

* c) In the table below, distinguish between examples of theoretical approaches to the dimensions of appraisal in emotion. Note how many appraisal dimensions are identified in each approach, and provide some examples of appraisal dimensions with their corresponding emotions. (See also Tables 11-2 and 11-3.) (388-389)

Theory	Appraisal Dimensions and Related Emotions
Plutchik's "primary emotions" approach	
Roseman's "primary appraisal dimensions" approach	
Smith & Ellsworth's "multiple dimensions" approach	

* 5. Discuss some of the clinical implications of the cognitive appraisal analysis of emotion along each of the following lines: (389-390)

—Freud's concept of repression:

—Brenner's views on emotional development:

—the effects of past experience:

6. a) Zajonc (pronounced "zye-aunce") has offered an alternative to Lazarus's notions concerning the role of cognitive appraisal in emotional experience. Cite some everyday examples that suggest that emotion may occur without cognition. (390)

166   Chapter 11

*   b) Discuss Zajonc's idea from the perspective that there may be two kinds of emotional experiences (those with cognitive appraisal and others that are "precognitive") possibly supported by functions of the amygdala in the brain. (390)

    c) What is your authors' reconciliation of these differing points of view regarding the role of cognitive appraisal in emotional experiences? (390)

EXPRESSION AND EMOTION

* 1. a) Cite some evidence obtained by Ekman to support the assertion that certain facial expressions appear to have meanings that are not culture–specific? (391)

*   b) How does the universality of expression support Darwin's evolutionary analysis of emotion? (392)

*   c) Are all facial expressions and gestures clearly innate? Explain and cite some examples of the effects of culture on emotional expression obtained by Klineberg. (392)

    d) Give some examples of display rules in effect in different cultures. (392)

2. a) What do the facts of universality and cultural specificity in emotional expression suggest about the underlying neurology? (393)

*   b) Discuss three lines of evidence to suggest that the right cerebral hemisphere is where emotional expression is localized. (393)

    c) Outline some evidence on even more specialized levels of localization obtained from the study of prosopagnosics and from electrical stimulation of the brain. (393)

* 3. a) What is another way in which emotional expression is communicated? Cite three dimensions along which this information is conveyed. (393)

    b) Where is this function localized in the brain, and how do we know? (393)

* 4. a) Discuss the key aspects of Tomkins's facial feedback hypothesis. (393)

    b) Cite two sources of support for this theory. (393-394)

*   c) Outline the idea that facial expressions may determine the quality of emotions. How does this possibility relate to the James–Lange theory presented earlier in this chapter? (394)

* 5. a) Discuss Zajonc's proposal for a bodily mechanism by which facial expressions may determine the positivity or negativity of emotion. (394)

    b) Describe an innovative study that provided some preliminary evidence on Zajonc's temperature hypothesis. (394)

GENERAL REACTIONS TO BEING IN AN EMOTIONAL STATE

* 1. What three reactions accompany emotional states? (395)

2. a) Can you cite a personal example to illustrate the relationship between level of arousal and performance efficiency? (Hint: Have you experienced a difference in studying for an examination days in advance versus hours before?) (395)

    * b) How does the degree to which a task is well–learned affect the performance–arousal relationship? (395)

    * c) Cite evidence to show that individual differences constitute another variable in the performance–arousal function. (395)

    d) What may happen when intense emotion problems are not resolved quickly? (395)

* 3. a) Illustrate both of the following assertions with experimental results. (395-396)

    —we tend to pay more *attention* to events that are congruent with our mood than those that are not:

    —*learning* is also a function of congruence of moods with material to be learned:

    b) Discuss the memory mechanisms by which congruence between mood and material may affect learning. Use an example. (396)

* 4. a) Cite the evidence with respect to the effects of mood states upon judgments we may make in the following cases: (396-397)

    —evaluations of people and objects:

    —estimation of frequency of risks:

    —specific mood effects:

    b) What do your authors mean when they say that "the general consequences of a mood serve to perpetuate that mood"? (397)

AGGRESSION AS AN EMOTIONAL REACTION

1. Illustrate by example the meaning of the term "intent" in the definition of aggression. (397)

* 2. Discuss two critical aspects of the frustration–aggression hypothesis. Which is especially controversial? (398)

* 3. a) What is one implication of the notion that aggression is really a basic drive? Discuss the changing views on this issue and the current status of the evidence obtained by Goodall and others. (398)

*   b) Outline the evidence on biologically based aggression in both of the following species. (398)

—cats:

—laboratory rats:

*   c) Contrast the above findings on the biological control of aggression in lower mammals with higher mammals, considering the role of the cortex: (399)

—monkeys:

—humans:

d) What hormone may be related to aggression in humans? Cite the evidence and your authors' view of the certainty of this relationship. (399)

4. According to social–learning theory how do people come to select certain behavior patterns over others? (399)

* 5. After reading this subsection, indicate two respects in which social–learning theory differs from both of the following alternative approaches to aggression. (See also Figure 11-7.) (399-400)

—strict behaviorism:

—psychoanalytic theory:

* 6. Why do your authors say that "it is no surprise that social–learning theory rejects the concept of aggression as a frustration-produced drive"? Apply the social–learning view to the case of aggression in a frustrating situation. (400)

* 7. a) Outline the methods, results, and conclusion of the classic Bandura study of aggressive behaviors in nursery–school children. (400-401)

*   b) Discuss the observations made by Patterson and his coworkers on the role of consequences for aggression and counteraggression. (401-402)

8. How does research on catharsis relate to the issue whether aggression is an unlearned drive or a learned response? (402)

* 9. a) Summarize several research results that favor the view that acting aggressively fosters aggression rather than catharsis. (402)

b) Similarly, outline some observations made in a real–life situation that make the same point. (402)

c) Is there *any* instance in which behaving aggressively may reduce its subsequent occurrence? How do your authors account for this observation? (403)

* 10. a) Outline the results of studies on the effects of viewing television violence on children's behavior in natural settings. (403)

*   b)   Does televised violence influence aggression, or is it simply the case that children who are more aggressive already prefer to watch violent television programs? Discuss the methods of a study designed to evaluate this important issue. (403-404)

*   c)   What results were obtained in this experiment that specifically addressed the issue raised in 10b)? (See also Figure 11-10.) (404)

*   d)   Discuss the differences in the effects of viewing violence on girls versus boys. How do these differences reflect on the catharsis hypothesis? (404)

11.   a)   What are some additional causes of anger and aggression? (404)

*   b)   Indicate your authors' summarative statement on the relationship between frustration and aggression. (404)

170   Chapter 11

Sample Quiz 11.1

1. With respect to the six components of emotion: a) all components come together to create an emotion; b) a systems theory of emotion is evolving in which the components of an emotion are seen to have reciprocal effects on each other; c) one of the key questions for modern theories is to what extent the components of emotion help to differentiate emotions; d) all of the above.

2. The process in which we interpret events or actions in terms of our personal goals and well-being is termed: a) vicarious learning; b) goal setting; c) cognitive appraisal; d) goal structuring.

3. Cognitive appraisal theories are notable for their suggestion that: a) the experience of emotion is based on bodily reactions; b) people's appraisals of situations lead to the experience of emotion; c) appraisal is a right–hemisphere process that enables the recognition of facial expression; d) we learn emotional behaviors through observation of others.

4. The amygdala is: a) the seat of instinctual drive in Freud's theory; b) the portion of the autonomic nervous system that functions to conserve energy; c) a structure of the brain that has importance in the recognition of faces; d) none of the above.

5. The types of emotions and related behavior that people should have in various situations are specified in: a) precognitive emotions; b) instinctual action tendencies; c) display rules; d) facial feedback signals.

6. Evaluations of people and estimation of frequency of risks are two: a) general effects of emotional moods; b) specific functions of the amygdala; c) types of stimuli for specific emotions mentioned in your text; d) forms of display rules.

7. At the level of higher mammals, such as monkeys and humans, patterns of aggression appear to be controlled by: a) the cortex; b) experience; c) the hypothalamus; d) both a and b.

8. Which of the following is an important aspect of social–learning theory? a) vicarious learning; b) environmental contingencies; c) cognitive processes; d) all of the above.

9. Which of the following exemplifies catharsis? a) "I blew up at my boyfriend and felt better afterwards." b) "I got caught in traffic, and it made me really irritable." c) "I was so mad at Mother that I kicked the cat." d) "I was so anxious the night before the exam that I couldn't study."

10. Which of the following is *true*? a) Girls are no less likely to imitate aggression than boys. b) The main factor determining violence in young adults appears to be having an aggressiveness nature in childhood. c) Televised violence, even in the form of cartoons, appears to increase interpersonal aggression in children. d) There is no relationship between high exposure to violence on television at a young age and later aggressiveness, say, after 10 years.

Sample Quiz 11.2

1. The physiologist who argued that the autonomic nervous system could not be important in enabling the differentiation of emotions was: a) William James; b) Walter Cannon; c) Carl Lange; d) Charles Darwin.

2. Which of the following is *not* a reason given by your authors why the influence of the Schacter & Singer experiments may have been unjustifiable? a) Not all of the results reached statistical significance. b) There is no evidence that injection of epinephrine produces physiological arousal. c) Autonomic arousal in the happy and angry conditions may not have been the same. d) The placebo control group did not react in accordance with the experimenters' hypotheses.

3. Which of the following best characterizes the James–Lange view of emotion? a) stimulus -----> physiological arousal -----> experience of emotion; b) stimulus -----> cognitive appraisal -----> experience of emotion; c) appraisal of stimulus -----> experience of emotion; d) facial expression -----> experience of emotion.

4. Cognitive appraisal theory would predict that: a) the degree to which a situation evokes an emotion does not depend upon past experience; b) a person's emotional sensations may not change greatly across life; c) a person must experience an emotion to react consistently with it; d) none of the above.

5. Precognitive emotions have been identified with the: a) sympathetic nervous system; b) amygdala; c) right cerebral hemisphere; d) parasympathetic nervous system.

6. Your authors' position on whether or not we can have emotion without cognition is that: a) we cannot; b) all cognitions have an emotional component; c) emotional experiences without cognitive appraisal may be relatively undifferentiated positive or negative feelings; d) all emotion must be accompanied by activity in the amygdala.

7. We would expect that your performance on a unit quiz would be lowest when your level of emotional arousal is: a) high; b) moderate; c) low; d) both a and c.

8. Being in an emotional state: a) determines judgments we make about the world; b) affects what we attend to and what we learn; c) energizes or disrupts behavior; d) all of the above.

9. Intention is an important aspect in identifying: a) anger; b) anxiety; c) depression; d) happiness.

10. Social–learning theory views aggression as a: a) frustration–produced drive; b) specific reaction to the experience of frustration; c) learned response like any other; d) biological reaction that is largely not affected by imitation and reinforcement.

Answer Key, Chapter 11

Important Names

1. William James
2. Walter Cannon
3. Charles Darwin

Vocabulary and Details

COMPONENTS OF AN EMOTION

1. subjective experience; bodily responses; cognitions; facial; global reactions; action tendencies
2. systems

AROUSAL AND EMOTION

1. sympathetic
2. parasympathetic
3. James–Lange

COGNITION AND EMOTION

1. Cognitive appraisal
2. appraisal theory
3. amygdala
4. precognitive emotions

EXPRESSION AND EMOTION

1. communication
2. display rules
3. right cerebral hemisphere
4. prosopagnosic
5. subjective experience; facial feedback hypothesis

GENERAL REACTIONS TO BEING . . .

1. moderate; high or low

AGGRESSION AS AN EMOTIONAL . . .

1. aggression
2. psychoanalytic; drive
3. frustration–aggression hypothesis
4. social–learning theory
5. vicarious learning; models
6. catharsis

Sample Quiz 11.1

1. d, 378-379
2. c, 383
3. b, 388
4. d, 390
5. c, 392
6. a, 396
7. d, 398-399
8. d, 399-400
9. a, 401
10. c, 404

Sample Quiz 11.2

1. b, 382
2. b, 387
3. a, 388
4. b, 389-390
5. b, 390
6. c, 390
7. d, 395
8. d, 395
9. a, 397
10. c, 400

Individual Differences

Learning Objectives

1. Be able to specify the difference between reliability and validity and why each is necessary for an intelligence or personality test to be trustworthy.

2. Be familiar with the development of tests of intellectual ability and the general format of the Stanford–Binet and Wechsler Intelligence Scales. Know how scores are interpreted.

3. Be able to describe how factor–analytic techniques were used by Spearman and Thurstone to separate the different abilities that contribute to intelligence.

4. Be familiar with the information–processing approach to analyzing performance on intelligence test items and the componential model of Sternberg.

5. Be familiar with factor–analytic methods of determining personality traits, the factors arrived at by Cattell and Eysenck, and the criticisms of the trait approach.

6. Be familiar with the tests used to assess personality traits, including use of the criterion–keyed method to develop personality inventories. Know what is meant by a projective test and the problems encountered in interpreting the results of the Rorschach and TAT.

7. Understand what a heritability estimate does and does not tell, and be able to counter some misunderstandings about heritability. Be familiar with the twin studies evidence for genetic contributions to intelligence.

8. Be prepared to define the three dynamic processes of personality–environment interactions (reactive, evocative, and proactive) and to give examples of each.

9. Be able to discuss the evidence for continuity of personality provided by the two longitudinal studies described in the text. What characteristics showed the strongest continuity?

10. Be prepared to explain, with examples, how the three processes of personality–environment interaction influence the continuity of personality.

11. Be able to distinguish between the cumulative consequences and the contemporary consequences of personality characteristics and to provide examples of each from the longitudinal studies of ill–tempered or dependent children.

Important Names

1. The first attempt to develop tests of intellectual ability was by the nineteenth–century naturalist and mathematician _____. (413)

2. The first psychologist to devise what by contemporary standards would be considered a test of "intelligence" was the Frenchman _____. (413)

3. The most familiar revision of Binet's test, the Stanford–Binet Intelligence Test, was first adapted and standardized by the American psychologist _____. (414)

4. One of the first intelligence tests designed to measure separate abilities was first designed in the 1930s by _____. (414)

5. The originator of factor analysis and the concept of a general intelligence factor was _____. (417)

6. The psychologist _____ objected to Spearman's notion of general intelligence and argued that intelligence consists of a number primary abilities. (417)

7. The psychologist who applied factor analysis most extensively to the study of personality traits and distinguished between 16 different factors is _____. (422)

8. Another psychologist who uses factor analysis in the analysis of traits, but who has arrived at fewer dimensions than Cattell, is _____. (422)

Vocabulary and Details

1. The biological and environmental factors that individualize us and make us different from one another are termed _____. (411)

ASSESSMENT OF INDIVIDUAL DIFFERENCES

1. Tests that rely heavily on the objective assessment of individual differences—especially differences in cognitive or intellectual abilities—are termed _____ or _____ tests. (411)

2. Tests are said to be _____ when they are give reproducible and consistent results. (411)

3. In one way of measuring reliability, when a correlation is obtained between two administrations of the *same* test we speak of _____ or _____. (411)

4. In a second measure of reliability, when a correlation is determined between two different *forms* of a test, we speak of high _____. (412)

5. A third measure of reliability is _____, the degree to which the separate items on a test all measure the same thing. (412)

6. A fourth way of measuring reliability is _____ or _____, a method that is used when correlations are obtained between raters or judges of subjective responses of individuals. (412)

7. The extent to which a test measures what it is intended to measure is termed _____. (412)

8. One form of validity is _____ or _____, obtained by correlating a test score with some external criterion. (412)

9. Another form of validity is called _____, the extent to which a test measures some theoretical concept or construct. (412)

10. The first test of intellectual ability adapted for American schoolchildren early in this century was the _____. (414)

11. Alfred Binet and his colleague, Théophile Simon, distinguished between the scaled age at which a child could solve problems on the intelligence test, called _____, versus the actual age of the child taking the test, called _____. (414)

12. Terman adopted an index of intelligence called the _____ which expresses intelligence as _____ (cite the formula). (414)

13. The most recent version of the Stanford–Binet test uses _____ instead of IQ scores, which show the _____ of subjects in the standardization group falling above or below a given score. (414)

14. The intelligence test devised by David Wechsler, the _____ (abbreviated _____), separates abilities into two divisions using a _____ scale and a _____ scale. (414)

15. A version of the WAIS for children is called the _____ (abbreviated _____). (414)

16. Spearman designed a mathematical technique called _____ to determine the minimum number of abilities, or _____, required to explain an observed pattern of correlations for an array of tests. (416-417)

17. Spearman proposed that all individuals possess a factor called the _____ or _____, that is, the general determinant of performance on intelligence tests. (417)

18. In addition, Spearman called factors that are specific to particular abilities or tests _____ or _____. (417)

19. By contrast, Thurstone argued that intelligence, rather than general in nature, actually consists of a number of _____. (417)

20. In his search for primary abilities, Thurstone (like Spearman) used the _____ approach. (417)

21. Since the 1960s, an alternative to the factorial approach is the attempt to understand intelligence in terms of cognitive processes, termed the _____ approach. (418)

22. The distinctive and characteristic patterns of thought, emotion, and behavior that define an individual's personal style of interacting with the environment constitute _____. (421)

23. When describing an individual's personality, we usually use terms that refer to relatively persisting personality _____—such as "intelligent," "extraverted," or "conscientious." (421)

24. A questionnaire in which a person reports reactions or feelings in certain situations in order to measure one or several dimensions of personality is called a _____. (423)

25. In the _____ method of test construction, items are administered to groups of people known to differ from the norm on some criterion, and only those questions that discriminate between the groups are retained. (424)

26. The most popular of all personality inventories is the _____ (abbreviated _____), consisting of 550 items aimed at determining serious deviations from the norm group for a number of personality dimensions. (424)

27. A recently revised version of the MMPI is the _____, standardized with a larger and more representative population. (425)

28. A personality inventory designed to assess more "normal" personality traits than the MMPI, such as dominance and responsibility, is the _____, (abbreviated _____). (425)

29. In the _____ method for personality trait assessment, a rater (sorter) is given a set of cards containing personality statements and asked to describe an individual by placing the cards into stacks ranging from least to most descriptive. (426)

30. Tests used in psychoanalytic assessment that present ambiguous stimuli and allow for a broad range of responses are called _____. (426)

31. One projective test is the _____, named after its developer, in which a series of 10 cards depicting complex inkblots are presented; a subject responds by indicating what each stimulus resembles. (426-427)

32. Another projective test is the _____ (or _____), devised by Henry Murray. It is a test that consists of ambiguous pictures of persons and scenes, and a subject responds by telling a story about each picture. (427)

INTERACTION BETWEEN NATURE AND NURTURE

1. The proportion of a trait's variation accounted for by genetic differences among individuals in a population is termed _____. (430)

2. Two humans who develop from a single fertilized egg are called _____, or said to be _____. Twins who develop from different egg cells are called _____, or said to be _____. (431).

3. In the interaction between genotype and the environment, termed _____, different individuals exposed to the same environment experience it, interpret it, and react to it differently. (434)

4. In the second form of interaction between genotype and the environment, termed _____, an individual's personality evokes distinctive responses from others. (434)

5. In the third form of interaction between genotype and the environment, termed _____, individuals select or create environments of their own. (435)

CONTINUITY OF PERSONALITY ACROSS THE LIFE COURSE

1. Studies that observe or assess the same persons over time are called _____. (437)

2. The processes of interaction may shape the life course through _____, the consequences that arise when an individual's early personality channels him or her into particular life paths. (440)

3. Alternatively, we speak of _____ when early personality carries forward into adult life in the form of current personality to evoke distinctive responses from the environment. (440)

Ideas and Concepts

ASSESSMENT OF INDIVIDUAL DIFFERENCES

1. Cite examples of the two uses of tests in the study of individual differences in psychology: (411)

   —aptitude or ability tests:

   —tests for assessing interests, attitudes, or personality traits:

* 2. Outline the procedures used in each of the following forms of reliability measurement. Cite examples when possible. (411-412)

   —test–retest reliability (temporal stability):

   —alternate form reliability:

   —internal consistency:

   —interrater agreement (interjudge reliability):

* 3. a) What should be the value of the reliability coefficient for objective tests? For personality tests or subjective judgments? (412)

* b) How can we increase the reliability of a test's total score? By analogy, how can we increase the reliability of measurement of subjective judgments? (412)

* 4. a) Does high reliability guarantee that a test measures what it is intended to measure? Explain the difference between reliability and validity, and illustrate. (412)

*Basic Ideas and Concepts

b) Provide examples of two forms of validity: (412-413)

—criterion (empirical) validity:

—construct validity:

c) Is it always possible to compute a single coefficient for criterion validity? Why or why not? (413)

*   d) Relatedly, what is the "criterion problem" in personality psychology, and how is it dealt with? (413)

*   5. a) What did Galton believe about differences between families and how did he conceptualize intelligence? (413)

b) Outline Galton's methods for supporting his conception and the obtained results that disappointed him. (413)

*   6. a) What was Binet's task and how did he go about achieving his aims? (413)

*   b) Discuss the reasoning by which Binet came to develop the notion of mental age. (413-414)

*   7. Using Terman's formula for IQ, determine the value for each of the following hypothetical unknowns: (414)

—MA = 9, CA = 10, IQ =

—IQ = 100, CA = 5, MA =

—IQ = 120, MA = 12, CA =

*   8. a) What changes in scoring of the Stanford–Binet test have been made in the most recent revision? How is IQ now calculated? (414)

b) What current view of intelligence is now reflected in the Stanford–Binet, and how is it reflected in the revised test? (414)

    9. a) Be able to distinguish the kinds of items used on the WAIS. (See also Table 12–2.) (415-416)

*   b) For what would a discrepancy between verbal and performance scores on the WAIS or WISC prompt an examiner to look? (415)

* 10. a) Distinguish between *individual ability tests* and *group ability tests*. (415)

*   b) Cite two kinds of group tests of general ability (including their abbreviations) that are familiar to many college–bound students. What kinds of changes have been instituted recently in each of these tests and why? (415-416)

*   c)   What is the relationship between scores on the Scholastic Aptitude Test (SAT) and performance in college? (416)

* 11.   a)   Discuss the views of intelligence held by Alfred Binet and David Wechsler. (416)

      b)   What is the contrasting view of many other psychologists concerning the nature of intelligence? (416)

* 12.   What is the basic idea behind factor analysis and what does the factor analysis of an array of data tell us? (416-417)

* 13.   a)   According to Spearman, what determines whether a person is, say, generally bright or generally dull? (417)

      b)   Cite some examples of Spearman's *s* factors. (417)

* 14.   a)   What has become of Thurstone's theory of primary mental abilities? Use the term ***Test of Primary Mental Abilities*** and comment on its predictive power. (417)

      b)   Cite two reasons why Thurstone's hope that he could factor analyze intelligence into its elements was not fulfilled. (417)

  15.   What has led to doubt about the factorial approach? Is it still in use? (417)

* 16.   a)   List three questions raised in the information–processing approach to research on intelligence. (418)

*   b)   What does the information–processing model assume regarding individual differences on a task? (418)

*   c)   Indicate the goal of the information–processing model and the kinds of measures employed in seeking that goal. (418-419)

  17.   a)   List the five classes of components identified by Sternberg's ***componential model*** of intelligence. (419-420)

*   b)   Give an illustration of Sternberg's model in action using the specific components ***encoding process*** and ***comparison process*** in your answer. (419-420)

      c)   Discuss in detail the kinds of individual differences that appear in research on skilled and less–skilled performers on analogy problems. (420)

  18.   Discuss the ways in which a factorial and an information–processing approach can be used together to yield complementary interpretations of intelligence test per–formance. (420)

* 19.   a)   List the six kinds of intelligence offered by Gardner. What three have been emphasized, and what three deemphasized in Western society? (420)

*   b)   In Gardner's view, what particular intelligence has been more important than logical-mathematical intelligence throughout human history? (420)

c) Define the two classes of personal intelligence in this approach. (420-421)

* d) In terms of the predictive ability of conventional IQ tests, why might some people who succeed in college not do well in later life, and vice-versa? Does this mean that standard intelligence tests are not useful in society at large? Explain. (421)

* 20. a) Historically, what approach have personality psychologists taken in describing and measuring personality? (421)

* b) Specify three ways in which personality theorists go beyond everyday trait conceptions. (421)

21. a) Describe the approach used by Allport & Odbert to obtain a set of human personality traits, and give the number obtained. (422)

* b) What technique did Cattell apply to Allport and Odbert's list of traits, and what was the result in terms of numbers of traits obtained? (422)

* c) Discuss Eysenck's variation on the application of factor analysis to the problem of personality traits. Be able to distinguish among the various types defined by his dimensions of personality. (422)

—*introversion–extraversion*:

—*stable–unstable (neuroticism)*:

* 22. a) Identify three reasons why there is such a large discrepancy among the various trait theorists in terms of the numbers of traits they assign to people. (423)

* b) What consensus regarding numbers of traits appears to be emerging and what are the dimensions? (423 and Table 12-5)

23. Describe personality inventories in terms of characteristics of their items and how the items are arrived at in test construction. (423-424)

* 24. Describe the MMPI in terms of: (424-425 and Table 12-6)

—method of development:

—general nature of the *content scales* and *validity scales*:

—an advantage and a disadvantage of the criterion–keyed method:

—criticisms:

—overall value and a limitation:

* 25. What was the purpose for construction of the California Psychological Inventory? Illustrate with some of its scales. (558)

* 26. a) In what respect is a Q sort different from rating individuals on rating scales? (426)

b) How can two Q sorts be compared with one another for two individuals? For the same individual at two different times? When two raters do the judging? (426)

c) Describe how a Q sort could be used as the basis for an adjustment score. (426)

27. a) What is a particular interest of psychoanalytically-oriented personality psychologists, and to what form of assessment does this lead them? (426)

b) Why is the term "projective" used? (426)

28. a) Along what dimensions is the Rorschach Test scored? (427)

* b) Have the scoring systems for the Rorschach been shown to have predictive value? On what do many psychologists base their interpretations? (427)

* 29. a) What are stories on the TAT designed to reveal? Use the term *apperception* in your answer. (427)

b) What do psychologists look for when using the TAT? (428)

* 30. a) Indicate the general outcome of reliability and validity assessments of the Rorschach Test. (428)

* b) Similarly, how has the TAT fared in evaluations of reliability? (428)

* c) In terms of validity, what may be a difficulty with using the TAT in assessment? Cite an example. (428)

d) In what terms do users of projective tests such as the Rorschach and TAT defend these instruments? (428)

INTERACTION BETWEEN NATURE AND NURTURE

1. a) Be able to describe the material in Figure 12-4, and define the terms *frequency distribution*, *mean*, and *variance*. (429-430)

b) What happens in the exam score example in Figure 12-4 when the variable—study time—is fixed? (429-430)

* c) Based on the example in 1b), in general, what happens to variance when we hold constant any variable that "makes a difference"? What happens to the mean of the distribution under these conditions? (430)

* 2. a) What is the relationship between the number of individual differences on a trait due to genetic differences and the value of heritability? Give an example. (430)

* b) What is the problem if we wished to ask the question, how much of the variance in students' exam scores is due to genetic differences? In what way does the study of twins, identical and fraternal, address this issue? (430-431)

Individual Differences   183

3. a) Across many twin studies, what is the value of heritability found in IQ scores? Similarly, in other twin studies, what value of heritability was obtained for the traits of extraversion and emotional stability? (431)

* b) What is one difficulty in interpreting the results of twin studies and an ideal solution to the problem? Indicate the actual results obtained when the solution was implemented in a study in which a wide range of personality variables were assessed in identical and fraternal twins. (431)

* c) Indicate the levels of heritabilities found in measures of ability, of personality, and of beliefs regarding politics, religion, or vocation. (431)

* 4. Discuss what is known about heritability in terms of its relationship to misconceptions about: (432-433)

—measures on an individual:

—fixed attributes of a trait:

—the source of mean differences between groups:

—the effects of environmental changes on the mean level of a trait:

* 5. a) Explain and give some illustrations of your authors' contention that there is a "built–in correlation" between genotype and environment: (434)

—positive correlation between environment and genotype:

—negative correlation between environment and genotype:

b) Whether the correlation is positive or negative, what is the pertinent point? (434)

* 6. a) For each of the forms of environment–genotype interactions in the table below, be able to cite some examples. (434-435)

Examples

reactive interaction	
evocative interaction	
proactive interaction	

184   Chapter 12

b) How does the relative importance of the three forms of personality–environment interactions change over the course of development? (435)

* 7. a) Indicate some puzzling issues relative to personality comparisons between identical and fraternal twins. (435)

b) Give a reason why the personalities of identical twins may be so similar, and cite an example. (435)

* c) What is an important feature of personality–environmental interaction processes as they may operate in identical twins? Illustrate and contrast with the case of fraternal twins and siblings. (435-436)

* 8. a) Discuss a surprising result that has emerged from studies of the role of environment in personality differences. (436)

* b) Outline the explanation offered by your text for this controversial finding and what this explanation may imply regarding the design of future research. (436-437)

CONTINUITY OF PERSONALITY ACROSS THE LIFE COURSE

1. What is a basic task for the study of personality and development? (437)

* 2. a) Note the fundamental procedures of two large–scale longitudinal studies begun in California at the Institute of Human Development (IHD) in the 1920s. (437)

* b) Outline the results of these longitudinal studies, indicating especially the features of personality that show the strongest continuities: (437-438)

—strongest continuities:

—weaker continuities:

—weakest continuities:

* 3. a) Is it the genotype itself that directly produces continuity? Explain in terms of the relevant factors, and cite some examples. (438)

* b) Discuss the results of another IHD (Berkeley Guidance) study that investigated whether spouses who were alike would produce greater continuity in personality in one another than those who were not so alike. (439)

* 4. a) To illustrate some of the coercive ways that reactive, evocative, and proactive interaction can sustain maladaptive personality patterns, cite an example of the potential *cumulative* consequences of childhood personality. (440)

* b) Alternatively, discuss this example from the standpoint of *contemporary* consequences of current personality. (440)

* 5. a) Outline the procedures for the study of cumulative and contemporary consequences of the personality trait of *ill–temperedness*, as traced in the IHD archive of the Berkeley Guidance Study. (440)

Individual Differences   185

   *   b) With respect to male subjects in this study, in detail, what were the life course factors studied, and what was the "path" that the trait of ill–temperedness took from childhood to adulthood? Use the term *path analysis* in your answer, and be able to relate different paths to differential significance of correlation coefficients. (440-441)

   *   c) What variables showed the effects of cumulative consequences and contemporary consequences, respectively, in this study? How do we know? (441)

           d) What other aspect of these men's lives were influenced by the ill–temperedness factor? (441)

6. a) With respect to the women in the Berkeley Guidance Study, why could the same analysis not be applied to determine whether the persistence of childhood ill–temperedness into adult life reflected cumulative or contemporary consequences? (441)

   *   b) Was ill–temperedness shown to persist for these women? What features of the women's lives in the Berkeley study appeared to correlate with this personality characteristic? (441-442)

7. a) Give three reasons why ill–tempered children do not inevitably become ill–tempered adults. (442)

           b) What is another frequent source of pressure for personality change across the life course? (442)

           c) Briefly indicate the procedures of a Berkeley study of childhood dependency that further explored the possibility discussed in 7b). What question was asked in this study? (442)

   *   d) Outline the main results of this study noting both of the following effects: (442)

—the relationship between childhood dependency and adult personality for men:

—the relationship between childhood dependency and adult domestic behaviors for men:

Sample Quiz 12.1

1. Which of the following is *true*? a) The value of the reliability coefficient for objective tests should be .90 or above. b) We can increase the reliability of a test by adding reliable items. c) High reliability does not guarantee that a test measures what it is intended to measure. d) All of the above.

2. The extent to which a test measures some theoretical concept is termed: a) empirical validity; b) internal consistency; c) construct validity; d) temporal stability.

3. The most recent version of the Stanford–Binet test uses: a) IQ scores; b) mental age; c) Standard Age Scores; d) special factors.

4. The information–processing approach asks the question: a) what types of mental representation of information do intellectual cognitive processes act upon? b) how rapidly are cognitive processes carried out in the performance of intellectual activities? c) what mental processes are involved in the various intelligence tests? (d) all of the above.

5. Personality terms like "intelligent," "extraverted," or "conscientious" are commonly used to refer to: a) primary abilities; b) examples of reactive interaction; c) special intelligence factors; d) traits.

6. Raymond Cattell is noted for: a) extensive use of the factorial approach; b) identification of two main factors in personality traits; c) the first intelligence test to measure separate abilities; d) both a and b.

7. A consensus regarding traits is emerging that agrees: a) on how to name the factors; b) on how to interpret the factors; c) that there are five factors; d) that factor analysis is an inappropriate approach.

8. Theoretically, if we hold constant any variable that makes a difference in the values of scores in a distribution: a) the variance of the distribution will be reduced; b) changes in the mean of the distribution will always be reduced; c) under some conditions, the variance could diminish to zero; d) both a and c.

9. In reactive interaction: a) different individuals exposed to the same environment experience it differently; b) individuals create environments of their own; c) an individual's personality produces different reactions from others; d) genetic differences solely determine personality reactions.

10. Path analysis of variables that relate ill–temperedness in men with later aspects of life show that: a) an erratic adult worklife is a cumulative consequence of childhood ill–temperedness; b) low occupational status is a cumulative consequence of ill–temperedness; c) an erratic worklife causes low occupational status; d) both a and b.

Sample Quiz 12.2

1. Internal consistency is: a) the correlation between two administrations of the same test; b) when correlations are used to determine the degree that items on a test all measure the same thing; c) the correlation between two forms of a test; d) when correlations are obtained between raters.

2. A discrepancy between verbal and performance scores on the Wechsler test would lead to: a) development of a new test; b) examination of the individual for specific learning disabilities; c) assignment of an IQ score in terms of verbal scores only; d) assignment of IQ in terms of performance scores only.

3. The information–processing approach: a) was originally used in the design of the first intelligence test; b) is a recent alternative to factor analysis in the attempt to understand intelligence; c) is the underlying model in the development of projective tests; d) was the theoretical approach used in test construction of the MMPI.

4. In the view of Howard Gardner, a critic of current intelligence testing: a) musical ability has been more important than logical-mathematical ability throughout most of human history; b) current IQ tests tend to tap primarily practical intelligence and to ignore aspects of academic intelligence; c) Western societies have tended to emphasize spatial, musical, and bodily–kinesthetic aspects of intelligence; d) all of the above.

5. The most popular of all personality inventories is the: a) Stanford–Binet; b) CPI; c) MMPI; d) Rorschach Test.

6. If we were to use the TAT, we would ask: a) subjects to answer 550 items of a personality inventory; b) subjects to write stories about ambiguous pictures; c) a client to indicate what some inkblots represent; d) a client to sort cards containing personality statements.

7. Which of the following statements regarding heritability is *false*? a) Heritability is not a measure on an individual. b) Heritability does not tell us about the source of mean differences between groups. c) Heritability is not a varying attribute of a trait. d) Heritability does not tell us about the effects of the environment on the mean level of a trait.

8. Which of the following best states the effects of the family environment on the personalities of two children from the same family? a) They will be no more alike than any two children drawn randomly from the population. b) They can be expected to be very similar. c) They will be more dissimilar than two children drawn randomly from the population. d) Any of the above may be true depending upon socioeconomic factors.

9. When interactive processes result in early personality channeling an individual into particular life paths, we speak of: a) longitudinal interaction; b) contemporary consequences; c) channeling consequences; d) cumulative consequences.

10. Childhood dependency in boys is correlated with: a) a warm, nurturant personality in adulthood; b) high divorce rates in adulthood; c) dissatisfaction among wives in adulthood owing to continued dependency; d) both b and c.

Answer Key, Chapter 12

Important Names

1. Francis Galton
2. Alfred Binet
3. Lewis Terman
4. David Wechsler
5. Charles Spearman
6. Louis Thurstone
7. Raymond Cattell
8. Hans Eysenck

Vocabulary and Details

1. individual differences

ASSESSMENT OF INDIVIDUAL . . .

1. aptitude; ability
2. reliable
3. test-retest reliability; temporal stability
4. alternate form reliability
5. internal consistency
6. interrater agreement; interjudge reliability
7. validity
8. criterion validity; empirical validity
9. construct validity
10. Stanford–Binet Intelligence Scale
11. mental age (MA); chronological age (CA)
12. intelligence quotient (IQ); IQ = MA/CA x 100
13. Standard Age Scores; percentage
14. Wechsler Adult Intelligence Scale (WAIS); verbal; performance
15. Wechsler Intelligence Scale for Children (WISC)
16. factor analysis; factors
17. general intelligence factor; *g*
18. special factors; *s*
19. primary abilities
20. factorial
21. information–processing
22. personality
23. traits
24. personality inventory
25. criterion–keyed
26. Minnesota Multiphasic Personality Inventory (MMPI)
27. MMPI–2
28. California Psychological Inventory (CPI)
29. Q sort
30. projective tests
31. Rorschach Test
32. Thematic Apperception Test (TAT)

INTERACTION BETWEEN NATURE . . .

1. heritability
2. identical twins; monozygotic; fraternal twins; dizygotic
3. reactive interaction
4. evocative interaction
5. proactive interaction

CONTINUITY OF PERSONALITY . . .

1. longitudinal studies
2. cumulative consequences
3. contemporary consequences

Sample Quiz 12.1

1. d, 412
2. c, 412
3. c, 414
4. d, 418
5. d, 421
6. a, 422
7. c, 423
8. d, 430
9. a, 434
10. b, 441

Sample Quiz 12.2

1. b, 412
2. b, 415
3. b, 418
4. a, 420
5. c, 424
6. b, 427
7. c, 432-433
8. a, 436
9. d, 440
10. a, 442

Personality

Learning Objectives

1. Be able to state the two tasks of personality psychology and how theories have gone beyond the trait approaches in addressing the many relevant processes in personality.

2. Be familiar with the key concepts of Freud's psychoanalytic theory, including his assumptions about personality structure, dynamics, and personality development.

3. Be able to discuss the theories of later psychoanalysts and to evaluate the psychoanalytic approach in terms of its portrait of human personality and criticisms of the theory.

4. Understand the basic assumptions of the behavioristic, most notably the social–learning, approach to personality, including the role of operant and classical conditioning and the person variables that account for individual differences in behavior. Be familiar with the research methods of this approach.

5. Explain what is meant by the consistency paradox, and be prepared to discuss the possible reasons why studies find low correlations between measures of the same trait in two different situations or between personality test scores and situational measures of a trait.

6. Be prepared to discuss the solutions to the consistency paradox offered by aggregated measures, the person–centered approach, and interactionism.

7. Be able to describe the behavioristic portrait of personality and to evaluate the contributions of this approach.

8. Understand how the phenomenological approach differs from psychoanalytic and social–learning approaches. Be familiar with the basic assumptions underlying the humanistic theories of Carl Rogers and Abraham Maslow, and the more cognitive view of George Kelly.

9. Be familiar with the concept of the self and how real–ideal self–congruence is measured in Rogers's theory. Similarly, be able to discuss the Role Construct Repertory Test in the context of Kelly's theory.

10. Be able to describe the phenomenological portrait of human personality and to evaluate this approach.

Important Names

1. The creator of the psychoanalytic theory of personality was _____. (447)

2. A *social cognitive* theory that emphasizes reciprocal interactions among variables has been put forth by _____. (456)

3. The individual whose views on "actualization" and whose nondirective therapeutic methods grew out of the principles of humanistic psychology was _____. (464)

4. Another important humanistic psychologist who became known for his notion that individuals behave in accordance with a hierarchy of needs was _____. (466)

5. A third notable phenomenological psychologist, whose "personal construct" approach emphasizes individualistic dimensions for interpreting (or construing) the world, was _____. (467)

Vocabulary and Details

1. The distinctive and characteristic patterns of thought, emotion, and behavior that define an individual's personal style of interacting with the environment constitute _____. (447)

PSYCHOANALYTIC APPROACH

1. In the *psychoanalytic approach*, essentially, the attempt to explain personality in terms of unconscious processes, the method in which a patient is instructed to say everything that comes into awareness is termed _____. (447)

2. In the psychoanalytic view, the small portion of the human mind of which we are currently aware is the _____; the information that is not immediately in awareness but that can be brought into consciousness is called the _____; and the largest portion of impulses, memories, and wishes that are inaccessible to consciousness is termed the _____. (448)

3. The doctrine (influential in the psychoanalytic approach) that all thoughts, emotions, and actions have causes is known as _____. (448)

4. In the psychoanalytic view, personality is composed of three systems or structures, the most primitive of which is the _____, consisting of the basic biological impulses or drives. (448)

5. The id is said to operate on the _____ principle, striving immediately to obtain pleasure and avoid pain. (448)

6. The second personality system is the _____, which attempts to mediate between the impulses of the id and the demands of society to behave appropriately. (448-449)

7. The ego obeys the _____ principle, delaying gratification until it can be obtained in socially appropriate ways. (449)

8. The third structure of personality is the _____, the internalized representation of the values of society that prompts a person to adhere to moral standards. (449)

9. Each person's image of the morally ideal person is called their _____. (449)

10. In Freud's *personality dynamics*, the psychic energy for personality is called _____, reflecting his view that the _____ drive was primary. (449)

11. Freud used the term _____ for the ego's strategies by which a person can avoid or reduce the anxiety attendant upon expressions of the id. (450)

12. The most basic of these strategies is termed _____, in which unacceptable thoughts or impulses are pushed by the ego out of consciousness and into the unconscious. (450)

13. Freud referred to the developmental periods in which the impulses of the id focus on different areas of the body as _____. (450)

14. During the phallic psychosexual stage, a conflict emerges, called the _____, in which a young boy is attracted to his mother and regards his father as a rival for her affection. (450)

15. Freud also maintained that an individual could be stopped or _____ at a given stage of psychosexual development, with later consequences for personality. (451)

BEHAVIORISTIC APPROACH

1. The approach to personality that stresses environmental variables and assumes that behavior is the result of continuous interactions between personal and environmental variables is termed the _____, or, in its contemporary form, the _____. (455)

2. Social-learning theorists emphasize three forms of learning in the development of personality: a) _____, in which behavior is a function of its consequences; b) _____, in which people learn by observing the actions and consequences of others' behavior; and c) _____, in which the relationships between conditioned and unconditioned stimuli play a role. (455-456)

3. The _____ refers to the paradox that intuitively we feel that individuals are consistent in their behavior across situations, while research tells us that they are not. (458)

PHENOMENOLOGICAL APPROACH

1. The approach to the study of personality that focuses on the individual's *subjective experience,* that is, the personal perception and interpretation of events in the environment, is termed the _____. Central to this approach is the subdiscipline _____. (463)

2. From the standpoint of Rogers's brand of humanistic psychology, the basic motivating force of the individual is the tendency toward _____. (464)

3. Rogers's method of humanistic therapy assumes that the individual will strive toward growth and has the ability to decide personally on the direction for change; this technique is called _____. (464)

4. The central concept in Rogers's approach, termed the _____ or _____, consists of all the ideas, perceptions, and values that characterize the individual concept of "I" or "me." (464)

5. From this perspective, how a person would *like* to be is called that individual's _____ self; thus, how the person actually *is* may be termed the _____ self. (465)

6. Maslow's concept of a _____ proposes that needs are organized so that the more basic ones must be satisfied before increasingly more complex, psychological needs will influence action. (466)

7. Maslow used the term _____ to describe individuals who have made extraordinary use of their potential. (466)

8. According to Maslow, moments of happiness and fulfillment that may accompany self–actualization are termed _____. (466-467)

9. Kelly's theory emphasizes the dimensions that individuals use to interpret themselves and their social worlds. These dimensions are the individual's own _____, and the approach is called _____. (467)

10. A measuring instrument devised by Kelly for eliciting an individual's personal constructs is called the _____ or _____. (468)

Ideas and Concepts

1. a) What is one task of personality psychology? (447)

   b) Is the trait approach to personality a theory? Explain and indicate what this has meant for the development of theories of personality and a second task for this field. (447)

   c) Why do your authors state that most personality psychologists today are not "pure" adherents to any of the three approaches to personality discussed in this chapter? (447)

PSYCHOANALYTIC APPROACH

1. Describe the early development of Freud's approach. (447-448)

* 2. Using the iceberg metaphor, outline the relationship between Freud's concepts regarding levels of consciousness. Use the early term *topographic model* in your answer. (448)

* 3. According to psychoanalytic theory, what causes most psychological events, and what are some manifestations? (448)

*Basic ideas and concepts

* 4. a) Use examples to ensure that you can distinguish among the id, ego, and superego. (448-449)

* b) What happens if the moral standards of the superego are violated, and how is this result experienced? Describe a case of an overdeveloped superego and of a weak superego. (449)

c) Do the three structures of personality coexist peacefully? Discuss. (449)

* 5. a) Discuss the influence of the view of energy conservation on Freud's notions regarding personality dynamics. (449)

* b) By this view, what happens if forbidden impulses are suppressed? Give an example. (449-450)

* 6. Describe events in each of the following psychosexual stages of personality development, and indicate the age at which they occur. (450-451)

	Age	Description
oral stage		
anal stage		
phallic stage		
latency period		
genital stage		

* 7. Outline the sequence of events in the development of a male child's Oedipal conflict. Use the term *castration anxiety*. (450)

* 8. a) Describe a normal case in which the Oedipal conflict is resolved successfully. (451)

* b) Describe the consequences of fixation at a stage of psychosexual development. Illustrate with the personality attributes that would result from fixation at two different stages. Use the terms *oral personality* and *anal personality*. (451)

9. a) In what respect was Freud flexible in his thinking? Cite two examples. (451)

* b) In what respect was Freud not so open to revisions, and on what topic was that especially apparent? (451)

Personality   195

*   c) Indicate the result of Freud's dogmatism upon the field of psychoanalytic theory, and name some representative individuals who developed rival theories. (451)

*   d) On what aspect of Freud's theory have more recent psychoanalytic theorists concentrated their efforts? Cite some instances, including *object relations theory*. (451)

10. Similarly, outline the ways in which Erikson's important theory of *psychosocial stages* (discussed in Chapter 3) represents a departure from Freud's views. (452-453)

11. a) Compare Freud with Copernicus and Darwin in terms of how the views of each have challenged time–honored notions of the preeminence of the earth and of man. (453)

*   b) What stand does classic psychoanalytic theory take on each of the following issues? (453-454)

—personality as determined:

—personality as evil:

—personality as fixed and passive:

—personality and psychological health:

* 12. a) Is psychoanalytic theory "true or false"? Explain and indicate three major contributions of Freud's theory to our understanding of human behavior. (454)

*   b) In contrast, discuss the shortcomings of the concepts of psychoanalytic theory. Use examples when they are helpful. (454)

*   c) Among the criticisms of Freud's approach, which is the most serious? Discuss and relate to current concerns regarding childhood sexual abuse. (454)

    d) What has been the general outcome of empirical tests of Freud's theories? Describe efforts to relate adult personality to psychosexual events in childhood. (454)

13. On what population did Freud base many of his observations, and how did this relate to cultural biases of his time? (454-455)

* 14. On what dimensions has Freud's theory survived experimental tests, and on what dimensions has it not proved viable? (455)

BEHAVIORISTIC APPROACH

* 1. a) Characterize the behavioristic approach and its contemporary formulation, the social–learning approach, in terms of emphases, forms of relationship between person and situation, and bases for prediction of behavior. (455)

196   Chapter 13

b) To what approaches in psychology is social–learning theory most related? (455)

* 2. a) What do your authors mean when they say that social–learning theory adopts the basic tenet of operant conditioning? (455)

* b) Is direct reinforcement or punishment necessary for learning in this approach? Explain and indicate another way in which people may learn. (455)

* 3. a) Describe the three forms of reinforcement that are said to control the expression of learned behavior. Provide an example for each. (455)

  —*direct reinforcement:*

  —*vicarious reinforcement:*

  —*self–administered reinforcement:*

* b) Describe the role that *generalization* and *discrimination* play in the cross-situational variability of behavior. Give an example. (455-456)

* c) Based on your answer to 3b), what is the position of social–learning theorists on the role of traits in personality? (456)

* 4. To what kinds of behavior do social–learning theorists view classical conditioning to be relevant? Give an example and use the terms *unconditioned stimulus*, *conditioned stimulus*, and *conditioned response* in your answer. (456)

5. Contrast trait theories, psychoanalytic theory, and the social–learning approach to personality in terms of their ability to specify the variables on which people differ from one another and the processes of personality functioning. (456)

* 6. Describe Mischel's social–learning approach through an explanation of how each of the following person variables is said to function in person–environment interactions. (458-462)

Functions in Person–Environment Interactions

competencies	
encoding strategies	
expectancies	
subjective values	
self–regulatory systems and plans	

7. Discuss the research methods that characterize the social–learning approach to personality in the following settings. (457-458)

—naturalistic settings:

—therapeutic settings:

—research settings:

8. a) Outline the forms that the assumption of cross–situational consistency takes in type and trait theories, psychoanalytic theory, and phenomenological theory. (458)

* b) Describe the procedures, results, and conclusion of the classic Hartshorne and May investigation of consistency in personality in the 1920s. (458)

* c) What similar results and conclusion did Mischel present in the 1960s, based on his review of the related literature? (458)

* 9. Review the main subsections in the *Consistency Paradox* section, then state in your own words what is meant by each of the following terms as they refer to solutions to the paradox. (458, 460-462)

—*aggregation solution:*

—*person–centered solution:*

—*interactional solution:*

10. a) Provide several illustrations of your authors' statement that "a more accurate estimate of cross–situational consistency would be obtained if investigators combined several behavioral measures of the same trait to arrive at an aggregated score." (460)

b) What additional paradox is resolved by the aggregation solution? (460)

* 11. a) Distinguish between the trait–centered and the person–centered strategies for dealing with the consistency paradox. (460)

* b) Give an example to illustrate Allport's person–centered solution to the consistency paradox. What is the "fallacy of the trait–centered approach"? (460-461)

c) Use another example to show that our intuitions appear to follow the person–centered approach to consistency in behavior. (461)

198   Chapter 13

* 12. Discuss three forms of interactions to show how personal dispositions and situational variables may come together to account for apparent consistency in personality across situations. (461-462)

—*reactive interaction*:

—*evocative interaction*:

—*proactive interaction*:

13. Why do your authors say that "psychologists who use only the laboratory to study personality will never see its major manifestations"? (462)

* 14. Contrast the social–learning approach with other approaches to personality on the following issues: (462-463)

—determinism:

—human beings as good or evil:

—modifiability of personality:

—passive/active role of the individual:

* 15. Summarize some of the contributions and one possible shortcoming of the social–learning approach. (463)

PHENOMENOLOGICAL APPROACH

* 1. In what notable respects does the phenomenological approach differ from other approaches to personality? (463)

* 2. Prior to the 1960s, essentially, what were the two "forces" in psychology? Be familiar with the four principles associated with the so–called "third force" that emerged: (463-464)

—primary interest:

—preferred topics of investigation:

—selection of research problems:

—the ultimate value:

* 3. a) Discuss the nature of the basic motivating force of the human individual from the perspective of Rogers. (464)

b) In client–centered therapy, what is the role of the therapist, and how does this differ from the therapist's approach in psychoanalytic therapy? (464)

4. a) Does a person's self–concept necessarily reflect what he or she "is" or "does"? Give an example. (464-465)

*   b)   Discuss Rogers's view of the role of the self–concept in relation to how people want to behave and what happens if their reality is not congruent with their potential. Relatedly, what results when this incongruence is too great? (465)

c)   Characterize the well–adjusted person from this perspective. (465)

*   5.   a)   In terms of the "real" and the "ideal" self, how is fulfillment realized, and what accounts for unhappiness and dissatisfaction? (465)

*   b)   Therefore, based on your answer to 5a) and your discussion in 4b), what are two kinds of incongruence in Rogers's system? (465)

*   6.   a)   Distinguish between the following two fundamental ways in which parents and others may relate to a child and the consequences in terms of the child's self–concept: (465)

—*unconditional positive regard:*

—*conditional positive regard:*

b)   Illustrate the experiential effects of conditional positive regard by example, and cite Rogers's suggestion for the best approach in such cases. (465)

7.   a)   Be able to describe the procedures for the Q–sort method of personality assessment (described more fully in Chapter 12). (465)

*   b)   Indicate the use of the Q–sort method by Rogers. What are the two categories in which clients are asked to sort self–statements? (465-466)

*   c)   What is meant by *self–ideal discrepancy* in the context of Rogers's Q set? Indicate some of the related results obtained over the course of therapy. (466)

d)   In what two ways may the self–ideal discrepancy be reduced? (466)

*   8.   a)   Be familiar with the relative kinds of motives reflected in the levels of Maslow's hierarchy of needs. (466)

*   b)   What is the highest motive in this conceptualization? Give some examples of individuals that Maslow believed had attained this level of self–expression. (466)

*   c)   Be able to characterize the self–actualizer and the kinds of activities that permit this level of self–fulfillment. (466)

9.   In what terms do people describe their peak experiences, and during what kinds of activities do they occur? Can you think of peak experiences of your own? (466-467)

*   10.   a)   From Kelly's standpoint, what should be the goal of the psychologist? (467)

*   b)   In Kelly's approach, in what sense may people be considered to be "scientists," and in what ways does this impact on their beliefs? (468)

c) Relatedly, what is the purpose of therapy from Kelly's approach, and what technique, in particular, may be useful in achieving this end? Provide an example. (468)

11. Describe in detail the method for administration of the Role Construct Repertory Test. Note a type of result that leads your authors to state that the test "is designed to assess the individual's constructs, not the psychologist's." (468-469)

* 12. a) In terms of determinants of behavior and psychological health, what portrait does the phenomenological approach paint of the human personality? Are individuals basically good or bad in this perspective? (469-470)

    b) Discuss the "radical" political implications of the humanistic movement, noting by way of illustration its relationship to feminist views in particular. (470)

* 13. From your authors' perspective, evaluate the phenomenological approach to personality along each of the following dimensions: (470-471)

    —contributions:

    —empirical methods and quality of the evidence:

    —population for study:

    —fundamental human values:

Sample Quiz 13.1

1. In the psychoanalytic view, the largest portion of the human mind is the: a) conscious; b) preconscious; c) unconscious; d) ego.

2. Which of the following is *true* of the psychoanalytic approach? a) Most psychological events are caused by unsatisfied drives and unconscious wishes. b) The three structures of personality do not coexist in peace. c) There is a constant amount of psychic energy for any individual called the libido. d) All of the above.

3. Which of the following best characterizes the behavioristic approach? a) a focus on the individual's subjective experience; b) continuous interactions between personal and environmental variables; c) an attempt to explain personality in terms of unconscious processes; d) a striving toward growth and self-actualization.

4. Albert Bandura is noted for his theory that emphasizes: a) nondirective therapy; b) a hierarchy of needs; c) reciprocal interactions among variables; d) personal constructs.

5. From Mischel's perspective, people who differ in self–regulatory systems differ in: a) intellectual abilities and social skills; b) assignment of values to outcomes; c) personal standards and rules for behavior; d) the way they selectively attend to information.

6. The person-centered solution to the consistency paradox maintains that: a) if enough measures were taken and combined, we would find that people's traits would be more stable; b) we intentionally select and create situations in which we can behave in ways that are comfortable to us; c) the focus should be on the unique patterning of traits within the individual; d) none of the above.

7. A shortcoming of the behavioristic approach may be that it: a) fails to show how reinforcement can affect behavior; b) does not take into account the phenomena of observational learning; c) views people as fundamentally good but inflexible; d) overemphasizes the importance of situational variables.

8. Dimensions that individuals use to interpret themselves and their social worlds are called: a) personal constructs; b) ego defense mechanisms; c) interpretational experiences; d) object relations.

9. Rogers is to the Q sort as Kelly is to: a) free association; b) the Role Construct Repertory Test; c) the hierarchy of needs; d) vicarious learning.

10. Critics feel that the phenomenological approach: a) ignores too much the role of private experiencing; b) is too much built on observations of healthy, well–functioning people; c) is fundamentally incompatible with American ideology; d) all of the above.

Sample Quiz 13.2

1. A method in which a patient is instructed to say everything that comes into conscious awareness is: a) vicarious learning; b) free association; c) the Rep Test; d) self-actualization.

2. The id: a) consists of the basic impulses and drives; b) operates on the reality principle; c) strives to delay gratification until it can be obtained in socially–appropriate ways; d) both a and b.

3. In Freud's view, the internalized representation of society's moral standards is termed the: a) id; b) ego; c) superego; d) libido.

4. The stage in which children must resolve the Oedipal conflict is the: a) phallic stage; b) oral stage; c) genital stage; d) psychosocial stage.

5. Which of the following terms best describe the portrait of human nature painted by the psychoanalytic approach? a) deterministic, good, active; b) free, evil, active; c) free, good, passive; d) deterministic, evil, passive.

6. In the social–learning approach, seeing someone else receive a reward is the form of reinforcement of learned behavior termed: a) vicarious reinforcement; b) direct reinforcement; c) self–administered reinforcement; d) conditioned reinforcement.

7. We intuitively feel that people behave the same way from one situation to the next when, in fact, they do not. These observations constitute the: a) intuition hypothesis; b) self-actualization problem; c) Oedipal conflict; d) consistency paradox.

8. In the phenomenological view, how a person would *like* to be is called the: a) ego ideal; b) ideal self; c) peak personal construct; d) topographic model.

9. That meaningfulness must precede objectivity in the selection of problems to be investigated in psychology is a principle of the: a) phenomenological approach; b) behavioristic approach; c) trait approach; d) psychoanalytic approach.

10. Which of the following statements regarding phenomenological theories is *false*? a) The self-ideal discrepancy would be expected to increase during the course of client–centered therapy. b) Self–actualization is attained before all other needs are fulfilled. c) The central concept in Rogers's theory is the personal construct. d) All of the above.

Answer Key, Chapter 13

Important Names

1. Sigmund Freud
2. Albert Bandura
3. Carl Rogers
4. Abraham Maslow
5. George Kelly

Vocabulary and Details

1. personality

PSYCHOANALYTIC APPROACH

1. free association
2. conscious; preconscious; unconscious
3. psychological determinism
4. id
5. pleasure
6. ego
7. reality
8. superego
9. ego ideal
10. libido; sexual
11. defense mechanisms
12. repression
13. psychosexual stages
14. Oedipal conflict
15. fixated

BEHAVIORISTIC APPROACH

1. behavioristic approach; social–learning approach
2. operant conditioning; observational (or vicarious) learning; classical conditioning
3. consistency paradox

PHENOMENOLOGICAL APPROACH

1. phenomenological approach; humanistic psychology
2. actualization
3. client–centered therapy
4. self; self–concept
5. ideal; real
6. hierarchy of needs
7. self–actualizers
8. peak experiences
9. personal constructs; personal construct theory
10. Role Construct Repertory Test; Rep Test

Sample Quiz 13.1

1. c, 448
2. d, 448-449
3. b, 455
4. c, 456
5. c, 457
6. c, 460
7. d, 463
8. a, 467
9. b, 468
10. b, 470

Sample Quiz 13.2

1. b, 447
2. a, 448
3. c, 449
4. a, 450
5. d, 453
6. a, 455
7. d, 458
8. b, 465
9. a, 463
10. d, 466-467

Stress, Health, and Coping

Learning Objectives

1. Be able to give general definitions of stress, stressors, and the related fields of behavioral medicine and health psychology.

2. Be prepared to describe five general characteristics of stressful events and know how predictability and controllability affect the severity of stress. Be able to cite studies in which the ability to control a stressor influenced the degree of stress experienced.

3. Be familiar with the various psychological and related emotional reactions to a stressful situation including post–traumatic stress disorder and learned helplessness.

4. Know the physiological reactions to a stressful situation, including the complex responses of the two neuroendocrine systems controlled by the hypothalamus.

5. Be able to outline research showing the effects of chronic overarousal on the cardiovascular system and on the body's immune system as studied in the field of psychoneuroimmunology.

6. Be prepared to discuss three theoretical perspectives as applied to why some people are more likely to appraise events as stressful. In this context, understand specific kinds of cognitive attributional styles and the nature of the hardy individual.

7. Note the characteristics of the Type A personality, and be familiar with the research relating heart disease to Type A behavior and to occupational and social stress.

8. Distinguish between problem–focused coping and emotion–focused coping, giving examples of each.

9. Be familiar with Freud's concept of repression and the defense mechanisms that aid repression. Explain how the defense mechanisms of rationalization and intellectualization differ from rational and intellectual thinking and how reaction formation and projection differ in their defense against an undesirable trait.

10. Be able to summarize two major classes of techniques for managing stress and several varieties of these methods as well as specific applications of each method.

Vocabulary and Details

1. _____ is a state that occurs when people are faced with events they perceive as endangering their physical and psychological well–being. (477)

2. In stress, the events that are perceived as threatening are called _____; the person's reactions to these events are called _____. (477)

3. The study of how stress and other social, psychological, and biological factors come together to contribute to illness is known as _____ or _____. (477)

CHARACTERISTICS OF STRESSFUL EVENTS

1. A drop in the electrical resistance of the skin, termed the _____ (abbreviated _____), is a measure of autonomic arousal that often is used to assess anxiety. (479)

2. One well–known measure of stress in terms of life changes is the _____, also termed the Holmes and Rahe _____. (480 and Table 14-1)

3. When a person must choose between incompatible or mutually exclusive goals or actions, we speak of _____. (481)

PSYCHOLOGICAL REACTIONS TO STRESS

1. A persisting syndrome called _____ includes a) emotional numbness and a sense of estrangement, b) intruding memories and dreams of the trauma, and c) sleep disturbances, difficulty concentrating, and over–alertness. (483)

2. The _____ hypothesis assumes that whenever a person's effort to reach a goal is blocked, an aggressive drive motivates behavior to inflict injury on the cause of the frustration. (484)

3. When aggressive emotional reactions are directed away from a source of frustration, we may speak of _____ aggression. (484)

4. When organisms are exposed to repeated unavoidable and inescapable aversive events, they may fail to respond to avoidable aversive stimuli in later situations; this phenomenon is termed _____. (484)

PHYSIOLOGICAL REACTIONS TO STRESS

1. The entire innate complex of internal and external responses to stress prepare an organism to fight or flee; this has been called the _____. (486)

2. The part of the brain that has been called the "stress center" is the _____. (486)

3. The hypothalamus activates two neuroendocrine systems in response to an emergency. In one case, it activates the _____ system of the autonomic nervous system resulting in the arousal of a wide range of physiological stress responses. (486)

4. In the other case, the hypothalamus signals the _____ as the first step in a complex of events within the _____ system. (488)

5. A critical hormone in the adrenal–cortical system, sometimes called the body's "major stress hormone," is _____ (abbreviated _____). (486)

6. Physical disorders in which emotions are believed to play a central role are termed _____. (488)

HOW STRESS AFFECTS HEALTH

1. One of the potential diseases due to chronic overarousal in stress is _____ (abbreviated _____), a disease that occurs when the blood vessels that supply the heart muscles are narrowed or closed due to the buildup of plaque. (488-489)

2. The study of the relationship between psychological variables and the body's immune system is called _____. (490)

3. The quality of an individual's immune functioning is termed _____. (490)

4. Behaviors that influence the body's general functioning and its ability to fight disease are termed _____. (492)

APPRAISALS AND PERSONALITY AS MEDIATORS OF STRESS RESPONSES

1. The process of evaluating an event with respect to its significance for a person's well–being is termed _____. (493)

2. Psychoanalysts term "reasonable" anxiety in response to a harmful situation as _____; anxiety that is out of proportion to the actual danger posed by threat is called _____. (493)

3. Causal explanations that people give for important events are termed _____. (493)

4. _____ are consistent styles of making attributions for the events in people's lives. (494)

5. People who are most resistant to stress, in the sense that they do not become physically or emotionally impaired in the face of stressful events, are said to possess the characteristic of _____. (494)

6. Behavior patterns relevant to heart disease are those of people who are rushed, competitive, aggressive, and achieving, termed the _____ pattern; by contrast, behaviors of people who are more relaxed and feel less pressure are termed the _____ pattern. (495)

COPING SKILLS

1. The process by which a person attempts to manage stress is called _____. (497)

2. When a person focuses on a problem or situation and tries to find some way of changing or avoiding it, we speak of _____. (497)

3. If, on the other hand, a person attempts to deal with stress–induced emotions without dealing directly with the stressful situation, we speak of _____. (497)

Stress, Health, and Coping   207

4. Freud called unconscious strategies that defend a person against negative emotions by changing the perception of reality in some way _____. (499)

5. In Freud's view, the most basic and important of defense mechanisms is _____, the exclusion of painful or frightening impulses from consciousness. (500)

MANAGING STRESS

1. In the procedure called _____, a person is given information (feedback) about a physiological response (such as muscle contractions or blood pressure) and then attempts to alter the response. (503)

2. In one type of _____, a person progressively tenses and then relaxes individual muscles in succession. (504)

3. Any sustained activity that increases heart rate and oxygen consumption is termed _____. (504)

4. Methods that attempt to help people identify the kinds of stressful situations that produce their physiological or emotional symptoms and to alter the ways in which they cope may be subsumed under the heading _____. (504-505)

Ideas and Concepts

1. When are stress reactions adaptive, and when can they become maladaptive? (477)

CHARACTERISTICS OF STRESSFUL EVENTS

1. From your own knowledge and experience, can you think of examples of each of the categories of stressors covered in this section? (477-478)

   —traumatic events (general):

   —major life events (individual):

   —hassles:

   —conflicting motives or desires:

* 2. Outline and illustrate the series of psychological reactions following trauma. (478)

* 3. What are three characteristics of events (that also serve as the headings of the following subsections) that lead to their being perceived as stressful? Indicate a fourth factor that influences the perceived stressfulness of an event. (478)

* 4. a) What is the relationship between apparent *controllability* of an event and the degree to which it is perceived as stressful? (478)

* b) Discuss two interesting demonstrations of the effects of the *perception* of controllability upon human stress reactions. In the first study, what relationship was shown between the perception of controllability and anxiety? (479)

*Basic ideas and concepts

208   Chapter 14

* 5. a) What is the relationship between *predictability* of the occurrence of a stressor and the severity of stress? (479)

* b) Show with laboratory examples that both animals and people prefer predictable to unpredictable aversive events. (479)

c) In what two ways can the effects of predictability be understood? (In the second case, use the term *safety signal* in your answer.) Give examples. (479)

d) Cite some real–life examples of the serious effects of unpredictability on human health. (479-480)

* 6. a) Use final exams to illustrate how some events, though controllable and predictable, still are experienced as stressful. Why is this the case? (480)

b) To further make your case, illustrate how positive events can be stressful as well as negative ones. (480)

* 7. a) Describe how Holmes and Rahe put together their Life Events Scale. (480-481)

b) Outline some of the research findings related to differences between effects of positive and negative events and to some individual differences in patterns of responding to the Life Events Scale. (481)

* 8. Discuss the way in which serious internal conflicts may evolve in each of the following motive clashes: (481-483)

—independence versus dependence:

—intimacy versus isolation:

—cooperation versus competition:

—impulse expression versus moral standards:

PSYCHOLOGICAL REACTIONS TO STRESS

* 1. What is the most common emotional response to a threatening situation? Provide an experiential definition of this emotion. (483)

2. In what respect may guilt play a role in post–traumatic stress disorder? (483)

* 3. a) Cite some data to show that post–traumatic stress disorder may last a long time after a traumatic event. (483)

* b) When was post–traumatic stress disorder recognized as a diagnostic category, and why? (484)

c) Give some statistics to show the high prevalence of substance abuse and interpersonal problems among Vietnam veterans. (484)

Stress, Health, and Coping   209

*   d) Cite some possible reasons for the high prevalence of post–traumatic stress disorder among Vietnam veterans. (484)

*   4. Discuss each of the following situations involving aggressive responses to stressors. Use examples when they are helpful: (484)

—responses to laboratory stressors:

—frustration:

—direct versus displaced aggression:

*   5. Besides active aggression, what is another common (but opposite) response to stress? (484)

*   6. a) Outline the procedures and results of animal experiments dealing with the kind of apathy called learned helplessness. (484-485)

*   b) To account for some human reactions to uncontrollable events, how must the concept of learned helplessness be expanded? (485)

    c) Give some illustrations to show that the original learned helplessness theory nevertheless may be useful in accounting for reactions of people to difficult events. (485)

*   7. a) Discuss two sources of cognitive impairment during stress. (485)

*   b) Use the term *test anxiety* to exemplify the relationship between stress and cognitive functioning. (485)

    c) What kinds of behavior patterns result from cognitive impairment during stress? Relatedly, to what kinds of behaviors do people resort under stress? Illustrate and see if you can think of an instance from your own life. (486)

PHYSIOLOGICAL REACTIONS TO STRESS

1. Describe some of the common physiological responses in emergency situations and their biological advantages. (486)

—glucose levels:

—metabolism:

—activation and inhibition of bodily processes:

—painkillers:

—other:

210   Chapter 14

* 2. In the tables below, indicate the functions of each of the portions of the physiological stress response. Be sure you can trace the relationships among the respective systems, organs, and hormones. (See also Figure 14-1.) (486–487)

Sympathetic System   Functions

adrenal medulla	
epinephrine	
norepinephrine	

Adrenal-Cortical System   Functions

pituitary gland	
ACTH	
adrenal cortex	

* 3. Why do stress researchers argue that many activities included within the fight–or–flight response are not very adaptive in the modern–day environment? (486-487)

* 4. a) What can be the positive effects of repeated exposure to intermittent stressors? Use the term "physiological toughness," and cite some related data. (487-488)

* b) Which aspects of the physiological stress response and of behavior appear to be beneficial, and which appear to be harmful? (488)

HOW STRESS AFFECTS HEALTH

1. a) To what outcome can chronic stress lead and why? (488)

* b) Are people with psychophysiological disorders really "sick" and in need of medical attention? Explain. (488)

c) What hypothesis was advanced originally with regard to the role of attitudes in certain disorders, and what has been the outcome of efforts to research those relationships? Is there any exception? (488)

* 2. What is meant by the "direct effects" of stress on health? Indicate two ways in which direct effects can occur. (488)

Stress, Health, and Coping   211

* 3. a) What is the leading cause of death and chronic illness in the United States, and what are some of the variables that promote this type of disease? (489)

*   b) Indicate the two main psychological factors that contribute to the stressfulness of jobs. Cite the results of one study of these factors in the work place. (489)

        c) Outline the relationships for women between cardiovascular health, working, and raising children. (489)

        d) Indicate one group of Americans who are particularly susceptible to high blood pressure, and give some of the reasons why. (489)

*   e) Discuss an animal study that linked disruptions of the social environment to cardiac disease factors. Which animals in particular showed the largest effects in this study? (489-490)

* 4. What is the immune system, and what does it do? (490)

    5. a) Outline the procedures of an "unusual" study of immunocompetence in which healthy volunteers were exposed to cold viruses. (490)

*   b) What were the principal results of this study in terms of the relationship between stress and immunity? (490)

*   c) Summarize the results of a number of other studies that related the effects of stressful events to immune responses. (491)

* 6. a) Indicate a psychological factor that can *reduce* the effects of stress on immune functioning. (491)

*   b) Outline the procedures of a series of animal studies designed to study the role of controllability of electric shock in stress responding. (See also Figure 14-3.) Be sure you understand what is meant by the term *yoked control*. (491)

*   c) What are *T–cells*? Discuss the effects of controllability on T–cells found in one study using the yoked control design outlined in 6b). (491)

        d) Discuss the effects of controllability in another study in which tumors were implanted into rats. (492)

    7. Provide some additional evidence to show the role of perceptions of control in *human* immune functioning. (492)

* 8. What recent discovery has been made that implicates the nervous system in immune functioning, and why is this discovery important? (492)

* 9. How does stress impact health behaviors in ways that may negatively affect the body's immune system? (492)

APPRAISALS AND PERSONALITY AS MEDIATORS OF STRESS RESPONSES

* 1. For each of the following theoretical approaches to the appraisal of stressful events, discuss one or more applications and provide related everyday examples where possible. (493-494)

Approach	Application to Stress	Everyday Example(s)
Psychoanalytic Theory		
Behavioral Theory		
Cognitive Theory: Attributional style		
Cognitive Theory: Hardiness		

2. a) Outline the modifications of learned helplessness theory that extend its application to human situations. (493-494)

b) Discuss a study designed to show the effects of attributional styles on student attitudes at exam time. (494)

* c) Similarly, review a study linking attributional style to physical illness and two possible reasons for the relationship that was found. (494)

* d) How does attributional style affect health? Indicate two mechanisms by which a pessimistic outlook may have a negative impact and a related study. (494)

* 3. a) Outline the methods and results of the Kobasa study on the role of hardiness in reactions to stress. (494)

b) What is one issue that was left unanswered by this study, and how was it addressed in subsequent research? What three variables emerged as significant, and which was the most important? (494-495)

* c) Discuss how the three characteristics of the stress–resistant (hardy) individual interrelate with other factors dealt with in this chapter: (495)

—commitment:

Stress, Health, and Coping   213

—control:

—challenge:

4. Be able to characterize in detail the Type A and Type B behavior patterns that have been correlated with coronary heart disease: (495)

—Type A:

—Type B:

* 5. a) Outline the methods and results of an early large–scale study of the role of Type A behaviors in heart disease. (495-496)

* b) What characteristics that were said to define the Type A individual were *not* supported in recent studies of the role of Type A behaviors in heart disease, and what variable *was* implicated? Cite two studies of professional populations that further implicate this variable. (496)

* c) Discuss the possible role of hostility in heart disease from the standpoint of the sympathetic and parasympathetic nervous systems. (496-497)

COPING SKILLS

1. a) Be able to list a variety of strategies that people use in problem–focused coping. Cite a specific example. (497)

* b) What relationships have been found between depression and the use of problem–focused coping? (497)

* 2. a) Why do people use emotion–focused coping when under stress? (497)

* b) Distinguish by example between the following two forms of emotion–focused strategies: (497-498)

—behavioral strategies:

—cognitive strategies:

3. a) Discuss an example to show the role of social support as a cognitive strategy for coping with the negative emotions related to breast cancer. (498)

* b) Is social support necessarily always positive in its impact on health? Explain and cite examples. (498)

* 4. a) What is *rumination*? Discuss the relationships obtained between depression and ruminative styles for coping found in two longitudinal studies. (498-499)

b) Are people who engage in ruminative coping more likely to solve their problems because they are more sensitive to their own feelings? Discuss the results of several related studies. (499)

5. a) What do your authors mean when they say that all defense mechanisms involve some "self–deception"? (499)

214   Chapter 14

b) Indicate one difference between defense mechanisms and coping strategies. (499-500)

*   c) Be sure that you can recognize each of the defense mechanisms in the following table by providing a definition for those listed in bold type and examples for all. (500-502)

Defense Mechanism	Definition	Example
repression	(Also see *Vocabulary*.)	
rationalization		
reaction formation		
projection		
intellectualization		
denial		
displacement		

* 6. a) Distinguish between repression and *suppression*. (500)

    b) Did Freud think that repression was always effective? Explain and indicate the relationship with the use of other defense mechanisms. (500)

*   c) How do we characterize the style of people who repress or suppress painful thoughts and emotions? What effects of this tendency and its opposite, confiding in others, has been found in recent research in this area? (500)

*   d) Discuss two reasons for how repression or suppression may contribute to poor health. Use the term *rebound effect* in your answer. (500)

7. What may be a positive effect of verbally expressing traumas and emotions? Indicate three reasons why this may be true. (501)

MANAGING STRESS

* 1. Provide examples to show that sharing stress with others can reduce the effects of stress in the case of personal loss or community disasters, but that sometimes families or friends can have the opposite impact. (502-503)

Stress, Health, and Coping   215

2. a) For purposes of organization, list two major classes of techniques for man-aging stress and three related subclasses. (503-504)

   —i:
      —a:
      —b:
      —c:
  —ii:

*   b) Describe the biofeedback procedures used in efforts to control tension headaches. (503)

c) Similarly, describe the application of biofeedback to the control of blood pressure and heart rate. Indicate one specific stress–related disorder to which such methods are applied. (504)

*   d) What appears to be the most important variable in using biofeedback and relaxation training in the treatment of tension headaches and hypertension? Does everyone respond the same to these two forms of stress management? Explain. (504)

3. Discuss some of the physical benefits of aerobic exercise and one of the reasons why exercise is becoming a standard part of stress management programs. (504)

* 4. a) What additional benefit may cognitive behavior therapy have over biofeedback and relaxation training in the management of stress? (504-505)

*   b) Your authors list five steps in the process of cognitive therapy. List these steps, and apply them to the case of a man with tension headaches. (505)

5. Describe a recent study aimed at determining the beneficial effects of modifying Type A behavior, including (a) the specific behaviors that were targeted for change and (b) the outcome in terms of the critical dependent variable. (505)

Sample Quiz 14.1

1. Stress reactions may become maladaptive when: a) it is possible to flee or attack a stressor; b) when stressors are chronic; c) when stress is uncontrollable; d) both b and c.

2. Which of the following is *true* with regard to predictability and controllability? a) The perception of controllability is not as important to the stressfulness of events as is their actual controllability. b) Whereas animals prefer predictable over unpredictable stressors, people appear to prefer unpredictability. c) The ability to predict the occurrence of stressful events usually reduces the severity of stress. d) Both a and c.

3. A measure of stress in terms of life changes is the: a) Life Events Scale; b) Social Readjustment Rating Scale; c) GSR; d) both a and b.

4. Which of the following was *not* mentioned in your text as an area of potential conflict that produces stress? a) generativity versus self–absorption; b) independence versus dependence; c) cooperation versus competition; d) impulse expression versus moral standards.

5. A recent discovery regarding the immune system that is particularly important is that: a) it operates independently of perceptions of control; b) the immune system operates independently from other physiological systems; c) lymphocytes are equipped to receive messages from the nervous system and may therefore be sensitive to negative emotional states; d) none of the above.

6. We speak of emotion–focused coping when a person: a) tries to find a way to change a stressful problem; b) behaves in an aggressive, rushed manner; c) tries to cope with the effects of stress without dealing with the stressful situation; d) experiences sleep difficulties and distressing dreams.

7. In response to why she doesn't exercise to help reduce her stress, a fellow student states, "I have too many other things to do." This is an example of the defense mechanism: a) rationalization; b) projection; c) denial; d) intellectualization.

8. A behavioral technique for managing stress is: a) biofeedback; b) relaxation training; c) aerobic exercise; d) all of the above.

9. The most important factor in using biofeedback and relaxation training in the treatment of tension headaches and hypertension is: a) duration of treatment; b) learning how to relax; c) type of response that is trained (e.g., heart rate versus blood pressure); d) age.

10. When applied in the context of managing stress, cognitive behavior therapy would aim at: a) encouraging strong expression to opposite motives; b) identifying stressful situations; c) developing effective ways to displace anger onto safe targets; d) both a and c.

Sample Quiz 14.2

1. The study of how stress and other factors come together to contribute to illness is the definition given in your text for: a) psychoneuroimmunology; b) cognitive behavior therapy; c) health psychology; d) psychophysiology.

2. Post–traumatic stress disorder is characterized by all *except* which of the following symptoms? a) emotional numbness; b) sleep walking; c) over–alertness; d) repeatedly reliving trauma.

3. The frustration–aggression hypothesis predicts that aggressive responses will be: a) directed at the cause of the frustration; b) displaced away from the source of frustration; c) motivated by an underlying aggressive drive; d) all of the above.

4. The critical hormone in the adrenal–cortical system is: a) Type A hormone; b) ACTH; c) GSR; d) CHD.

5. Which of the following statements regarding cardiovascular disease is *false*? a) High blood pressure is a serious problem among African–Americans. b) Employed women in general are at a higher risk of heart disease than women who are homemakers. c) People in jobs that are demanding in terms of responsibilities but that provide little control are at greater risk for heart disease. d) As a result of animal research, we expect higher rates of heart disease in dominant males in unstable social conditions.

6. Evaluating events for their significance for well–being is the process defining: a) appraisals; b) attributions; c) attributional styles; d) Type A behaviors.

7. The fact that students with pessimistic attributional styles report more illnesses and visit the health center more often than optimistic students is used by your authors to document the contribution of _____ in the understanding of appraisal in stress. a) behavioral theory; b) psychoanalytic theory; c) cognitive theory; d) biological theory.

8. With respect to cognitive strategies for coping: a) positive social support may help people to adjust to stress emotionally by reducing rumination; b) people with a high degrees of conflict in their social networks show poorer physical health following a major stressor; c) people who engage in ruminative coping are less likely to engage in active problem–solving during stress; d) all of the above.

9. The most basic and important of the defense mechanisms is: a) repression; b) denial; c) reaction formation; d) none of the above; all defense mechanisms are equally important in Freud's system.

10. Cognitive behavior therapy may have an advantage over biofeedback and relaxation training in terms of: a) changing an individual's reactions in actual stressful situations; b) how much treatment is required; c) reducing overall physiological symptoms of stress; d) changing the focus of awareness from identifying and modifying stressful situations to altering bodily reactions.

Vocabulary and Details

1. Stress
2. stressors; stress responses
3. behavioral medicine; health psychology

CHARACTERISTICS OF STRESSFUL . . .

1. galvanic skin response (GSR)
2. Life Events Scale; Social Readjustment Rating Scale
3. conflict

PSYCHOLOGICAL REACTIONS TO . . .

1. post–traumatic stress disorder
2. frustration–aggression
3. displaced
4. learned helplessness

PHYSIOLOGICAL REACTIONS TO . . .

1. fight–or–flight response
2. hypothalamus
3. sympathetic
4. pituitary gland; adrenal–cortical
5. adrenocorticotrophic hormone (ACTH)
6. psychophysiological disorders

HOW STRESS AFFECTS HEALTH

1. coronary heart disease (CHD)
2. psychoneuroimmunology
3. immunocompetence
4. health behaviors

APPRAISALS AND PERSONALITY . . .

1. appraisal
2. objective anxiety; neurotic anxiety
3. attributions
4. Attributional styles
5. hardiness
6. Type A; Type B

COPING SKILLS

1. coping
2. problem–focused coping
3. emotion–focused coping
4. defense mechanisms
5. repression

MANAGING STRESS

1. biofeedback
2. relaxation training
3. aerobic exercise
4. cognitive behavior therapy

Sample Quiz 14.1

1. d, 477
2. c, 479
3. d, 480
4. a, 481-483
5. c, 492
6. c, 497
7. a, 501
8. d, 503-504
9. b, 504
10. b, 504-505

Sample Quiz 14.2

1. c, 477
2. b, 483
3. d, 484
4. b, 486
5. b, 489-490
6. a, 493
7. c, 494
8. d, 498-499
9. a, 500
10. a, 504

Abnormal Psychology

Learning Objectives

1. Know the four criteria that may be used in defining abnormality as well as the characteristics that are considered indicative of normality.

2. Understand the advantages and disadvantages of classifying abnormal behavior into categories. Be familiar with the DSM–IV system of classification, including the variables covered in an individual diagnosis and some of the major categories.

3. Be able to describe four types of anxiety disorders, and show how their symptoms either express anxiety directly or reflect attempts to control anxious feelings.

4. Be able to explain the development of anxiety disorders from the standpoint of psychoanalytic, behavioral, and cognitive theories. Know what research on biological factors has contributed thus far to our understanding of these disorders.

5. Be prepared to describe the two major mood disorders and to compare psychoanalytic, behavioral, and cognitive theories of depression.

6. Be familiar with the evidence indicating that genetic and biochemical factors play a role in mood disorders.

7. Know the defining characteristics of schizophrenia, and give examples of each characteristic.

8. Be familiar with the research on the causes of schizophrenia; be able to discuss the probable contributions of genetic, biochemical, social, and psychological factors.

9. Understand the role of vulnerability and stress in the development of mental disorders; be prepared to describe how studies of children at risk for schizophrenia are investigating these two factors.

10. Be able to define personality disorders; know the defining characteristics and probable causes of antisocial personalities and borderline personality disorder.

Important Names

1. An influential cognitive theory of depression, devised by _____, emphasizes the role of negative thoughts and cognitive distortions in thinking as the cause for the disorder. (529)

Vocabulary and Details

ABNORMAL BEHAVIOR

1. Literally, behavior that is "away from the statistical norm" is _____; but a more satisfactory definition must take into account a number of additional criteria, including deviation from social norms, maladaptiveness, and personal distress. (510)

2. The classification of mental disorders used by most mental health professionals is the _____, more commonly cited by its abbreviation _____. (512)

3. Traditionally, the term _____ referred to a group of disorders characterized by serious anxiety, unhappiness, and maladaptive behaviors, but DSM–IV separates such disorders into several categories. (512, 514)

4. Traditionally, the term _____ applied to more serious mental disorders characterized by disturbance of thought processes, loss of contact with reality, inability to cope, and requiring hospitalization. (514)

5. Rather than a category of disorders called psychoses, DSM–IV recognizes that people with serious disturbances may exhibit _____ during their disorder. (514)

6. Psychotic behaviors may include (a) _____, false sensory experiences, such as voices or visions, and (b) _____, that is, false beliefs. (514)

7. The _____ model considers the interaction between a predisposition that makes a person vulnerable for developing an illness and stressful conditions the person encounters in the environment. (515)

ANXIETY DISORDERS

1. Disorders in which anxiety is the main symptom or is experienced when the individual attempts to control certain maladaptive behaviors are called _____. (516)

2. _____ is characterized by constant tension and worry, somatic complaints, and difficulty in concentration. (516)

3. Episodes of acute and overwhelming apprehension and terror recur in the disturbance called _____. (516)

4. Intense fear to a stimulus or situation that most people do not consider dangerous is called a _____. (517)

5. When a person's life is dominated by repetitive acts or thoughts, we speak of an _____ disorder. (518)

6. Persistent intrusions of unwelcome thoughts or images are called _____; irresistible urges to carry out certain acts or rituals are called _____. (518)

7. The idea that organisms are predisposed biologically to be more readily classically conditioned to some stimuli than to others is termed _____. (521)

8. The tranquilizers Valium and Librium are in the class of antianxiety drugs called the _____. (523)

MOOD DISORDERS

1. When a person is severely depressed or manic (wildly elated), we speak of _____. (524)

2. In one form of mood disorders, called _____, the individual is extremely sad and dejected without mania. (524)

3. In the other form of mood disorders, called _____ (or _____), periods of severe depression alternate with periods of mania, usually with a return to a normal state in between. (525)

4. The likelihood that two twins will have a characteristic, such as depression, given that one twin does is called the _____. (530-531)

5. Two neurotransmitters believed to have a role in mood disorders are _____ and _____, both in a class of compounds called _____ localized in emotion–regulating areas of the brain. (531)

6. Two major classes of antidepressant drugs that influence the effects of norepinephrine and serotonin are _____ (or _____) inhibitors and _____. (531)

SCHIZOPHRENIA

1. The term _____ applies to a group of disorders characterized by severe personality disorganization, distortion of reality, and an inability to function in daily life. (533)

2. Beliefs that society would disagree with or regard as misinterpretations of reality are called _____. (534)

3. When it is falsely believed that one's thoughts are having an undue influence on others or that one's thoughts, feelings, and actions are caused by external forces, we speak of _____. (534)

4. Also frequent in schizophrenia, beliefs that others are threatening or plotting against one are called _____. Less common, false beliefs that one is powerful or important are termed _____. (535)

5. A person who has delusions of persecution is said to be _____. (535)

6. The most common hallucinations in schizophrenia are _____ (visual/auditory). (535)

7. The neurotransmitter _____ is active in the limbic system of the brain, an area that is implicated in the regulation of emotion. (538)

8. The _____ proposes that schizophrenia is caused by too much dopamine at certain synapses in the brain. (538)

9. It is believed that the drugs called _____ relieve the symptoms of schizophrenia by affecting the usable dopamine in the brain. (539)

PERSONALITY DISORDERS

1. Long–standing and inflexible patterns of maladaptive behavior that impair the individual's ability to function are called _____. (542)

2. Among the 11 types of personality disorders categorized in DSM–IV, _____ refers to the type of individual who is preoccupied with fantasies of success, who constantly seeks admiration and attention, and who is insensitive to the needs of others. (542)

3. Another personality disorder is _____, characterized by a passive orientation, indecisiveness, irresponsibility, and requiring continual support from others. (542)

4. The individual classified as having an _____ shows little guilt for misdoings or concern with others' needs, is impulsive, seeks thrills and excitement, and may be often in trouble with the law. (543)

5. A personality disorder characterized by instability of mood, self–concept, and interpersonal relationships is termed _____. (547)

Ideas and Concepts

ABNORMAL BEHAVIOR

* 1. a) Is there general agreement on the meaning of "abnormal behavior"? (510)

* b) Discuss the applications of each of the following four criteria to the definition of abnormal behavior, indicating limitations where possible. Which of these criteria provides a satisfactory description of abnormality? Explain. (510-511)

—deviation from statistical norms (use the term *statistical frequency*):

—deviation from social norms:

—maladaptiveness of behavior:

—personal distress:

*Basic terms and concepts

224   Chapter 15

* 2. Similarly, describe six criteria for normality. Do these characteristics make sharp distinctions between normal and abnormal behavior? Explain. (511-512)

* 3. Discuss three advantages and two disadvantages of classifying abnormal behavior. (512)

4. a) What does DSM–IV provide for the task of diagnosis of an individual? (512)

* b) Outline the five axes of DSM–IV. (Why were axes I and II separated?) (512)

* 5. a) Discuss the reasons why DSM–IV does not include the traditional categories of neuroses and psychoses among the classified disorders. (514)

* b) Indicate the categories of DSM–IV that now include the disorders formerly called neuroses and the disorders formerly called psychoses. (514)

6. a) From Table 15–2, note the prevalence of several serious forms of disorders. Which are the first and second most common disorders in the group, respectively? (514)

b) Cite some additional statistics on the prevalence of serious abnormal behaviors in the population, noting sex and age differences. (514)

c) Do all cultures recognize the same mental disorders as outlined in DSM–IV? Explain. (514 and 515, Table 15-3)

* 7. a) Distinguish among the following perspectives on the causes and treatments for mental disorders. (514-515)

—biological perspective:

—psychoanalytic perspective:

—behavioral perspective:

—cognitive perspective:

b) Using illustrations, indicate one way of integrating psychological and environmental factors in mental disorders. (515)

* c) Does being vulnerable guarantee that a person will develop a disorder? What is the key point of the vulnerability–stress model? (515-516)

ANXIETY DISORDERS

* 1. After reading this section, organize the scrambled terms below into an outline to help you to recall the several forms of anxiety disorders in DSM–IV. (516-519)

social phobia	obsessive–compulsive disorders
panic disorders	simple phobia
generalized anxiety	phobias
agoraphobia	obsessions, compulsions

2. When is anxiety considered abnormal? (516)

* 3. a) What is the main symptom of generalized anxiety and panic disorders? (516)

   b) What is the source of the bodily symptoms that occur in panic attacks? (516)

* c) Why is the anxiety in generalized anxiety and panic attacks called "free–floating"? (517)

* 4. Do persons with phobias realize that their anxiety is irrational? What is the effect of this knowledge in terms of what the person feels and does? (517)

* 5. a) Define and provide an example of each of the following kinds of phobias. After reading this subsection, indicate the treatability of each kind. (517-518)

   —*simple phobia:*

   —*social phobia:*

   —*agoraphobia:*

   b) Describe the history typical of agoraphobia and the variety of related fears. What personality characteristic may accompany this disorder? (518)

6. What is the central feature of obsessive–compulsive disorders? (518)

* 7. a) Can you think of obsessive thoughts or ritualistic behaviors of your own? What distinguishes between these and the activities that define obsessive–compulsive disorders? Give examples. (518)

* b) What kinds of topics provide the content for obsessive thoughts? Give some examples of changes in the topics of obsessions across time. (518)

8. a) Indicate the relationship between the presence of obsessive thoughts and the presence of compulsions. (519)

* b) Define the terms **washing** and **checking**, and provide examples. What is the common theme behind all compulsions? (519)

9. Discuss some of the similarities and differences between obsessive–compulsive disorders and the following two other classes of disorders. (519)

   —phobic disorders:

   —obsessive–compulsive personality:

* 10. For each of the following perspectives on anxiety, state the general approach in your own words, and, where possible, indicate how the view would apply to generalized anxiety, phobias, and obsessive–compulsive disorders. Use examples when they are helpful. (519-524)

Perspective	Description	Applications to Disorders
psychoanalytic perspective		
behavioral perspective		
cognitive perspective		
biological perspective		

* 11. a) Using examples, discuss the application of the classical conditioning paradigm in the behavioral perspective on phobias. What problems emerge with this approach? (520-521)

* b) How are such problems handled with the notion of prepared conditioning? Illustrate with examples. (521)

* c) Discuss two experiments that demonstrated prepared classical conditioning of fears in human subjects. (521)

d) How does the notion of prepared conditioning also account for the course of extinction of certain fears? Cite another related experiment. (521)

* 12. From the behavioral perspective, indicate a source of phobias in addition to direct classical conditioning. (521-522)

* 13. Turning to the biological perspective, do anxiety disorders tend to run in families and to what degree? Does this prove that anxiety disorders are hereditary? Explain. (522)

* 14. a) In what biochemical ways can panic attacks be initiated? Discuss the role of the brain chemical *cholecystokinin* in panic disorder. (522-523)

b) Despite the enthusiasm of biological theorists, does your answer to 14a) necessarily imply that panic disorder is strictly biochemical in origin? Discuss the notion of cognitive misinterpretation including a mechanism for this possibility. (523)

*   c)   What conclusions may be drawn regarding the debate about a biochemical cause for panic disorders? (523)

*   15.   a)   What recent evidence supports the likelihood that generalized anxiety involves the complex interactions of neurotransmitters in the brain? (523)

*   b)   Discuss three specific effects at the benzodiazepine receptor site that implicate the role of natural substances in both anxiety and the inhibition of anxiety. (523-524)

   16.   Cite other findings that suggest a biological basis for obsessive–compulsive disorders, including a related treatment effect. (524)

MOOD DISORDERS

*   1.   a)   What are common precipitators of "normal" depression, and what two characteristics define abnormal depression? (524)

*   b)   Describe the four sets of symptoms of depression. Which set is the most salient? (524)

     —emotional (mood) symptoms:

     —cognitive symptoms:

     —motivational symptoms:

     —physiological symptoms:

*   2.   Discuss the data on the duration and recurrence of depression. (525)

*   3.   a)   Describe the characteristics of the mildly and severely manic individual. (525-526)

*   b)   Indicate the prevalence of mania by itself and of bipolar disorders generally. (528)

*   c)   How does manic–depression differ from other mood disorders? (528)

* 4. For each of the following perspectives, indicate the theoretical source(s) of depression, and illustrate with an example or related observation. (528-531)

Perspective	Sources of Depression	Examples or Observations
psychoanalytic perspective		
behavioral perspective		
cognitive perspective		
biological perspective		(See item 9 below.)

* 5. a) In the psychoanalytic approach, what complicates the reaction to loss in people who are prone to depression? Give an example. (528)

   b) Discuss the psychoanalytic view on the role of self–esteem in depression. (528)

* c) Indicate the status of evidence with regard to the psychoanalytic perspective on depression. (528)

* 6. Discuss the "vicious cycle" of activities and rewards outlined by the behavioral perspective on depression. (528-529)

* 7. a) Characterize the cognitions of depressed persons according to Beck's theory, including the degree of conscious control and awareness that may be present during negative thoughts. (529)

* b) Be able to discuss and provide examples for each of the three categories of Beck's *cognitive triad*. (529)

—negative thoughts about the self:

—negative thoughts about present experiences:

—negative thoughts about the future:

c) When are a person's negative self–schemata formed? Be familiar with the five types of *cognitive distortions* Beck argued could characterize depressed persons. (529 and 530, Table 15-5)

* 8. Discuss the three dimensions that contribute to depression in the attributional approach. Is attributional style alone enough to account for depression? Explain. (529-530)

* 9. a) Does research clearly show that depressive cognitions cause depression? Discuss the outcomes of studies showing each of the following. (530)

—correlations between depressive thinking and depression:

—the relationship between depressive cognitions and effects of a depressive episode:

—the role of depressive cognitions in recovery from depression:

* b) What is another variable that may account for depression more effectively than the interpretation of negative events? (530)

* 10. a) Cite the concordance rates for manic–depressive disorder and depression. Therefore, which disorder appears to have a stronger genetic component? (530-531)

* b) Discuss the hypothesis that implicates norepinephrine and serotonin levels in depression and mania. Cite some related observations. (531)

* c) Similarly, discuss the possible mechanisms by which two classes of drugs, the MAO inhibitors and the tricyclics, may exert their antidepressant effects. (531)

* d) Do the antidepressant drugs produce their effects by modifying the *levels* of relevant neurotransmitters? Discuss the emerging evidence regarding the long–term effects of antidepressants. (531)

11. On what issue concerning mood disorders is there no doubt, and what is one question that remains unresolved in this area? (531)

* 12. a) Discuss the concept of *vulnerability* in relation to depression, indicating two classes of variables that may be important. (532-533)

b) List other factors that may play a role in vulnerability. Which of these may be the most important in women, and how do we know? (533)

SCHIZOPHRENIA

1. a) Describe schizophrenia in terms of prevalence, who is affected, and patterns of onset. (533)

b) Why might African–Americans be more often misdiagnosed as having schizophrenia? (533)

* 2. Summarize the characteristics of schizophrenia outlined in each of the following subsections of your chapter: (534-536)

—disturbances of thought and attention (use the terms **word salad** and **loosening of associations**, and note the general difficulty in schizophrenic thought):

—disturbances of perception:

—disturbances of affect:

—motor symptoms and withdrawal from reality:

—decreased ability to function:

* 3. Cite examples to show disturbances in the *content* of schizophrenic thought in terms of lack of insight and delusions. (534)

4. a) In what sense are the visual hallucinations of schizophrenia not far from ordinary experience, and what does this suggest regarding a neural basis for this aspect of the disorder? (535)

b) Similarly, indicate the possible origins of auditory hallucinations in ordinary thought. In general, what is "central" to the experience of the schizophrenic? (536)

* 5. a) Discuss evidence on the genetic risks of developing schizophrenia from studies of related and unrelated persons. What result obtained with identical twins also shows the importance of nongenetic variables? (536-537)

*   b) Discuss evidence concerning the way that schizophrenia may be transmitted genetically. (537)

6. a) Describe a new technique that enables a search for the specific genes involved in schizophrenia. Use the term *DNA* in your answer. (537-538)

b) Given the mixed data, what are two possibilities with respect to the genetic bases for schizophrenia, and what one thing is clear? (538)

* 7. a) In line with the dopamine hypothesis for irregularities in the brain chemistry of schizophrenics, indicate two possible reasons for excess dopamine in certain areas of the brain in this disorder. (538-539)

*   b) Discuss two sources of evidence relative to antipsychotic drug effects that lend support to the dopamine hypothesis. (539)

*   c) Relatedly, how does evidence on the effects of amphetamines favor the dopamine hypothesis? (539)

8. What conclusions may be drawn with respect to the dopamine hypothesis for schizophrenia? (539)

* 9. a) Outline new methods by which possible structural problems in the brains of schizophrenia sufferers are studied in the search for alternative explanations for this group of disorders. Use the terms *CAT* and *MRI* in your response. (539)

* b) What results have been obtained to date with these techniques, and what may we infer? (539)

* 10. a) Discuss the recent hypothesis for Type I and Type II schizophrenia from the standpoint of the following aspects. (539-540)

—symptoms *(positive* versus *negative):*

—biological differences:

b) Is this distinction supported by all of the evidence? Explain. (540)

* 11. a) From the social and psychological perspective on schizophrenia, what observation has been made consistently on the incidence of the disorder? Discuss the following two explanations for this fact. Which has been supported? (540)

—social selection--downward mobility:

—social causation--adversity and stress:

b) What has been a major problem in the attempt to study the psychological factors in schizophrenia by focusing on relationships within families? (540)

c) Discuss the results of a related study on family communication problems. (540-541)

12. a) Outline the procedures of another study that attempted to address the problem indicated in 11b). (541)

* b) Indicate the results of this research noting in particular the characteristics of parents in those families in which the highest incidence of schizophrenia occurred. (541)

* c) Why do your authors say that the causal variables for schizophrenia in family interactions are still not clear from this research? Nevertheless, what is known? (541)

* 13. a) How are children who are at high risk for schizophrenia usually defined? Describe the methods of a number of longitudinal studies of such children conducted in efforts to determine the role of vulnerability and stress in the disorder. (541-542)

* b) Discuss four ways in which the subjects who developed schizophrenic symptoms differed from matched control subjects in these studies. (542)

1. In what respects do personality disorders differ in general from mood and anxiety disorders or schizophrenia? (542)

* 2. a) What was the former term for "antisocial personality"? Why is either term somewhat misleading when applied to most people who display antisocial behaviors? (543)

*   b) Among the features of antisocial personality (or "sociopaths") discussed in your text, which two stand out as the most characteristic? (543)

3. a) List the three areas of research on "understanding antisocial personalities" that serve as headings for the next three subsections. (543)

   b) With respect to biological factors in the development of the antisocial personality, what are some lines of evidence for genetic influences? (543)

*   c) Similarly, discuss an experiment demonstrating evidence of low arousability in persons with antisocial personality. How do these results relate to the effects of punishment for people afflicted with this type of personality disorder? (543-544)

* 4. a) What type of evidence supports the possibility that antisocial personality disorder is relating to difficulty in inhibiting impulsive behavior in childhood? (544-545)

*   b) What is your authors' conclusion with regard to the role of genetic and environmental factors in the development of antisocial personality in children? (545)

* 5. a) With respect to parental factors in antisocial personality, what is one of the best predictors of children's conduct disturbances? Discuss the related observations. (545)

*   b) How might biological factors coincide with parental factors in determining behavior patterns related to antisocial personality? Cite your authors' conclusion. (545)

6. With respect to personality factors in antisocial personality, discuss the cycle of interactions that maintains and encourages aggressive and antisocial behaviors in children. (545-546)

7. a) What does "borderline" refer to in the term borderline personality disorder? (547)

*   b) Indicate the key feature of borderline personality disorder. Describe some of the related manifestations of this type of abnormal behavior. (547-548)

   c) Cite some of the data on suicide, prevalence, and use of mental health services by persons afflicted with borderline personality disorder. (548-549

* 8. a) For each of the following perspectives on borderline personality disorder, state the general approach in your own words, and describe the related behaviors that characterize this type of disorder and the forms of treatment used. (549-550)

Perspective	Description of Approach	Behaviors/Treatment
biological perspectives		
psychoanalytic perspectives		
cognitive perspectives		

b) Indicate one other source for borderline personality disorder suggested by recent research. (550)

234   Chapter 15

Sample Quiz 15.1

1. Which of the following criteria provides a satisfactory description of "abnormality" by itself? a) deviation from social norms; b) deviation from statistical norms; c) maladaptive behavior; d) none of the above.

2. The key point of the vulnerability–stress model of abnormal behaviors is that: a) vulnerability guarantees that a person will develop a mental disorder; b) certain stressors will cause a disorder under nearly all conditions; c) specific stressors will cause a disorder if the person has a biological vulnerability; d) neither stress nor vulnerability are sufficient to predict whether a person will develop a mental disorder.

3. In DSM–IV, relatively nonsituational and constant tension, somatic complaints, and difficulty concentrating are symptoms of: a) phobias; b) panic disorders; c) generalized anxiety; d) mood disorders.

4. Irresistible urges to carry out rituals are to persistent intrusions of unwelcome thoughts as: a) phobias are to neuroses; b) panic disorders are to phobias; c) compulsions are to obsessions; d) psychoses are to mood disorders.

5. An antidepressant drug that influences relevant neurotransmitters is: a) MAO inhibitor; b) serotonin; c) epinephrine; d) both b and c.

6. Which of the following statements regarding depression is *false*? a) Depression has a larger genetic component than bipolar disorder. b) Antidepressants appear to have their effects by modifying the brain's *sensitivity* to norepinephrine and serotonin rather than the levels of these neurotransmitters. c) There is no doubt that mood disorders involve biochemical changes in the nervous system. d) Of all the factors important in determining vulnerability to depression among women, the most important appears to be not having a close relationship with another.

7. A mental patient believes that her actions are caused by external forces in the form of messages beamed down by aliens. She is manifesting delusions of: a) persecution; b) influence; c) grandeur; d) power.

8. With respect to the role of the family in schizophrenia: a) the highest incidence occurred in families in which the adolescent was treated negatively; b) family disorganization is an important variable; c) it is not clear whether family problems are a cause or a result of a member being schizophrenic; d) all of the above.

9. Personality disorders are defined as: a) severe personality disorganization, distortion of reality, and an inability to function in daily life; b) disturbance of thought processes, loss of contact with reality, and auditory hallucinations; c) long-standing, inflexible patterns of maladaptive behavior that impair function; d) periods of severe sadness in alternation with periods of extreme elation.

10. Instability of mood, self–concept, and interpersonal relationships characterizes: a) narcissistic personality disorder; b) borderline personality disorder; c) dependent personality disorder; d) antisocial personality disorder.

Sample Quiz 15.2

1. Psychotic behaviors may include: a) delusions; b) hallucinations; c) false sensory experiences; d) all of the above.

2. Which of the following is *true*? a) People with phobias usually do not recognize they are irrational. b) People with panic disorders may have a pretty good idea as to why they are frightened. c) Anxiety is considered abnormal only when it occurs in situations in which most people have no difficulty. d) All of the above.

3. The fact that we are more likely to become afraid of snakes than, say, knives (even though the latter are more likely to be dangerous) is explained by the notion of: a) cholesytokinin depletion; b) simple classical conditioning; c) the dopamine hypothesis; d) prepared conditioning.

4. The most salient symptoms of depression are: a) emotional; b) cognitive; c) physiological; d) motivational.

5. A theory of depression devised by Aaron Beck emphasizes: a) an unconscious reaction to loss and resulting low self–esteem; b) negative thoughts and cognitive distortions in thinking; c) lack of reinforcement; d) deficiencies of serotonin.

6. Which of the following is *not* one of Beck's cognitive triad categories for the thoughts of depressed people? a) negative thoughts about the future; b) negative thoughts about others; c) negative thoughts about present experiences; d) negative thoughts about the self.

7. A concordance rate specifies the likelihood that if one twin has depression, the other twin will have: a) depression; b) a mood disorder; c) excess epinephrine; d) both a and b.

8. The theory that too much of a specific neurotransmitter causes schizophrenia is the: a) dopamine hypothesis; b) vulnerability–stress model; c) serotonin uptake hypothesis; d) biogenic amine model.

9. One of the best predictors of conduct disturbances in children is: a) parental supervision; b) levels of serotonin in the brain; c) number of arrests; d) number of friends.

10. The term "borderline" in the personality disorder of the same name refers to: a) level of intelligence of those with the disorder; b) the vacillation between symptoms of neurosis and psychosis; c) the likelihood that the individual with this type of disorder will commit suicide; d) the severity of the delusions that characterize this disorder.

Important Names

1. Aaron Beck

Vocabulary and Details

ABNORMAL BEHAVIOR

1. abnormal behavior
2. Diagnostic and Statistical Manual of Mental Disorders, 4th edition, revised; DSM–IV
3. neuroses
4. psychoses
5. psychotic behavior
6. hallucinations; delusions
7. vulnerability–stress

ANXIETY DISORDERS

1. anxiety disorders
2. Generalized anxiety
3. panic disorders
4. phobia
5. obsessive–compulsive
6. obsessions; compulsions
7. prepared conditioning
8. benzodiazepines

MOOD DISORDERS

1. mood disorders
2. depressive disorders
3. bipolar disorders (manic–depression)
4. concordance rate
5. norepinephrine; serotonin; biogenic amines
6. monoamine oxidase (MAO); tricyclic antidepressants

SCHIZOPHRENIA

1. schizophrenia
2. delusions
3. delusions of influence
4. delusions of persecution; delusions of grandeur
5. paranoid
6. auditory
7. dopamine
8. dopamine hypothesis
9. antipsychotic drugs

PERSONALITY DISORDERS

1. personality disorders
2. narcissistic personality disorder
3. dependent personality disorder
4. antisocial personality
5. borderline personality disorder

Sample Quiz 15.1

1. d, 511
2. c, 515-516
3. c, 516
4. c, 518
5. a, 531
6. a, 532-533
7. b, 534
8. d, 541
9. c, 542
10. b, 547

Sample Quiz 15.2

1. d, 514
2. c, 516-517
3. d, 521
4. a, 524
5. b, 529
6. b, 529
7. d, 530-531
8. a, 538
9. a, 545
10. b, 547

Methods of Therapy

Learning Objectives

1. Be familiar with the historical background and current trends in the treatment of abnormal behavior.

2. Be able to specify the backgrounds and professional roles of the different specialists involved in psychotherapy.

3. Be able to describe the following approaches to psychotherapy, including the therapist's techniques and the patient's or client's experiences that are presumed to yield improvement:

    a) Psychoanalysis and psychoanalytic therapies.

    b) Behavior therapies.

    c) Cognitive behavior therapies.

    d) Humanistic therapies.

4. Be familiar with the techniques, advantages, and disadvantages of group therapy and family therapy. Understand what is meant by an eclectic approach to therapy.

5. Be prepared to discuss the difficulties involved in evaluating the success of psycho-therapeutic techniques. Know the factors common to the various psychotherapies that may be most important for behavior change.

6. Be familiar with the techniques, advantages, and disadvantages of the two forms of biological therapy; be able to describe the major classes of psychotherapeutic drugs.

7. Know the effects of culture and gender on such variables as rates of hospitalization, types of psychopathology, appropriate types of psychotherapy, and therapy dropout rates.

8. Be familiar with the variety of community resources being explored as ways of enhancing mental health and with the suggestions offered for promoting your own emotional well–being.

Important Names

1. As a more humane approach to mental disorders began to evolve in Europe, one notable individual was the Frenchman _____, who successfully unchained inmates in an asylum in Paris in the late 1700s. (554)

2. The individual most closely identified with classical psychoanalysis was _____. (558)

3. The famous humanistic psychotherapist who was responsible for the development of client–centered therapy was _____. (569)

Vocabulary and Details

HISTORICAL BACKGROUND

1. In the mental health field, the transition from treating mentally disturbed individuals in hospitals to providing treatment in the community is called _____. (556)

TECHNIQUES OF PSYCHOTHERAPY

1. The treatment of mental disorders by psychological means is termed _____. (558)

2. Psychoanalysts use the technique of _____ in which a client is encouraged to give free rein to thoughts and feelings without editing or censoring. (559)

3. In Freud's terms, when a client's unconscious exerts control over sensitive material during therapy, a form of blocking or _____ has developed which indicates an area to be explored. (559)

4. Another technique used in psychoanalysis is the exploration of dreams, called _____. (559)

5. The assumption of dream analysis is that the obvious, conscious or _____ content of dreams disguises an unconscious wish or fear, the so–called _____ content. (559)

6. The tendency for a client to make a therapist the object of emotional responses that relate to important people in the client's life is known as _____. (560)

7. A hypothesis that summarizes some portion of a client's behavior and provides an explanation for its motivation in an effort to provide client *insight* is termed an _____. (560)

8. Anxiety may be reduced and realistic problem solving may be developed in the psychoanalytic process of examining and reexamining conflicts and reexperiencing painful childhood emotions; this is termed _____. (560)

9. Psychotherapies that share Freud's conceptions of the role of unconscious conflicts and fears in mental disorders, but that differ from classical

240   Chapter 16

psychoanalysis along a number of dimensions, are called _____ or _____. (560-561)

10. A number of different therapeutic methods based on the principles of learning and conditioning collectively are called _____. (561)

11. One technique of behavior therapy is _____ in which an individual is taught to relax in the presence of imagined representations of situations that previously have caused anxiety. Closely related is _____, a procedure in which the client reaches a stage of desensitization in which the anxiety-producing situation is actually experienced. (562)

12. Common to the two forms of desensitization defined in item 11 is the gradual introduction of a ranked set or _____ of stimuli that more and more closely resembles the feared situation. (562)

13. Another behavior therapy procedure involving exposure to a feared stimulus is _____, in which the individual is exposed to real or imaginal material for an extended period of time without the opportunity to escape. (562)

14. While desensitization and exposure therapies are based on the principles of _____, alternative therapies may be based on the principles of _____, including the procedure in which reinforcement is given for desirable responses and withheld for others, termed _____. (563)

15. The process by which a person learns new behaviors by observing and imitating others (through observational learning) is called _____. (563)

16. Modeling is often combined with role–playing, also termed _____. (564)

17. Monitoring one's own behavior and using behavioral techniques such as self–reinforcement or self–punishment to effect change is known as _____. (565)

18. _____ refers to the class of treatment methods that use behavior modification techniques as well as procedures designed to change maladaptive cognitive factors, such as erroneous beliefs. (566)

19. Therapies that are based on the phenomenological approach to personality and that emphasize personal growth and self–actualization are termed _____. (568)

20. A form of humanistic psychotherapy that minimizes therapist intervention while helping clients to develop self–awareness and their own solutions to problems is called _____ . (569)

21. When psychotherapists do not adhere strictly to any single method of therapy, but rather select the ones they feel are most appropriate for a given client, they are said to adopt the _____ approach. (569)

22. When clients work out their problems by exploring attitudes and behaviors while interacting with others, we speak of _____. (571)

23. Two variants of group therapy are (a) therapy provided to couples, called _____ or _____, and (b) therapy for parents and/or their children, called _____. (572)

EFFECTIVENESS OF PSYCHOTHERAPY

1. The phenomenon called _____ refers to the fact that many people with psychological (as well as physical) problems improve without professional treatment. (573-574)

BIOLOGICAL THERAPIES

1. The _____ approach to treating abnormal behavior assumes that mental disorders are caused by biochemical or physiological dysfunctions of the brain. (577)

2. The most successful of the two main classes of biological therapies discussed in your text is the use of _____. (577)

3. Drugs that reduce anxiety, or _____ drugs, belong to the family called _____, commonly called _____. (577)

4. Most of the drugs that relieve the symptoms of schizophrenia, or _____ drugs, are in the family called _____. (577)

5. Drugs that elevate the mood of depressed individuals, or _____ drugs, include two major classes: _____ and _____. (579-580)

6. In the second main class of biological therapies discussed in your text, an electric current may be applied to the brain to produce a seizure and alleviate the symptoms of severe depression; this technique is called _____ (abbreviated _____), also known as _____. (580)

ENHANCING MENTAL HEALTH

1. A community resource in which patients who have been hospitalized can live while making the transition back to an independent life in the community is called the _____. (583)

2. Another community resource, termed _____, provides immediate help for individuals in such forms as 24–hour, walk–in services or telephone hot lines. (583-584)

3. Persons without advanced degrees who have been trained in assisting with professional services in community programs are called _____. (584)

Ideas and Concepts

HISTORICAL BACKGROUND

1. Trace the views of mental disorders that prevailed in ancient times, through the height of the Greek and Roman period, and into the Middle Ages. (554)

* 2. a) What was an important result of Pinel's intervention with respect to the inhumane treatment of inmates in an asylum in Paris? (554)

*Basic ideas and concepts

242   Chapter 16

*   b) Describe the mental deterioration that characterizes *general paresis*. What was the main consequence for the prevailing view of mental illness of the discovery that general paresis had a physical origin? (554-555)

    c) List the additional contributions to the changing attitudes toward mental illness that came through the efforts of Freud, Pavlov, and Beers. (555)

3.   a) Describe the range of facilities provided in mental hospitals today. (555-556)

*   b) Describe the impetus for deinstitutionalization in terms of the disadvantages of hospitalization and the advent of psychotherapeutic drugs. (556)

*   c) What was the national legislation in 1963 that was so important in the initiation of the dramatic trend toward deinstitutionalization, and what were some of the intended results? (556)

    d) Besides favorable consequences for some mental patients, what have been the less fortunate consequences for others of attempts to provide community–based care? Indicate an important ethical issue involved. (556-557)

* 4.   Discuss some of the legal issues that bear on the question of whether we should revert to more institutionalization of the mentally disturbed. (557)

* 5.   Distinguish among the mental health professionals listed in the following table in terms of their qualifications and usual role in psychotherapy. (557-558)

Mental Health Professional	Qualifications and Activities
psychiatrist	
psychoanalyst	
clinical psychologist	(Contrast the PhD and PsyD degrees)
counseling psychologist	
psychiatric social worker	
psychiatric nurse	

TECHNIQUES OF PSYCHOTHERAPY

* 1.   What do most methods of psychotherapy have in common? Discuss how this commonality is accomplished from the viewpoint of the client and the therapist. (558)

*   2.   a)   What is the assumption of the psychoanalytic theories of personality? Use the terms *id,* *ego,* and *superego.* (558)

         b)   Using an example, illustrate how unconscious conflicts beginning in childhood can persist to cause later maladjustment. (558-559)

*   c)   In terms of psychological treatment, what is a key assumption and goal of *psychoanalysis*? (559)

     3.   a)   What kinds of transference are possible during psychoanalysis? (560)

*   b)   In what period of life did Freud assume that the emotions in transference originate, and what did he attempt to do with the phenomenon when it occurred? (560)

*   4.   Beside client insight, for what purpose may interpretations be used, and why is the timing of interpretations so critical? (560)

     5.   How long does psychoanalysis often take and to what kinds of individuals is it generally limited for greatest effectiveness? (560)

*   6.   a)   Use the example of "ego analysis" to illustrate a more recent form of psychoanalytic (or psychodynamic) therapy. Indicate both the goal and strategy of the ego analysts. (560-561)

*   b)   Describe a number of ways that the techniques of psychoanalysis are modified in contemporary approaches. (561)

*   7.   a)   What is the assumption of behavior therapy and how does its focus differ from psychoanalysis? (561)

         b)   Cite an example to make the point of behavior therapists that insight may not be sufficient in achieving behavior change. (561)

*   c)   Indicate the kinds of goals and concerns of behavior therapy; contrast with those of psychodynamic therapy. (561)

*   d)   Outline the steps of behavior therapy, using examples when helpful. (561-562)

*   8.   a)   Describe the process of systematic desensitization and in vivo exposure in detail, indicating the several steps in the technique. Use the terms *counterconditioning* and *hierarchy*. (562)

         b)   Illustrate systematic desensitization, using the example of a client with fear of snakes discussed in your text. (562)

         c)   Using the same example, illustrate the process of in vivo exposure. How might modeling on the part of the therapist be helpful? (562)

*   d)   What is the suggestion of some researchers regarding the specific learning process in in vivo exposure? Specifically, how might this process work? Use the term *extinction*. (562)

* 9. a) Cite a case study to illustrate the regularized use of selective reinforcement in behavior therapy. Be sure to note both the reinforcement procedure and the specific behavioral effects. (563)

b) With an example, show how extinction may also be employed systematically in effecting behavior change. (563)

c) Be sure you understand the concept of the *token economy* as it is used in some mental hospitals. (563)

* 10. a) Describe the results of Bandura's study comparing various treatments for snake phobia. (564, Figure 16-2)

b) Why is modeling effective in overcoming fears and anxieties? Exemplify. (564)

* 11. a) How is modeling often combined with behavioral rehearsal? (564)

* b) Describe the process of *assertiveness training*, and show how behavior rehearsal might be helpful in this technique. (564)

* 12. a) When is self–regulation useful, and what is one advantage of these techniques? (565)

b) Cite some of the kinds of self–regulation techniques that may be used. (565)

c) Provide an example of self–regulation as applied to a person with alcohol dependency. (565)

d) Can you think of methods of self–reinforcement and self–punishment you could apply to help in the modification of your own study behaviors? (Table 16-2 may be helpful.) (565 and 566)

* 13. a) What has been the traditional attitude of behavior therapists toward cognition, and how has that view been changed at the hands of cognitive behavior therapists? (565-566)

b) Describe the application of cognitive behavior therapy to a case of depression. Specifically, what cognitive behaviors are identified in the depressed individual, and in what direction are these changed? (566-567)

* c) Show how the behavioral component of this type of therapy is utilized, and cite an example. (567)

d) Again by example, show how behavior modification may be combined with techniques for modifying negative thoughts. (567)

* 14. a) What do most cognitive behavior therapists argue is important in producing enduring changes in behavior? What is considered to be a more powerful way to achieve this effect than verbal methods alone? (567)

* b) Using Bandura's concept of *self–efficacy*, discuss the role of performance and success in developing a sense of personal mastery. (568)

Methods of Therapy   245

* 15. a) From the standpoint of humanistic therapies, why do psychological disorders arise, how are they manifested, and what is the goal of therapy? (568)

   b) In what respects are humanistic therapies like psychoanalysis, and how do they differ? (568-569)

* 16. a) Describe some of the characteristics of the therapeutic setting and therapist–client interaction in Rogers's client–centered therapy. (569)

   b) How does the therapist help the client toward self–insight in this method of therapy? (569)

*   c) Define each of the following qualities of an effective client–centered therapist: (569)

   —empathy:

   —warmth:

   —genuineness:

   d) Indicate some of the limitations of client–centered therapy. (569)

17. a) Provide some examples to illustrate the eclectic approach to psychotherapy. (569-570)

*   b) What is another approach to psychotherapy, closely identified with the eclectic model, that may be adopted when it is recognized that no single approach deals successfully with all problems? Cite an example. (570)

18. a) In what kinds of settings might group therapy be used? (571)

*   b) Describe the typical group therapy situation and some variations on this theme. (571)

*   c) Indicate several of the advantages of group therapy over individual psychotherapy. When is a group especially effective? (571)

   d) Traditionally, who leads groups, and what is an emerging trend in this area? Cite some examples. (571)

* 19. a) Why has marital (or couple) therapy been on the increase and what does the data show with respect to its effectiveness in solving interpersonal problems relative to individual therapy? (572)

*   b) Outline some of the emphases of marital therapy. Use the term *behavioral contracts* in your answer. (572)

* 20. a) Why did family therapy originate, and what is its premise? Use the term *family system* in your answer. (572-573)

   b) Indicate two typical problems within a family, and be able to provide examples. (573)

246   Chapter 16

c) Describe some of the methods used in family therapy. (573)

* d) Discuss an important application of family therapy in dealing with schizophrenia. (573)

EFFECTIVENESS OF PSYCHOTHERAPY

* 1. a) Why is it difficult to evaluate the effectiveness of psychotherapy? (573)

* b) In what respects is the term "spontaneous remission" not altogether appropriate when describing recovery from psychological problems? (574)

c) What are some of the specific resources other than professional help available to a person with psychological disorders? (574)

d) In view of the possibility of spontaneous remission, how must psychotherapy be evaluated and when is it judged to be effective? What ethical issue does this evaluation create, and how does one deal with it? (574)

* 2. a) Besides spontaneous remission, what is a second problem in evaluating psychotherapy? (574)

* b) What three independent measures should be included in the assessment of improvement? (574)

* 3. a) Describe the procedure used in a large scale analysis of psychotherapy evaluation studies. (574)

* b) What outcomes were obtained in this study? In addition, cite the data on improvement with psychotherapy as a function of numbers of sessions. (574-575)

* 4. a) Is therapy better than no treatment? Relatedly, what is the conclusion of most reviews of studies that have compared different psychotherapies? (575)

* b) Cite two reasons for the similar effects of different therapeutic methods. (575)

* 5. Describe each of the following factors common across different psychotherapies. Use examples when they are helpful. (575-576)

—interpersonal warmth and trust:

—reassurance and support:

—desensitization:

—reinforcement of adaptive responses:

—understanding or insight:

Methods of Therapy   247

*   1. What was the major impact of the discoveries of the drugs that relieved some of the symptoms of schizophrenia and depression? (577)

2. a) List three common tranquilizers by trade name, and indicate their effects on the central nervous system. (577)

*   b) Indicate some of the side effects and dangers of tranquilizers. (577)

3. a) Give the trade names of two common antipsychotic drugs. (577)

*   b) Why is the term "major tranquilizer" a misnomer when applied to an antipsychotic drug? What are some of their actual side effects? (577)

*   c) Discuss in detail an explanation for the effects of the antipsychotic drugs in terms of their impact on the dopamine receptors. Note also where these receptors are concentrated. (577-578)

*   4. a) What are the benefits of the antipsychotic drugs for treating schizophrenia, including their effects upon symptoms and relapse rate? Do these benefits mean that these drugs "cure" the disorder? (578-579)

*   b) Indicate some of the adverse side effects of the antipsychotic drugs. (579)

*   5. Describe the probable mechanisms for neurotransmitter action of the following two classes of antidepressant drugs. (Use the term **reuptake** when appropriate.) (579-580)

—MAO inhibitors (for example, Nardil and Parnate):

—trycyclic antidepressants (for example, Tofranil and Elavil):

6. a) Do the antidepressants produce their effects immediately? What is one implication of this fact? (580)

b) What advantages have been sought in the search for new drugs for depression? Cite two examples, and indicate some of their other effects in treating disorders. (580)

*   c) What drug has been found to be effective in treating bipolar disorders? (580)

*   7. Discuss your authors' view of drug therapy in terms of its benefits and limitations. (580)

8. a) Why is the use of ECT for depression now less common and when might it still be employed? (580)

*   b) List several reasons why the ECT procedure has been so controversial. (580-581)

c) Describe the current application of ECT. What is one side effect, and how is this effect alleviated? (581)

*   d)   Cite one possible explanation for how ECT works to relieve depression. (581)

THE EFFECTS OF CULTURE AND GENDER ON THERAPY

*   1.   Where possible and statistics are available, review this section and describe some of the differences among African–Americans, Native Americans, Asian–Americans, white Americans, and Hispanics in terms of: (581-582)

—rates of hospitalization:

—rates of major types of psychopathology:

—immediacy of tendency to seek mental health treatment:

—types of psychotherapy that might prove most acceptable:

—therapy dropout rates:

*   2.   Returning to earlier material in this section, with respect to gender differences, what are the data on hospitalization rates and related disorders? (582)

*   3.   Where do most people get their mental health treatment, and what are the gender differences with regard to seeking help for mental health problems? (582)

*   4.   a)   As discussed later in this section, what may matter more than specific forms of therapy where culture (and gender) differences are concerned? 582)

       b)   Does being from the same ethnic or racial group necessarily ensure the delivery of effective therapy? Explain. (582-583)

       c)   What should be done if a client wishes to be matched with a therapist in terms of ethnicity or gender? (583)

       d)   What is the importance of shared beliefs on the part of therapist and client insofar as the effectiveness of therapy is concerned? (583)

ENHANCING MENTAL HEALTH

*   1.   Describe three forms of community resources that have been developed in efforts to enhance mental health. (583)

*   2.   Discuss two forms of crisis intervention for people who need immediate help. (583-584)

     3.   a)   Exemplify the involvement of paraprofessionals in psychotherapy. (584)

       b)   Describe the Achievement Place residential mental health program, and indicate some of its positive outcomes. (584)

*   4.   List five ways that you can promote your own mental health. (584-586)

Sample Quiz 16.1

1. A psychiatric social worker: a) has a PhD degree; b) can prescribe medication; c) extends treatment to the home and community; d) all of the above.

2. The tendency for a client to make a therapist the object of emotional responses that relate to people in the client's life is termed: a) displacement; b) projection; c) transference; d) resistance.

3. Working through is: a) a process of examining conflicts and reexperiencing painful childhood emotions; b) a method in which a client is exposed to actual feared situations; c) a form of therapy that minimizes therapist intervention while clients discover their own solutions to problems; d) a class of treatment methods that uses behavior modification as well as procedures to change cognitions.

4. It has been suggested by researchers that the specific learning process in in vivo exposure is: a) discrimination; b) extinction; c) selective reinforcement; d) self-regulation.

5. We speak of eclectic therapy when: a) the therapist emphasizes growth and self-actualization; b) no single method is adhered to, but one is selected that seems best for the client; c) the principles of learning and conditioning are emphasized; d) in the effort to treat depression, electric current is applied to a patient's brain to produce a seizure.

6. Which of the following is *not* cited as an advantage of group therapy over individual therapy? a) Participants can do therapy on one another. b) A participant can learn vicariously by watching others. c) A participant can derive comfort from observing others with more serious problems. d) The therapist can use resources more efficiently.

7. With respect to the effects of psychotherapy: a) behavioral therapies are more effective than other types; b) there is little difference in effectiveness between therapies; c) psychotherapy produces greater improvement than no treatment; d) both b and c.

8. Drugs that relieve the symptoms of schizophrenia are in the family called: a) phenothiazines; b) monoamine oxidase inhibitors; c) tricyclics; d) benzodiazepines.

9. A halfway house is defined as a: a) type of clinic used for treatment of serious, chronic disturbances; b) place for transition from an institution back to the community; c) form of treatment in which patients receive counseling prior to admission into a long-term care facility; d) program that combines behavior therapy with drug therapy.

10. Which of the following is *not* a suggestion by your authors for how to promote your own emotional well-being? a) At the first sign of an emotional problem, seek professional help. b) Know your vulnerabilities. c) Develop your talents and interests. d) Accept your feelings.

Sample Quiz 16.2

1. Philippe Pinel was noted for: a) the development of client–centered therapy; b) efforts to provide more humane treatment for mental patients; c) principles of modeling in applications of cognitive behavior therapy; d) his role in classical psychoanalysis.

2. In psychoanalysis, interpretation: a) helps the client gain insight; b) offers an explanation; c) calls attention to resistances; d) all of the above.

3. The behavior therapy method in which a person is exposed to feared material without the opportunity for escape is termed: a) interpretation; b) free association; c) flooding; d) systematic desensitization.

4. Modeling is illustrated by a therapist who: a) asks a client to relax, then imagine handling a snake; b) upon hearing a client relate a recent terrifying incident with a snake, offers an interpretation in terms of childhood experiences; c) picks up a harmless snake and strokes its back; d) selectively reinforces behaviors that include the client's touching the snake.

5. Monitoring one's own behavior and using behavioral techniques to effect change defines: a) client–centered therapy; b) behavioral rehearsal; c) flooding; d) self–regulation.

6. Most cognitive behavior therapists agree that: a) it is important to alter beliefs to bring about permanent behavior change; b) behavioral procedures are the best way to alter beliefs; c) cognitive interventions are the most effective way to change beliefs; d) both a and b.

7. Spontaneous remission refers to: a) the reappearance of a response after it has undergone extinction; b) redevelopment of a disorder after it has been alleviated through therapy; c) improvement of a psychological problem without professional treatment; d) none of the above.

8. The most successful of the biological therapies is: a) the use of drugs; b) electroconvulsive shock therapy; c) crisis intervention; d) systematic desensitization.

9. Antipsychotic drugs: a) cure schizophrenia; b) alleviate hallucinations and confusion in schizophrenia; c) have few or no long–term side effects; d) appear to work by preventing the reuptake of serotonin and norepinephrine.

10. Culture and gender differences in mental disorders are reflected in the fact that: a) white Americans are more likely to be hospitalized in mental health facilities than African–Americans; b) white Americans are more likely to care for a member of the family with a mental disorder than Hispanics; c) women in the United States are more likely to be hospitalized for mental disorders than men; d) none of the above.

Answer Key, Chapter 16

Important Names

1. Philippe Pinel
2. Sigmund Freud
3. Carl Rogers

Vocabulary and Details

HISTORICAL BACKGROUND

1. deinstitutionalization

TECHNIQUES OF PSYCHOTHERAPY

1. psychotherapy
2. free association
3. resistance
4. dream analysis
5. manifest; latent
6. transference
7. interpretation
8. working through
9. psychoanalytic therapies; psychodynamic therapies
10. behavior therapy
11. systematic desensitization; in vivo exposure
12. hierarchy
13. flooding
14. classical conditioning; operant conditioning; selective reinforcement
15. modeling
16. behavioral rehearsal
17. self–regulation
18. Cognitive–behavior therapy
19. humanistic therapies
20. client–centered therapy
21. eclectic (or integrative)
22. group therapy
23. marital therapy; couple therapy; family therapy

EFFECTIVENESS OF PSYCHOTHERAPY

1. spontaneous remission

BIOLOGICAL THERAPIES

1. biological
2. psychotherapeutic drugs
3. antianxiety; benzodiazepines; tranquilizers
4. antipsychotic; phenothiazines
5. antidepressant; monoamine oxidase inhibitors (or MAO inhibitors); tricyclic antidepressants
6. electroconvulsive therapy (ECT) electroshock therapy

ENHANCING MENTAL HEALTH

1. halfway house
2. crisis intervention
3. paraprofessionals

Sample Quiz 16.1

1. c, 557
2. c, 560
3. a, 560
4. b, 562
5. b, 569
6. a, 571
7. d, 575
8. d, 577
9. b, 583
10. a, 586

Sample Quiz 16.2

1. b, 554
2. d, 560
3. c, 562
4. c, 563-564
5. d, 565
6. d, 567
7. c, 573-574
8. a, 577
9. b, 578-579
10. d, 581-582

Social Cognition and Affect

Learning Objectives

1. Be able to define social psychology in terms of its major emphases and viewpoints.

2. Be able to describe the three tasks that we as informal scientists perform in constructing our intuitive beliefs regarding human behavior. Give examples of the kinds of biases that influence our judgments at each stage.

3. Understand schematic processing. Show how it can lead to errors in processing social information and its role in memory. Note how the persistence of schemas and self–schemas in the face of disconfirming data impacts on social behavior.

4. Understand the function of stereotypes and show how they can be persistent and self–fulfilling.

5. Be familiar with the distinction between dispositional and situational attributions and the fundamental attribution error.

6. Be prepared to discuss self–perception theory, showing how some of the same processes that govern our judgments of others influence the judgments we make about ourselves. Note some related neurophysiological findings.

7. Be able to define attitudes and understand their three components.

8. Be familiar with the research on consistency among attitudes and beliefs and with five psychological functions of attitudes that affect their consistency.

9. Understand the relationships between attitudes and the prediction of behavior.

10. Be prepared to explain the results of induced–compliance experiments in terms of cognitive dissonance theory.

11. Be familiar with the four factors that determine interpersonal attraction, the dimensions of love, and two leading theories of love.

12. Be able to discuss the sociobiological view of pair bonding and its implications for distinctive behaviors of males and females, as well as limitations of the theory.

Important Names

1. The founder of modern attribution theory was _____. (602)

2. Self–perception theory was the proposal of the social psychologist _____. (602)

3. The influential psychologist notable, in part, for his important and heuristic theory of cognitive dissonance was _____. (613)

Vocabulary and Details

1. The study of how people perceive, think, and feel about their social world, and how they interact and influence one another, defines the field of _____. (593)

INTUITIVE THEORIES OF SOCIAL BEHAVIOR

1. The social information we attend to, estimate, and judge is influenced by the _____ of the information to which we attend; we are _____ (more/less) influenced by vivid than by nonvivid information of equal or greater reliability. (594)

2. The organized beliefs and knowledge we hold in memory structures about people, objects, events, and situations helpful in processing information are termed _____. (595)

3. Searching for the schema in memory that is most consistent with incoming data is called _____. (595)

4. Besides schemas of particular persons, we also have schemas of classes of persons, called _____. (595)

5. We even have a schema about ourselves, a set of organized self–concepts stored in memory, called a _____ (in a sense, a theory about oneself). (595)

6. In general, the first information we receive has the greater impact on our overall impressions; this phenomenon is called the _____. (596)

7. As intuitive scientists of social behavior, our attempts to detect "what goes with what" is the same as detecting correlation or _____. (598)

8. Because our stereotypes lead us to interactions with others that cause them to fulfill our expectations, we speak of _____ stereotypes. (601)

9. The process by which we attempt to interpret and to explain the causes of the behavior of other people is called _____. (601)

10. If we infer that something about a person is primarily responsible for their behavior, our inference is called an _____ or _____ attribution. If, however, we infer that a person's behavior has an external cause, we are using an _____ or _____ attribution. (601)

11. The bias toward dispositional attributions rather than situational attributions regarding the behavior of others has been termed the _____. (602)

12. According to Bem's _____ theory, we make judgments about ourselves using the same inferential processes (and making the same errors) that we use for making judgments about others. (602)

13. Studies in which incentives are used to obtain subjects' compliance with experimental procedures are called _____ experiments. (604)

ATTITUDES

1. One of social psychology's most central concepts is _____ or likes and dislikes—favorable or unfavorable evaluations of and reactions to objects, people, situations, or other aspects of the world. (606)

2. Social psychologists regard attitudes as a three–part system: Beliefs and perceptions are the _____ component; feelings are the _____ component; and actions are the _____ component. (607)

3. For example, negative beliefs and perceptions about a group (the cognitive component) are called _____; negative feelings about the group (the affective component) are called _____; negative actions against members of the group (the behavioral component) are called _____. (607)

4. That we strive to be consistent in beliefs, attitudes, and behavior is the basic premise of the _____ theories in social psychology. (607)

5. Attitudes that protect us from anxiety or from threats to our self–esteem are said to serve an _____ function. (609)

6. In the view of prejudice called the _____, it is held that negative attitudes toward minority groups sometimes serve an ego–defensive function, in which a prejudiced person's hostility takes the form of blaming the groups for personal and societal problems. (609)

7. According to the approach called _____, when a person's cognitions are mutually inconsistent, the discomfort produced by this dissonance motivates the person to remove the inconsistency and bring the cognitions into harmony. (613)

INTERPERSONAL ATTRACTION

1. Liking has been shown to be a function of a number of variables; among them are _____, _____, _____, and _____. (614)

2. Three dimensions that have been used in the assessment of romantic love in a scale constructed by Rubin are _____, _____, and _____. (618)

3. During romance, the state in which coexisting emotions are intense and often confused (for example, elation with pain, anxiety with relief) is called _____. (619)

4. In contrast, attachment to another person characterized by trust, caring, tolerance, and emotions of affection and warmth is called _____. (619)

5. A theory of love that divides it into three components—intimacy, passion, and commitment—is called the _____ of love. (621)

6. The application of evolutionary principles to social behavior is one aspect of the new discipline called _____. (623)

7. Sociobiologists contend that evolution is responsible for the tendency of people to engage in _____, that is, to form intense, long–term bonds with a partner that help to ensure that offspring survive to reproductive age. (623)

Ideas and Concepts

* 1. a) What is the basic observation of social psychology, and what two determinants of human behavior are emphasized? (593)

   b) What has research shown to be the more powerful of the two determinants of behavior? Is it the objective features of this determinant alone that are important? Explain. (593)

INTUITIVE THEORIES OF SOCIAL BEHAVIOR

* 1. a) What do your authors mean when they say that "we are all psychologists"? In what three basic tasks do we engage that are essentially the same tasks as those of the formal scientist? (Note that these also refer to the headings for the following sub–sections in your text.) Cite examples, including when we try to understand ourselves. (593)

   b) What would happen if our intuitive attempts to apply science to everyday life did not work? Does this result mean that we never make errors in social judgments? Explain. (593)

* 2. Discuss three sources of nonrepresentativeness and nonrandomness that may pervade the everyday collection of social data. (593-594)

* 3. a) Discuss a study of the effects of vividness of information on selection of psychology courses. What variable in particular influenced the students? (594)

   b) When does the vividness effect pose a special problem? Can you think of an example from your own experience? (594)

* 4. a) What do schemas and schematic processing enable us to do? (595)

   b) Are we actively aware of using schematic processing? (595)

   c) Cite a research observation to show that schemas help us to process information. (595)

* d) What is the *self–reference effect*? Give two reasons why it occurs. (595)

* 5. a) What is the "price we pay" for the efficiency gained through the use of schemas? Give an example of the related primacy effect in your answer. (595-596)

*Basic ideas and concepts

b) Illustrate the primacy effect as it applies to subjects who observed a student solve problems. (596)

* c) Of what is the primacy effect mainly a consequence? Explain. (596)

6. Why do your authors say that "There is truth to the conventional warning that first impressions are important"? Use an example in your answer. (596)

7. a) Provide an illustration for how schematic processing affects memory. (596)

* b) Discuss two reasons for effects of schema on memory. (597)

* c) Are memories always consistent with schema? Explain. (597)

8. a) Give examples of the persistence of schemas and of self–schemas. Use the term *perseverance effect* in the latter case. (597-598

* b) Discuss one explanation for the perseverance effect, and cite some related evidence. (598)

* 9. a) In general, does research show that are we good at detecting covariation? How does having and not having a theory, respectively, influence our estimates of covariation? (599)

* b) Discuss a study of clinical assessment with college student subjects plus a modified repeat of the study to demonstrate the difficulty that may be encountered when a person holds a preexisting theory regarding covariation. (599)

* 10. Using Figure 17-1 as the basis, be able to account for the persistence of the stereotype that gay men display effeminate gestures, citing various sources of contribution to this belief. Be sure to note the role of vividness in this illustration. (599-600)

* 11. To demonstrate that our schemas influence not only our perceptions and inferences but also our behavior, cite a study to show that prejudicial behavior towards others can, in turn, induce stereotyped reactions in them. (601)

* 12. Describe two sets of results of an experiment that showed that the stereotype held by one person that another person was attractive may have a self–fulfilling effect upon both parties. (601)

13. a) Distinguish by example between dispositional attributions and situational attributions in inferences regarding the behavior of others. (601)

* b) With respect to which of these two types of attributions people tend to favor, what did Heider contend and what is the trend of the evidence? (602)

c) Describe the outcomes of several studies demonstrating the power of the fundamental attribution error. (602)

* 14. Restate Bem's self–perception theory in your own words and provide some common illustrations. (602)

Social Cognition and Affect   257

* 15. a) Outline the procedures of a well–known "cognitive dissonance" experiment by Festinger and Carlsmith designed to show the effects of different sizes of incentives on self–perception in a task involving induced compliance. (604)

* b) In detail, what results were obtained in this study, and how would self–perception theory account for them? (604)

* c) How did the subjects in this study commit the fundamental attribution error? (604)

16. a) Describe another experiment in which subjects played the role of questioner or contestant in a contrived quiz game. How did both the contestant and an independent observer rate the general knowledge of the players in the game? (604-605)

b) What kind of judgment error do these results demonstrate? Discuss the implications of these findings for sex–role differences and for maximizing one's apparent knowledgeability in daily interactions with others. (605)

17. a) What two selves are represented in the process of self–perception? (605)

* b) Describe some experimental results obtained by Gazzaniga showing a possible structural basis for the observing and observed self in the functions of the two brain hemispheres. (606)

* c) In general, what do people do when asked to account for their preferences, behaviors, and emotional states? Cite some related observations. (606)

ATTITUDES

1. Be sure you understand the concept of attitudes by citing a few examples. (606)

2. a) Describe some examples of apparently disparate political and social attitudes that seem to be bound together by "psycho–logic." (607)

* b) From the standpoint of the cognitive consistency theories, what happens if there is inconsistency among attitudes, cognitions, and behaviors? (607)

3. a) As your authors point out, most of the research on consistency of attitudes has been conducted in laboratories with college students. By contrast, give some examples of *nonconsistency* outside the laboratory in the following areas. (607-608)

—social issues:

—political issues:

* b) What appears to be the norm (outside the laboratory) with respect to consistency of beliefs and attitudes? (608)

* c) What is an *opinion molecule*? Provide examples. (608)

* d) Cite three important social functions served by opinion molecules. (608-609)

258   Chapter 17

* 4. With respect to each of the following functions of attitudes, provide a definition in your own words and be able to cite one or more examples to demonstrate your understanding of each function. (609-611)

Function	Definition	Example(s)
instrumental function		
knowledge function		
value–expressive function		
ego–defensive function		
social adjustment function		

* 5. a) Discuss the Freudian concept of *projection* as it applies to attitudes that serve an ego–defensive function. (609)

   b) Cite the results of a study demonstrating ego–defensiveness in attitudes regarding homosexual people. (609)

* 6. a) Outline the views of the researchers contained in the book, *The Authoritarian Personality*, with respect to the nature of the home environments of anti–Semitic persons. (609-610)

* b) What are the characteristics of the *authoritarian personality*, and how are these expressed towards people in "outgroups"? (610)

   c) Indicate the current status of theory and research findings with respect to the authoritarian personality, noting especially an alternative view of the origins of this type of personality. (610)

* 7. a) Discuss Pettigrew's study of racial attitudes in the South showing that to the extent that attitudes serve purposes of social adjustment, they are likely to change as social norms change. Note specifically Pettigrew's findings with respect to the following: (611)

   —the role of authoritarianism:

   —changes in racial attitudes as desegregation progressed:

Social Cognition and Affect 259

    *   b) From these data, if attitudes cannot be legislated, what is the quickest path to changing "hearts and minds"? (611)

    *   8. a) What is a major reason for studying attitudes? Does this view have any support? (611)

             b) By contrast, describe a classic case in which attitudes and behaviors did not appear to be consistent. (611)

    *   c) What does the study outlined in 8b) illustrate, and what are two possible additional factors in attitude–behavior consistency? (611-612)

    *   9. For each of the four conditions under which attitudes are related to behavior, indicate the nature of the relationship, and be able to provide relevant examples: (612-613)

—strong and consistent attitudes:

—attitudes directly related to predicted behavior:

—attitudes based on direct experience:

—attitudes accessible through awareness:

    * 10. a) In what area has Festinger's cognitive dissonance theory generated especially provocative predictions? (613)

    *   b) Review the Festinger and Carlsmith experiment covered earlier in this *Study Guide* (item 15 in the previous section) for its implications regarding the role of dissonance in motivating attitude change. (613-614)

    *   c) What general conclusion may be drawn from the Festinger and Carlsmith study? Cite an additional observation on the role of amount of pressure used in inducing compliance in relation to attitude change. (614)

      11. What levels of support have the cognitive dissonance, self–perception, and impression management theories each received, and what should be the direction of future related research? (614)

INTERPERSONAL ATTRACTION

    *   1. a) How do people rank physical attractiveness in surveys of what is important in their liking of other people? Does the evidence support their expressed attitudes? Cite a related study that used a computer dating method to match subjects. (614-615)

             b) Is the importance of physical attractiveness related only to dating and to people of one's own age? Cite the evidence. (615)

    *   c) Give two reasons why physical attractiveness is so important. Discuss some studies to support the second reason, including a result that shows some limitations on the importance of attractiveness. (615)

d) Why is there still "hope for the unbeautiful"? (615)

* 2. a) Summarize the evidence obtained in a study of marriage license applications and in three other studies involving neighbors and roommates that demonstrate the importance of proximity in liking. (615)

   b) When does the proximity–liking relationship appear to fail, and why is this *not* likely to impact on most encounters between people? (615-616)

* 3. a) What is a major reason for the relationship between proximity and liking? Use examples to demonstrate the *familiarity breeds liking* phenomenon. (616)

   b) Cite a study showing that mere exposure to faces may affect liking. (616)

   c) In response to your authors' query, are you able to guess why people prefer reversed prints of themselves, whereas others prefer nonreversed prints of the same photos? (616)

   d) Cite additional evidence to support the relationship between familiarity and liking. (616)

* 4. a) While "opposites" may think they attract each other, what do the data show? Cite a number of related observations on the effects of similarity. (616-617)

   b) What role does physical attractiveness play in the effects of similarity as determined in a study of independent ratings of the attractiveness of couples? (617)

* 5. a) What is a major reason why people choose others of similar attractiveness for partners? (617-618)

   b) What other dimensions of similarity may be important in a relationship over the long term? Cite a study that provided some results that favored the importance of similarity in married couples. (618)

* c) Give two reasons why similarity produces liking, one of which is a repeat of a relationship discussed earlier. (618)

* 6. a) Despite the trends in the data discussed in items 4 and 5, under what conditions might opposites attract? Cite an example. (618)

   b) Is there much evidence for this "complementarity hypothesis"? Exemplify. (618)

* 7. In what way does one of the investigations by Rubin show that love is more than just intense liking? (618-619)

* 8. Cite some statistics to document the trend of attitudes with regard to the importance of romantic love in marriage over the past 25 years. (619)

* 9. a) Despite such attitudes as those discussed in item 8, which form of love in the *passionate/companionate* dichotomy of the love theory developed by Hatfield and Berscheid appears to be dominant in long–term relationships? Why does

Berscheid argue that the frequency of strong emotions in marriage is usually fairly low? (619)

    b) Discuss the results of a related study of marriages in two cultures that illustrate the true "drama" of love. (621)

*   c) Indicate the moral of passionate love. (621)

* 10. a) What is the paradox in the choice most people make in romantic and sexual partners? Then what may be the "spark" for passionate love? (621)

    b) Discuss three stages of Bem's *exotic becomes erotic* theory for choice of sexual partners, and cite supportive observations. (621)

* 11. a) Be able to define each of Sternberg's three components of love in the triangular theory. (621)

—*intimacy:*

—*passion:*

—*commitment:*

*   b) Using the information in Table 17-2, be able to distinguish between the two forms of passionate love, infatuated and romantic. Similarly, what distinguishes companionate love from liking? (622)

* 12. Discuss the relationship between childhood attachment styles and adult love styles, especially noting the different patterns of secure and avoidant adults. (622)

* 13. a) From the sociobiological perspective, indicate five problems in the process of pair bonding. (623)

*   b) Discuss other predictions from the sociobiological approach with respect to: (623-624)

—forming of long–term bonds:

—different roles and sexual behaviors of males and females:

—gender–related preferences for fertility and resources:

    c) Discuss some of the challenges to sociobiological theorizing regarding gender roles and a possible circularity in theoretical reasoning in this approach. (624)

    d) Does this mean that evolutionary thinking is not useful? Explain. (624)

Sample Quiz 17.1

1. When your text states that "We are all psychologists," what is *not* meant is that: a) we use standardized assessment methods; b) we collect data on human behavior; c) we try to infer cause and effect with regard to human behavior; d) we attempt to detect covariation in behavior—that is, what goes with what.

2. A self–schema is: a) a theory about oneself; b) a set of organized self–concepts stored in memory; c) helpful in processing information; d) all of the above.

3. If the first thing we hear about a person is that he or she is "kind", that will have a greater impact on our overall impressions than information received later. This phenomenon is the so-called: a) self–fulfilling stereotype; b) induced–compliance phenomenon; c) primacy effect; d) cognitive consistency phenomenon.

4. When your authors speak of the persistence of schemas, they are referring to the fact that: a) schemas tend to persist in the face of disconfirming data; b) people will tend to persevere in their belief that they have done well, but they will not continue to believe they have done badly in the face of evidence that their performance was unrelated to their behavior; c) people will persist in a belief even if it is contrary to their self-schema; d) all of the above.

5. If we infer that behavior has an internal cause we are using a(n): a) internal attribution; b) dispositional attribution; c) situational attribution; d) both a and b.

6. According to Bem's self–perception theory: a) we make judgments about ourselves using the same inferential processes that we use for making judgments about others; b) when a person's cognitions are mutually inconsistent, the discomfort motivates the person to bring the cognitions into harmony; c) negative attitudes toward some groups sometimes serve an ego–defensive function; d) evolution is a fundamental process in the understanding of human social behavior.

7. The norm with respect to attitude consistency appears to be that citizens: a) generally have the same beliefs in many different areas of their lives; b) generally have a consistent ideology that applies in many situations; c) do not organize their attitudes according to any overall ideology; d) both a and b.

8. Which of the following is *not* a condition under which attitudes tend to influence behavior most strongly? a) when they have powerful unconscious sources; b) when they are based on direct experience; c) when they are strong and consistent; d) when they are specifically related to the behavior.

9. Which of the following is a variable discussed in your text that is relevant to *liking*? a) a sense of attachment; b) a sense of caring; c) a sense of trust; d) none of the above.

10. The three components of the triangular theory of love are: a) proximity, similarity, and physical attractiveness; b) attachment, caring, and trust; c) intimacy, passion, and commitment; d) access to resources, fertility, and social status.

Sample Quiz 17.2

1. The self–reference effect: a) refers to the use of the self–schema to organize verbal information more efficiently; b) occurs because the self–schema serves to link in memory otherwise unrelated information; c) occurs because relating information to the self leads to more elaborate thinking; d) all of the above.

2. Self-perception theory is to _____ as cognitive dissonance theory is to_____. a) Fritz Heider, Leon Festinger; b) Daryl Bem, Leon Festinger; c) Leon Festinger, Daryl Bem; d) Fritz Heider, Daryl Bem.

3. Fritz Heider maintained that in looking for causes of other people's behavior, we tend to give more weight to: a) dispositional attributions; b) situational attributions; c) self–attributions; d) external attributions.

4. Experiments have shown that the interpreter or "observer" in self–perception may have neurophysiological parallels in activity of the: a) hypothalamus; b) right brain; c) left brain; d) brain stem.

5. According to your text, favorable or unfavorable evaluations of objects, people, or situations have all *except* which of the following components? a) cognitive; b) behavioral; c) genetic; d) affective.

6. If a negative attitude protects a person from anxiety, the attitude is said to serve a(n): a) instrumental function; b) ego–defensive function; c) value expressive function; d) social adjustment function.

7. *Not* characteristic of the authoritarian personality is the tendency to: a) be submissive and obedient to superiors; b) have the same political orientation in all societies; c) be contemptuous and aggressive toward those they consider inferior; d) have a moralistic and hierarchical family environment in childhood.

8. Evidence supports the observation that husbands and wives tend to be similar to one another in terms of: a) educational level; b) intelligence; c) physical features; d) all of the above.

9. In Bem's "exotic becomes erotic" view of sexual attraction, an important spark for romantic love is: a) a sense of attachment; b) dissimilarity; c) commitment; d) unusual beauty.

10. According to sociobiologists, the function of pair bonding is to: a) establish a sense of lasting attachment; b) ensure that offspring survive to reproductive age; c) provide a stable unit to ensure survival of the culture; d) provide a social unit for satisfying sexual relations.

Answer Key, Chapter 17

Important Names

1. Fritz Heider
2. Daryl Bem
3. Leon Festinger

Vocabulary and Details

1. social psychology

INTUITIVE THEORIES OF SOCIAL . . .

1. vividness; more
2. schemas
3. schematic processing
4. stereotypes
5. self–schema
6. primacy effect
7. covariation
8. self–fulfilling
9. attribution
10. internal or dispositional; external or situational
11. fundamental attribution error
12. self–perception
13. induced–compliance

ATTITUDES

1. attitudes
2. cognitive; affective; behavioral
3. negative stereotypes; prejudice; discrimination
4. cognitive consistency
5. ego–defensive
6. scapegoat theory
7. cognitive dissonance theory

INTERPERSONAL ATTRACTION

1. physical attractiveness; proximity; familiarity; similarity
2. a sense of attachment; a sense of caring; a sense of trust
3. passionate love
4. companionate love
5. triangular theory
6. sociobiology
7. pair bonding

Sample Quiz 17.1

1. a, 593
2. d, 595
3. c, 596
4. a, 597-598
5. d, 601
6. a, 602
7. b, 608
8. a, 612
9. d 614
10. c, 621

Sample Quiz 17.2

1. d, 595
2. b 602, 613
3. a, 602
4. c, 606
5. c, 607
6. b, 609
7. b, 610
8. d, 617
9. b, 621
10. b, 623

Social Cognition and Affect   265

Social Interaction and Influence

Learning Objectives

1. Be able to discuss the research on social facilitation and explain the findings in terms of drive level, mere presence, distraction–conflict theory, and self–presentation theory.

2. Understand how the concept of deindividuation explains mob behavior, including the variables assumed to contribute to and result from this hypothetical state.

3. Be familiar with the factors that determine whether a bystander will intervene in an emergency situation. Be able to differentiate between "pluralistic ignorance" and "diffusion of responsibility."

4. Be able to discuss the Asch studies on social norms and conformity; understand the factors that lead to conformity and those that reduce it.

5. Be able to describe the factors that enable a minority to influence the majority.

6. Be able to describe the Milgram studies on obedience to authority and the four factors that contributed to the high obedience rates.

7. Know the role of the fundamental attribution error in assessments of studies of conformity and obedience.

8. Understand the circumstances that can undermine obedience and produce rebellion as identified in the MHRC study.

9. Be prepared to describe cognitive response theory and show how it explains some of the phenomena of persuasion discussed in the text.

10. Be able to distinguish between the central and peripheral routes that persuasion can take in producing attitude and belief change. Understand the role of reference groups in enabling the transition from identification to internalization.

11. Know what is meant by group polarization. Be familiar with the related explanations in terms of informational influence and normative influence.

12. Be able to define groupthink; be familiar with the factors that set the stage for this process and with some of the safeguards that can be used to help avoid its effects.

Important Names

1. An important figure in the history of social psychology known, in part, for his classic research on conformity was _____. (636)

2. A more recent social psychologist who has contributed to our understanding of the factors that determine obedience to authority is _____. (640)

Vocabulary and Details

1. Direct and deliberate (as well as indirect and unintentional) attempts by others to change our beliefs, attitudes, or behaviors defines _____. (629)

2. When we publicly comply with the social influencer but do not necessarily change our private beliefs or attitudes, social psychologists speak of _____. In other cases, when we do change our private beliefs and attitudes, we speak of _____. (629)

3. Implicit rules and expectations that dictate what we ought to think and how we ought to behave are called _____. (629)

PRESENCE OF OTHERS

1. When a person's performance on a task improves (or declines) in the presence of another person who is working on the task, we speak of the influence of _____. (630)

2. Even the presence of a positive spectator—an _____ rather than a coactor—will often facilitate (or disrupt) performance. (630)

3. Enhancement of performance due to coaction or the presence of an audience is termed _____. (630)

4. In addition to the theory that the presence of others accounts for social facilitation, the _____ theory suggests that the presence of others distracts a person, causing conflict between attending to others or to the task and a resulting increase in *drive* reflected in performance. (631)

5. A third theory of social facilitation, the _____ theory, proposes that the presence of others enhances the person's desire to present a favorable image, with an increase in performance under some conditions. (631)

6. A state in which individuals feel that they have lost their personal identities and have merged into the group is called _____. (631)

7. The presence of other people may prevent bystanders from intervening in an emergency in two ways: The presence of others may (a) _____ as a nonemergency and (b) _____ for acting. (633)

8. We speak of _____ when everybody in the group misleads everybody else, for example, by defining a situation as a nonemergency. (633)

268   Chapter 18

COMPLIANCE AND RESISTANCE

1. Another term for complying with a source of social influence, such as the majority of a group, is _____. (636)

2. A set of beliefs and attitudes is an _____. (643)

3. To say that people overestimate the role of personal dispositions and underestimate the power of situational factors in controlling human behavior is to say that they make the _____. (645)

IDENTIFICATION AND INTERNALIZATION

1. In the area of persuasion, the theory termed _____ proposes that persuasion induced by communication is actually self–persuasion produced by the thoughts that the person generates while reading or hearing the communication. (648)

2. Beliefs that are so widely held that nobody thinks of questioning them are called _____. (649)

3. Persuasion can take two routes in producing belief and attitude change. In one, called the _____, the individual responds to the substantive arguments of a communication. (650)

4. In the other route to persuasion, called the _____, the individual responds to either (a) _____ cues or (b) _____ cues of a communication. (650)

5. According to the view called the _____ of persuasion, when an issue is of little personal relevance or when people are unwilling or unable to respond to the content of a communication, they will use simple heuristics, or _____, to judge its merits. (651)

6. If we respect or admire others, we may obey their norms and adopt their beliefs, attitudes, and behaviors in order to be like them, a process termed _____. (652)

7. Groups with whom we identify and refer to for evaluation and regulation of our opinions and actions are called _____. (652)

COLLECTIVE DECISION MAKING

1. When the decision of the group is in the same direction but more extreme than the average of the group members' initial positions, we speak of _____. (655)

2. Explanations for group polarization take two forms: In one, termed _____, people's thinking may become polarized when they learn new information and hear novel arguments relevant to the decision under discussion. (655)

3. In the other form of explanation for group polarization, termed _____, people may compare their own views with the norms of the group and adjust their thinking to conform to the majority position. (656)

4. A phenomenon in which members of a group are led to suppress their own dissent in the interests of group consensus is called _____. (657)

Ideas and Concepts

1. Provide examples of social influence, including some that are indirect or unintentional. (629)

2. Similarly, be sure you can cite examples of social norms. (629)

PRESENCE OF OTHERS

* 1. a) Describe Triplett's early observations of social facilitation and several more recent ones to demonstrate both coaction and audience effects. (629-630)

* b) In what two respects is this effect of social influence more complex than a simple facilitation of performance? (630)

* 2. a) Discuss Zajonc's motivational explanation for these different patterns of effects due to coactors and audiences. (630)

b) Outline some observations in support of this interpretation. (630)

* 3. a) Discuss some findings that suggest that the variable operating to produce social facilitation at the human level is a cognitive one rather than the mere presence of others. (630)

b) What is one problem with the type of studies discussed in 3a)? What procedures were used to address this difficulty in another experiment, and what results were obtained? (630-631)

* 4. What is the status of the research on the distraction–conflict theory and self–presentation theory and your authors' conclusion regarding all of the competing views? (631)

* 5. a) Outline LeBon's dim view of the influence of a mob or crowd on the behavior of the individual member. (631)

* b) Discuss the antecedents and consequences of the more modern counterpart to LeBon's theory proposed by Diener, the concept of deindividuation. In this view, of what is deindividuation the *direct* result? (631, 632, Figure 18-1)

* 6. a) Describe an experiment by Zimbardo that showed apparent effects of anonymity on aggression in college women. (631-632)

b) Outline another study that took advantage of the natural anonymity and deindividuation that occurs at Halloween. (632)

* c) Are the experiments discussed in 6a) and 6b) definitive? Discuss a follow–up to the Zimbardo study in 6a) that attempted to replicate his findings on anonymity, and also explore the effects of the roles that costumes confer on the wearer. Does anonymity necessarily enhance aggression? (632-633)

*Basic ideas and concepts

270   Chapter 18

* 7. Indicate a second qualification with regard to the deindividuation research and the variables that must be taken into account when predicting that deindividuation will take place. (633)

8. a) What aspects of the Kitty Genovese incident led to the notion of "bystander apathy"? (633)

* b) What are four reasons why the term "apathy" may not be accurate when applied to bystanders; that is, why it is surprising that "anyone should intervene [in an emergency] at all"? (633)

9. a) What is a common way to deal first with the ambiguity of many emergency situations? (633)

* b) What two forms may pluralistic ignorance take and which form may be more common? (633)

* c) Describe an experiment by Latané and Darley to demonstrate the effects of pluralistic ignorance in leading some subjects apparently to conclude that "where there is smoke there is not necessarily fire." (633-634)

d) What may have been another factor operating to produce the results of this study, and how was that possibility addressed in a subsequent experiment? (634)

* 10. Outline the methods and results of Latané and Darley's ingenious study that investigated the tendency for the presence of others to diffuse responsibility in an emergency. (634-635)

* 11. What happens to bystander intervention if pluralistic ignorance and diffusion of responsibility both are minimized in an emergency situation? Discuss a study with a more optimistic outcome that took place on a subway train. (635)

12. a) Describe a study demonstrating the role of models in enhancing bystander intervention. (635)

b) Besides actual models, what else may enhance the likelihood of people helping in an emergency? Again, cite a demonstration. (636)

c) Is getting the kind of information you have received in this section helpful in getting people to react in emergencies? Cite a related study. (636)

COMPLIANCE AND RESISTANCE

* 1. a) Describe the general procedures of the classic Asch experiments on conformity. (636-637)

* b) What startling results did Asch obtain and what was one line of explanation for why the subjects' confidence in their decision–making ability did not prevail? (637)

* 2. a) Discuss the impact of dissent from a majority and why it generates such strong pressures to conform in this type of situation. (637-638)

*   b) Indicate several additional observations made by Asch and his coworkers when a "dissenter" was added to the influencing group in some conformity studies. (638)

    c) Explain why Asch used a task in which the correct answer was obvious and why attempts to portray life more realistically are likely to yield less information regarding the critical variables in conformity. (638)

* 3. a) What has been a criticism by European investigators of American research on conformity? (638)

    b) In terms of experimental procedures, how have these researchers gone about making their point that minorities can influence majorities? (638)

*   c) What has been the general finding of these studies and others on minority influence? What characteristics of the minorities enhance these effects? (638-639)

*   d) Discuss an even more interesting outcome of this research, and cite one related demonstration. (639)

* 4. Cite your authors' general conclusions from these findings. (639)

* 5. a) Does an analysis of the people and events in Nazi Germany during World War II support a picture of a group of "psychopathic monsters" assembled to commit atrocities? Cite and discuss Arendt's controversial conclusion. (639-640)

*   b) What more recent event in Vietnam appears to provide additional support for this conclusion? (640)

* 6. a) Discuss in detail the procedures and the striking major result of the well–known Milgram experiments on obedience to authority. (640-641)

    b) What was Milgram's explanation for the general phenomenon of obedience? (641)

*   c) Discuss the following four factors that influence obedience, providing definitions in your own words, methods by which each factor was manipulated in Milgram's research, and related findings where possible. (641-643)

Factors in Obedience	Definition	Manipulation and Results (where possible)
social norms		
surveillance		
buffers		
ideological justification		

272   Chapter 18

* 7. Cite a demonstration of obedience to authority in everyday life. (643)

* 8. a) Discuss the additional results obtained by Milgram and in the study cited in item 5 in order to illustrate the fundamental attribution error on the part of "experts" and other commentators on these studies. (645)

   b) What additional aspect of the study described in item 5 shows yet another form of the fundamental attribution error? (645)

* 9. a) What is one reason that compliance experiments yield so much conformity and obedience? (646)

   b) Cite two variations on the Milgram experiments, providing some indication of variables that may counter obedience. (646)

* c) Discuss the MHRC experiment by Gamson and colleagues that went further in demonstrating substantial rebellion among participants. (646-647)

* d) What variable was probably operating to produce the differences between the results obtained in this study and those that were characteristic of Milgram's obedience studies? (647)

  10. Discuss in detail the meaning of your authors' contention that many of the subjects in the Gamson et al. study "were not choosing between obedience and autonomy but between obedience and conformity." (647)

IDENTIFICATION AND INTERNALIZATION

   1. Beyond mere conformity, what do most people who influence us want to change, and in what two general ways is this accomplished? (648)

* 2. a) What does cognitive response theory predict with respect to the process of persuasion under the following two conditions? (648)

   —the communication evokes supportive thoughts:

   —the communication evokes unsupportive thoughts:

   b) Cite some observations relative to this theory. (648-649)

* 3. Show how the cognitive response theory helps to integrate the findings relative to each of the following phenomena of persuasion: (649-650)

Phenomena	Findings	Explanation
one–sided versus two–sided communication		
inoculation against persuasion		
forewarning		

4. Describe a practical application of cognitive response theory to behaviors of seventh– and eighth–graders. (650)

* 5. Distinguish by example between noncontent cues and context cues in communication. (650)

* 6. a) When is the central route to persuasion followed and when is the peripheral route followed? (651)

* b) What is one factor that can influence which route to persuasion will be followed? Outline the procedures of a study by Petty and Cacciopo demonstrating the effects of high personal involvement in a communication. (Be sure you can explain the differential effects upon attitudes owing to strong as opposed to weak arguments.) (651-652 and Figure 18-8)

* c) Apply the heuristic theory of persuasion to the pattern of effects obtained in the Petty and Cacciopo study when the subjects had low personal involvement in the communication. (652 and Figure 18-9)

* 7. a) Discuss how the process of identification with a reference group can provide a bridge between compliance and internalization. (652-653)

b) Must we belong to a reference group for it to have an influence on us? Explain. (653)

* 8. Discuss the classic Bennington study of the impact of college on political attitudes, noting especially the effects of duration of exposure to the college environment on compliance and identification. (653)

9. a) Describe the process of "trying on" new sets of beliefs and attitudes in college. What is the real work of college? (654)

* b) Cite follow–ups of the Bennington study to show that one advantage of internalization over compliance is that changes in beliefs and attitudes tend to endure if internalized. Does this mean that further support for internalization is not needed? Explain. (654)

COLLECTIVE DECISION MAKING

1. a) Outline the methods used by Stoner in his study of dilemma resolution in groups. (654-655)

*   b) Summarize Stoner's results using the term *risky shift* in your discussion. (655)

*   2. a) Was the risky shift characterization of group decision making accurate? Discuss by summarizing the results of many more subsequent studies demonstrating what has come to be called group polarization. (655)

*   b) Describe the group polarization process in jury deliberations. When are juries most likely to show polarization? (655)

3. a) Give some examples of informational and normative influence. In the latter case, indicate the reason why members of a group are likely to become biased toward its initial position. (655-656)

    b) Is normative influence simply pressure to conform? Explain. (656)

    c) In the example cited in 3b), is just normative influence present? Which effect is typically greater, normative or informational? (656)

*   4. a) What were the "circumstances of the discussion" that led to the disastrous planning and pursuit of the Bay of Pigs invasion? (657)

*   b) Review the causes and consequences of Janis's groupthink phenomenon shown in Figure 18-10. What four conditions set the stage for and foster groupthink? When is groupthink particularly likely to develop? (657)

*   c) Discuss the "symptoms" of groupthink, noting especially the function of *mindguards* in the process. Provide an example. (657-658)

*   5. a) List Janis's suggested safeguards to avoid the hazards of groupthink. (658)

    b) Indicate two general criticisms of the groupthink theory. (658)

Sample Quiz 18.1

1. Which of the following regarding presence of others is *true*? a) Humans as well as other organisms typically perform better when others are present, either as coactors or as passive audience. b) Complex behaviors are more likely to show facilitative effects of others than simple behaviors. c) It is clear that complex cognitive processes are required to produce effects due to presence of others in all species. d) All of the above.

2. The distraction–conflict theory suggests that: a) the mere presence of others will facilitate performance; b) the person's desire to present a good image may enhance performance; c) it is an increase in drive that enhances performance when there is an audience; d) none of the above.

3. According to the text, when everybody in a group defines an emergency as a nonemergency, we speak of: a) group identity; b) pluralistic ignorance; c) majority influence; d) collective polarization.

4. Helping in an emergency can be facilitated by all of the following *except*: a) minimizing pluralistic ignorance; b) providing helping models; c) maximizing shared responsibility; d) receiving information about the conditions under which people are deterred from intervening.

5. Obedience is to _____ as conformity is to _____. a) Stanley Milgram, Solomon Asch; b) Daryl Bem, Stanley Milgram; c) Fritz Heider, Solomon Asch; d) Solomon Asch, Stanley Milgram.

6. European investigators have criticized American social psychological research because it: a) fails to adequately research the variables producing conformity; b) fails to take into account the influence of the minority on the majority; c) often does not provide appropriate control groups; d) spends too much time on variables that influence interpersonal attraction.

7. The fundamental attribution error occurs when: a) members of a group suppress their dissent in the interests of group consensus; b) people underestimate the role of personal dispositions in behavior; c) people learn new information relevant to an argument under discussion; d) people underestimate the importance of situational factors.

8. The theory that persuasion through communication is actually produced by the thoughts of the person while receiving the communication is called: a) cognitive response theory; b) social facilitation theory; c) conformity theory; d) self–presentation theory.

9. With respect to reference groups: a) they may aid in the transforming identification to internalization over time; b) one does not have to belong to one in order to be influenced by its values; c) most of us identify with several groups; d) all of the above.

10. Groupthink theory has been criticized for: a) not being sufficiently based on laboratory experimentation; b) failing to account for why groups tend to suppress dissent in order to obtain consensus; c) oversimplifying complex processes; d) both a and c.

Sample Quiz 18.2

1. When we change our private beliefs and attitudes in response to social influence, we speak of: a) compliance; b) conformity; c) internalization; d) identification.

2. Recent research on anonymity has shown that: a) anonymity necessarily leads to aggression; b) being in a group is a critical variable by itself in producing deindividuation; c) deindividuation can lead both to more aggression and more generosity in the same experiment; d) all of the above.

3. The presence of others may prevent bystanders from intervening in an emergency by: a) defining the situation as a nonemergency; b) increasing levels of anxiety with regard to the outcome; c) diffusing responsibility for action; d) both a and c.

4. The most important factor in Milgram's obedience experiments was the context in which it was performed, namely under the auspices of "science." This is the factor in obedience your text refers to as: a) ideological justification; b) surveillance; c) social norms; d) buffers.

5. Most individuals who attempt to effect social influence: a) are aiming at internalization; b) present a compelling message; c) present themselves as possessing expertise and trustworthiness; d) all of the above.

6. If a person already agrees with an argument to be presented, that agreement can be strengthened by presenting: a) a one-sided argument; b) a two-sided argument; c) a number of counterarguments; d) both b and c.

7. When we are persuaded to change a belief or attitude through context cues of communication, we speak of the: a) social influence route; b) central route; c) peripheral route; d) normative route.

8. Groups with whom we identify for evaluation and regulation of our opinions are defined in this chapter as: a) peer groups; b) regulative groups; c) reference groups; d) evaluative groups.

9. In normative influence: a) people may adjust their thinking to conform to the majority position; b) people may become polarized when they learn new information; c) people may be strongly influenced by their tendency to attribute behavior to dispositions; d) self–persuasion is the primary route to attitude change.

10. The stage for groupthink is set by all *except* which of the following factors? a) a divided group of decision makers without clear goals at the outset; b) isolation from external factors; c) a directive leader with a specific course of action; d) high stress.

Answer Key, Chapter 18

Important Names

1. Solomon Asch
2. Stanley Milgram

Vocabulary and Details

1. social influence
2. compliance; internalization
3. social norms

PRESENCE OF OTHERS

1. coaction
2. audience
3. social facilitation
4. distraction–conflict
5. self–presentation
6. deindividuation
7. define the situation; diffuse the responsibility
8. pluralistic ignorance

COMPLIANCE AND RESISTANCE

1. conformity
2. ideology
3. fundamental attribution error

IDENTIFICATION AND . . .

1. cognitive response theory
2. cultural truisms
3. central route
4. peripheral route; noncontent; context
5. heuristic theory; rules of thumb
6. identification
7. reference groups

COLLECTIVE DECISION MAKING

1. group polarization
2. informational influence
3. normative influence
4. groupthink

Sample Quiz 18.1

1. a, 630
2. c, 631
3. b, 633
4. c, 635-636
5. a, 636
6. b, 638
7. d, 645
8. a, 648
9. d, 653
10. d, 658

Sample Quiz 18.2

1. c, 629
2. c, 633
3. d, 633
4. a, 643
5. d, 648
6. a, 649
7. c, 650
8. c, 652
9. a, 656
10. a, 657

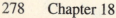